P9-CJV-402

Praise for *The Secret Life of Groceries*

"This book is at once a satisfying, enjoyable meal and a gla
water to the face. The modern shopper wants groceries that a
sustainable, humane, affordable, fresh, and convenient. But, a
covers, the costs of our demands are recouped from the bott
food chain: debt-ruined truckers, foreign slave labor, and WI
workers in our own communities—the people whose lives L
(and sometimes lived) for weeks or months. . . . *The Secret Life*
ies is a terrific read. The stories flow, and the hard truths are
with wit and hope."

—**Mary Roach,** author of *Stiff: The Curious Lives of Humar*

"A titanic achievement of reportage, insight, humor, and hum
Secret Life of Groceries will forever change the way you think
American food system. Lorr journeys deep into our troubl
chain with propulsive force and insight and brings us back th

—**Adam Chandler,** author of *Drive-Thr*
A Journey Through the Heart of America's Fast-Food

"In *The Secret Life of Groceries*, Benjamin Lorr demonstrate
lively and meticulous reporting how much the enthroneme
American consumer has cost workers. . . . With compassion a:
Lorr introduces us to very real people who constitute that al
we call the 'supply chain' and challenges us, in a thoughtful an
way, to consider the high price we pay for supermarket barga:

—**Timothy Noah,** author of *The Great L*
America's Growing Inequality Crisis and What We Can D

The SECRET LIFE of GROCERIES

The Dark Miracle of the American Supermarket

Benjamin Lorr

AVERY
an imprint of Penguin Random House
New York

AVERY

an imprint of Penguin Random House LLC
penguinrandomhouse.com

Most Avery books are available at special quantity discounts for bulk purchase for sales promotions, premiums, fund-raising, and educational needs. Special books or book excerpts also can be created to fit specific needs. For details, write SpecialMarkets@penguinrandomhouse.com.

Library of Congress Cataloging-in-Publication Data

Names: Lorr, Benjamin, author.
Title: The secret life of groceries : the dark miracle of the
American supermarket / Benjamin Lorr.
Description: New York : Avery, an imprint of Penguin Random
House, 2020. | Includes index.
Identifiers: LCCN 2020004949 (print) | LCCN 2020004950 (ebook) |
ISBN 9780553459395 (hardcover) | ISBN 9780553459401 (ebook)
Subjects: LCSH: Supermarkets--United States--Management.
Classification: LCC HF5469.23.U62 L67 2020 (print) |
LCC HF5469.23.U62 (ebook) | DDC 381.4/564130068--dc23
LC record available at https://lccn.loc.gov/2020004949
LC ebook record available at https://lccn.loc.gov/2020004950

Printed in the United States of America
1   3   5   7   9   10   8   6   4   2

Book design by Ashley Tucker

CONTENTS

Murray came out of an aisle and walked alongside Babette, just ahead of us. He took a twin roll of paper towels out of her cart and smelled it . . .

"This place recharges us spiritually, it prepares us, it's a gateway . . . The large doors slide open, they close unbidden. Energy waves, incident radiation. All the letters and numbers are here, all the colors of the spectrum, all the voices and sounds, all the code words and ceremonial phrases. It is just a question of deciphering, rearranging, peeling off the layers of unspeakability. Not that we would want to, not that any useful purpose would be served."

—Don DeLillo, *White Noise*

Between the Ice and You

In short, her shopping is primarily an act of love, that in its daily conscientiousness becomes one of the primary means by which relationships of love and care are constituted by practice. That is to say, shopping does not merely reflect love, but is a major form in which love is manifested and reproduced.... As Parker has noted, love for infants is inevitably accompanied by hatred and resentment.

—Daniel Miller, *A Theory of Shopping*

Let's look beneath the ice-chipped surface of a fish counter at a Whole Foods in New York City. This happens every other month after closing. The customers leave, the checkout crew changes into street clothes, the store goes into lockdown to prevent its own employees from robbing them. Shifts change and the ceaseless shitty Hall & Oates music stops and is replaced by silence. Night workers, a motley rainbow of low English, low skill, low smile workers, come in, kneepads over long pants, to restock the shelves like a reverse midnight harvest. They stoop over, heads down, in their KIND bar TM shirts, or whatever other functional and empowering edible shelled out sponsorship money, kneeling there, glumly stacking yogurts. At the fish counter, the seafood team begins. Fish are removed, latex gloves gripping them two at time—fillets and whole fish, sloppy little bastards—and tossed into the plastic tubs that are their nightly home. The mussels are bagged, the shrimp scooped together into mesh cages. Next the metal trays come up. These are little more than decorative housing, and are promptly sprayed down to remove a day's worth of sweat and oil and torn pieces of flesh that sloughed off from handling. Below the trays, a thin plastic webbing for grip, then a layer of ice: once individual chips, now grown hard as a skating rink from periodic thaws and re-icings during the day. The surface is littered with the typical debris: fish parts, crumpled-up stickers announcing WILD CAUGHT!, errant cockles, cracked mussels.

Usually that would be it. Aprons would be stripped off, giant foul garbage bags of fish guts and butcher paper would be lugged to the dumpsters in the back. But on this night, the one that comes every other month or so, the case itself is cleaned. An order has come down from high, seemingly at random. And so, for the entire length of the 38-foot case, the employees hack the ice into large chunks. It is exactly like shoveling snow in the winter and they use big thick shovels to do the job. Standing up on metal platforms to get leverage, they chop straight down, chiseling out 2' x 2' x 2' blocks that they then systematically take out like giant sugar cubes to be melted in the back. It is reasonably physical work and soon they are sweating. Once the top layer is removed, they begin anew on the layer below: gridding it out, chiseling, pulling out cubes. Beneath this second layer, the ice is more crunchy, less frozen. It's an old freezer and inconsistent and it only takes a few scrapes before you get to streaks of brown. A few more and the smell comes. It is horrible and not at all of decomposition but of fecal waste maybe sweetened slightly, thick in the air like you are exhuming something dangerous, which perhaps you are. Soon after the smell, the streaks of brown darken and the ice turns with entrails and smashed pieces of shell, the shovel uncovering squid tentacles, crab antennae, all two months old, rotten, buried under there, each scrape revealing some new purple color, and the odor is such that you really cannot breathe it long.

So neither team member does, instead spelling each other by rushing off to do other tasks like melting the giant cubes under hot water or just standing to the side and muttering how the fuck does it get like this?

Then, at a certain scrape of the shovel, the bottom of the case is revealed. Stainless steel. But it's streaked green with bile, gray with pancreatic froth, pink with clam flesh, all strung out and mashed in the ice slurry. To the extent that they are recognizable, the contents are inexplicable and vaguely horrifying. No shrimp were stored in this section of the case, so why the rotting pile of shrimp casings? No whole fish either, so why the set of red lacy gills? Months of slow melting and cracks in the ice and the chaos of retail have allowed it all to accumulate down there in a weird gutter of seafood waste compressed beneath four and a half feet of ice.

Eventually the ice and slime are removed and a high-blast hose with a separate nozzle for green concentrated soap is sprayed against the stainless-steel bottom. The water is hot, so there is steam, your glasses fog up, and the rot slithers down the drain. The shells cluster in cracked bits and are removed by hand. Finally, now somewhere closer to one a.m., the case bottom looks clean, even gleaming, and the team goes back to the giant ice machine along the north wall to return with heaping shovels of virginal white snow. Clean ice, the cleanest you've ever seen after that, and they pile it in heaps into the case, building back the buffer between the wet semi-rot that will be the bottom of the case and a top retail surface downy and clean. When they are finished, the ice sparkles. No more skate rink, each chip separate and glittering in the light; the perfect platform to sell good fish. The smell, once choking, is not just muffled but nonexistent. A very real and solid barrier has been erected. And once the floor has been sprayed down and mopped across with a giant squeegee, the entire scene will feel like a dream. Tomorrow morning the fish will be laid down again in their metal trays, cut parsley and trills of red peppers arranged on top. And it won't be unhygienic in the least. It will be undetectable and irrelevant. There will be a thick wall of ice separating the retail surface from the depths below. And in this way—the very real way the fish case at Whole Foods on the Bowery can be simultaneously appalling and perfectly hygienic and safe—it is a fitting metaphor for the grocery business as whole and a start to this book.

First, lest we get off on the wrong foot, a moment to state how underplayed that description of the opening smell was. Over the course of researching this book, I climbed aboard fishing boats littered with the debris of mashed fish and seaweed left for weeks at a time to roast in the sun. I necropsied chickens, pulling their guts apart looking for signs of disease as they radiated that lab-specific scent of ammonia and death. I snuck into industrial swine farms and chicken houses, wading through lagoons of feces in the process, and at one point, in Nakhon Si Thammarat, Thailand, on a ninety-degree summer day, I stood ankle-deep in rotten trash fish on the loading dock, ten thousand minnows piled up in silver ribbons, left for days, as they waited to be transformed into the protein base of the aquaculture pyramid. Those were some strong sniffs. And yet none of it—not the trash fish nor fecal lagoons—was as fundamentally gross and disturbing as the smell that came out of that fish case in Manhattan. In a Whole Foods. In one of the wealthiest neighborhoods in the wealthiest nation in the world. Which is to say, melodrama has its place in life, but not in my descriptions of smells. Maybe that's an odd note to start a book on, but this is nonfiction. Names have not been changed, except in the few places where I felt my writing might threaten a subject's livelihood. Characters have not been combined. Quotes are either from audio recordings or written down in the moment. And descriptions of smells have not been exaggerated for effect.

This book is about the grocery store. About the people who work there and the routes of supply that define it. It is the product of five years of research, hundreds of interviews, and thousands of hours tracking down and working alongside the buyers, brokers, marketers, and managers whose lives and choices define our diet. The five years were a time of dramatic upheaval. Walmart seized organics. Amazon seized Whole Foods. The promise of automation loomed over trucking. Minimum wage laws shifted, giving employees the promise of a new salary floor. Yet, what I found, whether talking to Whole Foods executives about the Amazon deal or to new Amazon employees as they stocked shelves, was that during this upheaval the most primal drives in the industry weren't so much disrupted as elevated and laid bare.

What emerged is a fascinating and largely hidden world. In 2018, Americans spent $701 billion at supermarket-style grocery stores, still our largest food expenditure by a wide margin; there are 38,000 of these stores across this land, and the average adult will spend 2 percent of their life inside one. They are the point of interface most familiar and least understood in our food system: bland to the point of invisibility, so routine they blur into background. And yet the grocery store exists as one of the only places where our daily decisions impact—make us complicit in—a system we have come in equal parts to scorn and see as savior. We've been happy to let more impersonal aspects of our food system—from industrialized slaughterhouses to farm bill subsidies— take up the lion's share of investigation and critique. But to understand how and why our food gets to us in the form it does, the grocery store is a powerful entry point. It is not only the way that most of us are introduced to the system, tagging along with Mom as she shops, it is perhaps the best opportunity to understand the system on the terms of the people who operate it on our behalf.

And their operation is something to behold. Grocery stores—and the supply chain that has grown up around them—are shockingly efficient. We spend only 10 percent of our budget on food, compared to 40 percent by our great-grandparents in 1900, and 30 percent by our grandparents in the 1950s. It is a number that has been decreasing the entire century along with the rise of mass supply chains. In the early republic, around the War of 1812, nearly 90 percent of the population worked to produce the nation's food; it was a grueling physical life, and in addition to being costly, the food produced was of uneven quality, in tightly limited supply, and could and did kill through disease. Now less than 3 percent of our population produces enough food to feed us all. It is easy to wax poetic about food before the rise of industry—about eating the way our grandmother's grandmother ate—but the fact is we spend less money than almost every other country in the world on food and we spend less time gathering that food than at any time in history. Somehow each year those numbers continue to shrink while the quality,[1] quantity, variety, and safety of the food available have gotten better and better.

So, within a century, we have cut rates of hunger and nutritional deficiency to historic lows, reduced food-borne illness to a rounding error, and democratized food that was once the height of luxury into fare for everyday consumption. And we have been so successful in all those endeavors that we now grapple with a series of problems entirely unprecedented in the history of humanity: of too much food, of using food to distribute ethical responsibility, of food as a proxy for control in our own increasingly detached lives.

---

1   Okay! I put this here to be argumentative. I am well aware that some modern tomatoes taste like mushy cardboard, and that you've never had a real avocado unless you blah blah blah. I too have traveled to third-world countries and rural American farm stands and bitten into [insert authentic version of otherwise ordinary food product here] and had a transcendent almost revelatory experience as the juices drooled down my throat. I am not convinced this means it's appropriate to lord these experiences over the entire system, or lament a bygone era where these moments were routine and food was not debased. Largely because I don't think these moments were ever routine. Quality between epochs is an incredibly hard thing to measure. Facets once highly desired, like the age of a hen at slaughter, fall out of fashion. The value of what we no longer have expands in our imagination. In the 1920s, fancy New York restaurants advertised their "food miles," proudly touting the distance each ingredient traveled on the menu as a symbol of sophistication. Now we see the same measure as a proxy for carbon footprint and wince.

All Those Facts Are Interesting but Not Why I Wanted to Learn About the Grocery Store

When I was nineteen, I went to Kenya and lived with no running water, no electricity, no communication with the outside world. I had signed on as a field researcher, studying blue monkeys, with binoculars and gum boots, racing around the literal jungle with a notebook trying to follow the arboreal path of what looked to my completely untrained eye like oversized gray cats grooming each other, humping, and hissing in angry confrontation. There were no phone lines strung to our field station, and this was before cell phones really existed except in movies as big brick-shaped devices signifying outrageous wealth, so our sole means of communication with the outside world began with a 1.5-mile walk from our forest hut to a tree, known as the "bicycle taxi stand," where we could commission an hour-long tandem bicycle ride over dirt roads, transfer to a motorized van at a cement junction, and then finally, after a half hour in the van, arrive at a town large enough to support a post office where we could buy aerograms for a few pennies to get word to an anxious mother that all was well.

Details from that summer flood in if I squint my eyes and try. They are wonderful when I can grab them. But the memory that comes to me unbidden, at odd moments, with eerie intensity—in fact, perhaps *the* definitional memory of my entire summer of being nineteen and in the Kenyan rain forest—didn't actually occur in Kenya. After months of this life, waking with the sun, going to sleep to the light of an oil lantern, my only external sounds from the rain forest itself, deafening, chaotic, and multi-paneled, the auditory equivalent of the ten thousand shades of blue you might see while staring out at the Mediterranean, after weeks of cooking the same cabbage dinner on a gas stove, of storing my cheese at room temperature, of learning the rhythms of the space—the daily thirty-minute equatorial thunderstorms whereby the air would transform into long translucent sheets of rain, flapping and whipping in the wind—a summer where I hitchhiked, bathed in rainwater, hand-washed my clothes, and wiped my ass with leaves, the single definitional memory of that summer, the one that is seared into my brain, came only when I arrived back home. It is a memory from my first night in New York, after wandering the streets in a daze, well past midnight and finding myself in the aisles of the Westside Market grocery store on 112th and Broadway. The memory is of my first night in that store. My body wandering down the aisles, eyes falling over the easy abundance, mind chewing over the scene like a dog gnawing on the very bone of Western civilization. I remember stepping in through the curtain of air-conditioning, pacing the cement waxed floors, my stretched reflection gleaming back like a shadow, my pulse slow and easy, my eyes scanning the cereal boxes banked high on both sides, the pontoons of two-liter soda bottles, and most memorably the cold counter of prepared foods, rows of chicken breasts, deli meats, and an oozing, seemingly never-touched giant bowl of octopus salad, serving spoon permanently wedged in its mayonnaise like the sword in the stone. I would puzzle over that octopus salad like a riddle. Like I was stoned out of my gourd, which I was most certainly not except in some metaphoric sense. I would stand there taking it in, almost feeling the store respire. The memory is crystalline in a way that feels false; a characteristic known as "flashbulb" memory, which I've since learned is associated with trauma. In my memory I am dazed and confounded and in love in that grocery store. A love like all love filled with doubt and rage and insecurity, but also overwhelming and blanketing, warm and intoxicating. It was a love of re-acclimation, of reabsorbing a childhood and birthright, of seeing myself and my country with new eyes, both fearful and reverent, and that—my definitional memory of a Kenyan summer full of memories—is where this book comes from.

A Secular Revelation

To almost everyone in the actual industry, food is just another CPG, or Consumer Packaged Good. This is true whether they entered the industry as a chef, a Harvard business school grad, or a cancer-survivor-vegan-doctor intent on change. It is true regardless of the rhetoric that graces their packages or the percent of their profits they donate to virtuous causes. It is true because that is what it means to enter the system. It is a necessary requirement of acting on scale. If you want to open even a single market fruit stand, you are suddenly dealing with a product that is flowing through you, that has been purchased and will be either sold or discarded as waste, and that is defined in your eyes by its economic properties alongside its nutritional, aesthetic, or ethical dimensions. When you expand to the scale of even a small grocery chain, the economic factors can't help but envelop everything else. Qualities like ethics and aesthetics get swallowed by the market, and reduced to price. The average store has 32,000 individuated products known as Shop Keeping Units, or SKUs. The biggest have more than 120,000 SKUs. Accordingly, the men and women who sell our food, who work amidst this volume, see our food differently than you or I. In particular, they see it as a line on a spreadsheet, with reams of qualities arrayed in columns, all weighted by various coefficients according to their particular proprietary model, that culminates in one or two numbers used to determine its value. The very same item they might have eaten for breakfast transubstantiates into something entirely non-ecological when they head to work, not really that different from thumbtacks or paper towels, though perhaps with slightly more fragile handling conditions.

This is something those on the inside are acutely aware of. Once, talking to a slaughter plant supervisor, a man who proudly declared he'd been present for the execution of 800 million chickens, I listened as he practically broke down describing the moments just after a chicken's death. The man was detailing the procession of events that leads to slaughter: after the catchers come through in their overalls, grabbing up the birds by hand, after they stuff the birds into their horizontal cages for transport, muddy cotton balls jammed against the steel, and after the cages are driven miles and miles to the plant, then removed by forklift, and the birds are yanked out—again by hand—and hung upside down on the line by their yellow scaly feet, they head toward a machine that will slice their carotid artery—140 birds a minute—while a man in a bloodstained smock looks on with raised knife, ready in case the machine misses and he has to step forward to finish the job; after the man and the neck slicing, the birds, still twitching, still warm, draining out—in short, still very much animals, though dying ones—are whisked into a dark metallic tunnel. This is the place. The place where the slaughter plant supervisor's voice wells up during his description. The tunnel continues through to a new room, but inside, encased in industry, invisible except on blueprints and design plans, something happens: the bird is blasted with hot steaming water, beaten by rubber flanges so its feathers fall off in ragged clumps; it is cleansed at an existential level, until on the other side of this tunnel the chicken emerges into a new room, now a decapitated, drained thing, all white pocked skin, a whizzing gleaming globe of meat racing forward on the line. There is a phase shift. The floors are now bloodless, men and women in white smocks stand at green plastic counters, and the whole area radiates with the high, reassuring notes of chlorine. "That is the precise point they go from living thing to food. You watch it happen," he says, his voice breaking—as into tears—but not in the remorseful or guilt-ridden sense; in the I am blessed and witness to the miraculous sense: "They come out and they are no longer an animal. They are food now." It is a fundamental rite of civilization, a moment where industry mimics the god, but rather than breathing new life into dust, a different consecration occurs, of sucking life out, an act of not just absolving murder but erasing the possibility.

A very similar process occurs in the retail store. Those deboned bulk chilled chicken breasts—or Granny Smith apples, or long fillets of frozen salmon, or whatever other food you want to imagine—arrive to the stores in their cardboard boxes, vacu-sealed in a marvel of plastic packaging, and when you click your box cutter down and reach to take them out, they cease being food. Another transformation has occurred; they are product now. Merchandise. SKUs. Listen to the retail managers and assistant managers talk among themselves: the word "food" doesn't come up; it is an irrelevant, unhelpful, even illogical way to discuss the work of a grocery. To these men it is always product. And so in the same way the fecal shrieking bird ceases being an animal and becomes food, an item within the grocery matrix loses its identity as food and becomes product. It is liberated; its transformation is no less critical to the project of civilization. Now it is defined by the cubic inches of its packaging, its price per unit, and the velocity of its sales. It is not until much later, the moment the customer comes pushing their cart down the aisle and reaches out for that Styrofoam tray, that our chicken becomes food again. It is a tenuous thing, but suddenly it has a new owner and a new meaning; now it will be eaten, and everything that matters about it has changed to reflect that fact.

Detailing these pivot points isn't just a weird exercise in categorization or linguistics. These shifts have material effects. As a culture we do a generally excellent to overzealous job thinking about food, a highly conflicted job thinking about its origins in the natural world as a living thing, and spend almost no time thinking about our groceries as retail product. It is simply elided in our brains, in our arguments, and in our attempts to intervene in the system as advocates. The men and women who work in the grocery industry do not actually speak another language when they discuss food, but the words they use refer to parallel attributes in the same thing.

And when you start digging into precisely how the people in grocery think, you find one thing open and waiting in the center: the maw. That voracious, devouring hole we feed three to thirty times a day, swallowing and salivating and stuffing, ceaseless in its demands right up to the point we lie in a hospital bed and it gets temporarily assisted by a polyurethane tube. The maw to me, like the sun above interfacing with the chloroplasts below the leaf, is more than just a mouth: it is a secular revelation, a complex of destruction and creativity, anchored in need. It is the sensory cells of the gut. The neuronal charge to acquire. The curiosities, comforts, and cravings we convince ourselves are necessities. It—like the Vedic concept of Self/self—comes in the universal as well as the personal, each of our unique pie holes mere tributaries to some more tremendous vortex right at the heart of the human project. And it is this maw more than anything that animates the wonks in the grocery back room, poring over their spreadsheets, deciding how to stock our shelves. More than greed, health, altruism, grocery wants to *serve*. The fact that we make serving that need so complicated, the fact that it ends in the contradiction that is the Whole Foods fish counter, beautiful and vile at the same time, should not be an invitation to scorn the system—or ourselves—but an opportunity for introspection and perhaps even growth. And ultimately it should upend our perception of grocery to remember it isn't about food, it never has been about food—food is the business of eating—grocery, we'll see, that's completely different; it's the business of desire.

PART I

Salad Days at Trader Joe's

These days, it's not enough to simply produce fruit; one must obtain fruit that is beautiful . . . good taste is not necessary—just beauty, gloss, and size. They are really more intended to dazzle the eye than to satisfy the palate.

—Gustave Rivière, writing in 1894

The Fourth Gibson Is Always Doom

Light glissando up the piano by the bar followed by the obligatory tapping of a single high note. A song has come to the end. This is late Friday afternoon, October 1965, at the Tail O' the Cock restaurant. Joe Coulombe, thirty-five, the smartest man in the room and just about every room he walks into, has gone jelly inside. Something bad is up. His friend and business partner, Merritt Adamson Jr., is mumbling, trying to gum up the courage to spit out some previously memorized line. The moment passes, and instead Joe watches Merritt lift a shy finger to the waiter, and order a fourth round of Gibsons.

The Tail O' the Cock is a weird Hollywood amalgam: English country-style restaurant, brown shingles, cozy fireplace, but rounded out with a grand piano and red leather booths. It is the type of place with a hat check next to the coat check, and cigarette girls with big hair and big smiles, where waiters have to do double duty during the holidays climbing up on the roof to put out reindeer and elves. A place that shells out for the best boozy Santa Claus in all Los Angeles to roam from table to table, creating roars of glee from the kids. It is white tablecloth and white people, excepting the attendants, casual old Hollywood magic that has somehow crept into the mid-1960s, frequented by Bogart and Gable, Bette Davis and Bela Lugosi. It is always swimming with booze, especially during the lunch hour.

Joe and Merritt meet there every month on a Friday. Always three Gibsons, always in the late afternoon. At this point, Joe is the owner of a small fleet of convenience stores, the Pronto Markets. They are folksy endeavors, staffed by men in red-and-white-checkered shirts that Joe buys from Sears on his weekends. Merritt owns the dairy that supplies Joe's milk. Theirs is the quintessential symbiotic grocer–supplier relationship. Merritt's cows keep producing and he needs to off-load the product quick. His business, like most dairy of the era, is anchored in home delivery—about 250 men running five hundred daily routes, six days a week. They're profitable lines when everything goes right: a threshold of housewives opt in, the route pays for itself; the milkman gets a middle-class job, and every bottle sold over threshold is lucre. But for the last five years, the business has turned sour. Routes once studded with every home on the block are now spotty. Refrigeration has gone mainstream and suddenly everyone demands their milk at seven a.m., no earlier, no later. Joe's convenience stores are both savior and drain here, their convenience the reason people are dropping home delivery, but their steady customer base offering Merritt a new venue to off-load product.

Merritt's dairy, Adohr Stock Farms, is the nation's largest: five thousand golden Guernsey cows munching on Pacific foxtail and purple needlegrass in the hills above Santa Monica. Although positively puny compared to the milking operations of 2020—those massive industrialized compounds with 100,000 cows shuffling around in dust—in 1965, Adohr's size is a liability. It produces more volume than Merritt can reasonably sell. Worse, the Guernseys themselves are trouble. As a breed, they eject an especially rich and creamy milk, about 30 percent fattier and 10 percent more queer looking: the gold in the Guernsey is the result of beta-carotene giving it an odd orange hue. For years, this combo marked the Guernsey as premium. But America's taste buds are changing; skim is the new rage, and so buyers across the industry are turning toward the less fatty, chalk-white milk of the Holstein.

The fourth Gibson arrives. Like all fourth Gibsons, it signals doom. Merritt gulps his down in silence.

Joe looks up at the man across from him suspiciously. Merritt Jr. is a bit of a golden Guernsey himself: blocky, wide shoulders, shy, with cud-chewing cheeks. He has the friendly reaching insecurity of the heir who knows he does not live up to the ambition or intellect of his forefathers, but who also—unlike them—might be a decent guy.[2] His face is perpetually flushed and a little sweaty.

---

2   And what an heir he is! In 1965, Merritt Jr. sits on the last crumbling vestiges of an empire. His father, "Smoke," a sheep rancher and self-described blood brother to the Havasupai tribe, made the match of the century, marrying Rhoda Rindge, sole inheritor of the entire Malibu coast. Purchased at $10 an acre from the original Spanish land grant, the Malibu Sequit amounted to 14,000 jaw-dropping acres—eventually becoming the single most valuable real estate holding in the country—all for the newlyweds to manage. Rather than try to develop the property, Rhoda and Smoke spent their lives trying to keep it pristine, chasing off road builders, real estate agents, and settlers of all stripes. They poured themselves into a series of quixotic/eccentric endeavors—using the local soil to make high-quality ceramics, keeping a personal zoo, and fighting the Pacific Coast Highway—that seemed to function as little more than spouts from which their fortune could drain. Eventually this steady efflux leaves them land-rich and cash-poor, and their sole functional for-profit business—the Adohr dairy, named after wife, Rhoda, hence the cheeky spelling—extremely vulnerable. Every time the cost of cattle feed spikes, the family is forced to sell a piece of its vast holdings below market value to prevent foreclosure. By 1965, less than 4,000 acres of the original land grant are left. Merritt Sr. and Rhoda are dead. The PCH exists and is roaring with autos. And so, Merritt Jr. decides, rather than fight sprawl, it is time to embrace it. To raise the money needed to develop Malibu into the paradise of Lamborghini dealerships and private beaches it is today, he's here, sequestered in a red leather booth at the Tail O' the Cock, confessing to Joe C. that . . .

Finally the gin hits home. Courage sloshing around his brain, Merritt blurts it out.

"Joe, I've sold Adohr. And I've sold it to Southland."

Both men know exactly what that means. Pronto Markets are going extinct. Joe, who used his entire life savings to buy the chain just three years ago, who is currently leveraged up to his nostrils in debt, and who has a pregnant wife and two young children to feed in a newly purchased home, understands that if nothing changes, he has, at best, two years before bankruptcy.

Southland is the parent company of 7-Eleven. The great rapacious Slurpee from the South: all Texas bravado, menace, and oil-backed capital, expanding like a rash over the map. Joe knows it well. He started his career studying it and opened Pronto Markets in its image. It's entirely fair to say his life in groceries up to this point has been a finely tuned study of Southland's 7-Eleven, cautiously riffing off it.

Born in Dallas from a series of ice docks, Southland invented the concept of the convenience store whole cloth. If that sounds absurd, get used to it. Innovations in grocery skirt an intellectual line where, on one hand, they seem so blindingly obvious you can't tell if it's abusive to true ingenuity to use the term "innovation" at all, or, on the other, whether they only appear that way because they have sprung so completely from the consumer unconscious that their absence is unthinkable once they are here.

Either way, it wasn't always thus, and in order to understand the behemoth that is Southland Corp in 1965, the innovation that is the convenience store, or the trajectory of Joe C. 's career, it is necessary to step back a moment to examine something even more primal to customer satisfaction than convenience. Comfort. In this case, a few cubes of ice amid the concussive heat of a Dallas summer.

Ice might feel like a modern luxury, but it's not. The Chinese have cut and stored it since at least 1000 BCE. The Romans kept it in covered pits, using horse-drawn carts to haul giant chunks down from the Alps. And in America, throughout the entire nineteenth century, there was a raging multimillion-dollar industry dedicated to manually carving up the small lakes of the Northeast, prying out giant blocks, hand-packing them in sawdust, and shipping them all over the world from Mexico to Calcutta. Ice was big business. The mammoth cubes were then stored in local depots, subdivided, and delivered straight to customers' homes via "the iceman"—a man who occupied no small amount of lore among housewives and their worried husbands, a man who would dutifully cometh, always bearing pleasure.

Southland was, in the verbiage of our times, a disrupter of this pre-existing industry. In 1890, it opened the first ice manufacturing plant in Texas, using the new technology of refrigerants to artificially freeze water that it then sold at its own proprietary chain of "ice docks." These were little more than elevated roadside stands to which husbands could trot their mule-drawn carts while a team of young men filled their order: hacking the ice, wrapping it up in blankets as insulation, and sliding the whole package right off the dock onto the waiting cart. Think of a full-service gas station, but before either cars or the pump.

The convenience store came to Southland in 1927, when John Jefferson Green, a fifty-five-year-old iceman, had a new realization about the Dallas summer. Nobody wanted to move during the brutal midday, much less trot up to a loading dock, so Green decided to broaden his hours to stay open longer during the margins of the day. Say from seven a.m. until eleven p.m. His customers appreciated the gesture. And when a neighbor lady rolled up to his dock one evening—after the general store had closed—and wished aloud that he could give her a quart of milk, the request stuck. He sought out an executive at Southland. If Southland would stake him money for milk, eggs, and bread, he'd sell them cheap, as a service to his customers, and they could split the profits.

The convenience store burst forth.

Even though the returns for Green's personal store were modest, the executives at Southland realized that replicating the service across all forty retail docks they controlled would be substantial. More, it complemented their summer business, providing a year-round core that allowed the ice docks to stay fully staffed, rather than frantically hire seasonal workers. And it diversified Southland from the ice business, which was rapidly losing its utility status, as freezing technology advanced, creating much lower barriers to entry.

The chain grew quickly, gobbling up Texas's ice docks and transforming them into food retailers. To wrangle all these sheds under a common name, and to emphasize their unprecedented accessibility, it was suggested that if all owners agreed to longer hours—à la Green—the chain could be called 7-Eleven. The label stuck. Giant pylons were driven into the ground with the number "7" and the word "ELEVEN" written across them. By 1951, it was Texas's largest retailer of beverages, milk, and bread, operating just under one hundred stores, earning $72 million in annual sales.

By 1965, with Joe sitting sot-faced in that red leather booth, it is a juggernaut.

Southland will open 398 new stores in 1965 alone, and by the end of the decade, another 2,261 more, collectively blowing through a billion dollars in sales. In contrast, since founding the Pronto Markets chain in 1957, Joe has opened about one new store a year, and teetered toward bankruptcy several times.

Merritt has not only sold Joe's sole source of milk and ice cream, he sold it to a competitor a thousand times greater in wealth. And this above all is why Joe knows he is doomed. Then, as now, convenience stores are essentially a real estate game. The best locations at the best rent determine the best profits in a business where everyone is selling essentially the same items. And real estate has only one rule: he with the biggest balance sheet wins. No sane landlord will side with a little guy like Pronto when comparing their lease applications to Southland. To add insult to injury, Joe had staked himself to a strategy of paying premium wages to his employees to attract the very best, a strategy that anyone who has ever visited a 7-Eleven knows intuitively and reflexively the chain has rejected.

And so, soaking with gin, foreseeing certain ruin, Joe responds the way only the greatest of entrepreneurs can: he holes up in a cabin with his wife and kids for a few days, then gets on a plane and flies as far away as possible.

The Genius of Joe

Joe isn't a handsome man, though it occurs to me quickly upon meeting him there is something far more compelling than handsome going on here. He is plain, a little goofy, even, with drooping aviator frames on a head as bald, speckled, and blooming as a white-cap mushroom. His voice is about three octaves deeper than his thin frame has any reason to suggest. The effect is grandfatherly to the extreme. He uses phrases like "every simple bastard" and "a bunch of kooks" and laughs at his own jokes in a bona fide chuckle, which is to say, with an easy, self-amused, reflective roll, as if he's astonished by a world so weird as to provide him this type of fodder. His eyes widen frequently but not theatrically. He leans in; he listens. He points out accepted industry-wide lies, calls his friends and competitors out on casual racism and sexism, and checks his own exaggerations immediately. He is the quintessential non–bullshit artist. And it is an art, this straight talk to the extreme. It is active and participatory and evoked *from* you, often despite you. Long before Silicon Valley titans strode into board meetings in hoodies and jeans, Joe was showing up to his financing meeting with Bank of America in the 1950s wearing tennis shoes and a plain white button-down with a Hussong's Cantina T-shirt blaring through underneath. He always got the money. In conversation, he employs the wink. And it is the rare wink that actually brings you closer, creates a channel of confidence eye to eye rather than feeling even remotely sketchy, forward, or hokey. It's infectious. But it's not a skill you should try to pick up; or at least, it went promptly sideways on me when I attempted one with a cabdriver after our first meeting. It is clear—in interview after interview with his former employees—he is ready to back up any random request with personal action. Joe never met a shelving unit he wasn't ready to install himself. He would often—long after expanding to double-digit stores—get down on his belly with a screwdriver to do just that. His wife once tells me, "This man is not a snob," and although a definition in the negative, and pretty damn limited, I underline it with black ink about fifty times and it strikes me as just about the truest thing anyone ever says about Joe. Which is to say, Joe might not be handsome, but he projects decency and integrity with a physicality that is striking in the same way extreme beauty strikes you. He projects this decency in a manner that I suspect he would agree is completely disproportionate to his actual integrity and decency; it is a quality he would call "an angle" that he can draw upon or "play" in negotiations. And his acknowledging this gulf only adds to the sense that he is fundamentally sound—grounded, even—about his foibles.

It all meant that, within minutes of meeting him, I liked Joe quite a bit. But I also didn't wholly trust that I liked him, or at least I recognized that it came attached to a very perceptive man who is much more capable than just likable. Joe is a man frequently described as a genius by other very smart men. When asking his employees and competitors and industry observers about him, I hear the word "visionary" so many times, it becomes wearisome. I hear he is brilliant. Incredible. Wise. Grown men tell me they are awestruck. Chilled. Giddy in his presence. Executives who worked for him, stuffed C-suite dullards of the grotesquely self-confident variety, will drop all pretense and describe wanting to wake up early in the morning to race to work because they can't wait to hear what Joe has to say. They tell me that he has a photographic memory. That he can read 1,200 words per minute. That he adds, multiplies, or divides lists of figures in his brain quicker than they could even scan them. That he knows the names of all his employees, and their spouses' names, and their dates of hire, and their birthdays and wedding anniversaries. But beyond all this awe—the steel-cage memory, the gymnastic cognitive quickness—the genius of Joe that impresses me most is his ability to project this integrity and decency when he wants to. He keeps you guessing exactly where the line lies between calculating businessman and wholesome self-taught founder in a way that allows almost everyone who meets him to underestimate his abilities yet simultaneously afford him huge amounts of respect. It is an awesome talent. Especially in a business built on negotiation, trust, and quick, decisive deals.

It is also the exact talent that has come to define the brand that shares his name, the products it sells, and the cultlike community of consumers drawn to them. Trader Joe's, just like trader Joe, has perfected the ability to project integrity while simultaneously offering a very similar class of mass-produced goods that its competitors offer. It is no accident that the real dynamite deals at TJ's have always been in the frozen aisle, or the canned goods, the jar of cookie dough spread, or the bacon-cheddar-flavored popcorn, those hyper-packaged exemplars of mass consumption that achieve the most special aura of all by appearing on Joe's shelf: decency.

A side effect of this is an image of him as CEO that many of his rivals, and a few of his successors, have bought into: that of a rube blindly pawing his way forward, stumbling and getting lucky, perhaps not so different from the way you or I might do it if we inherited our uncle's grocery store chain and decided to make a go of it, operating less from some strategic master plan, more out of our own image and sense of delight. And yet it is clear, once you get under the hood, this is exactly wrong. Joe may have stood on some tall shoulders, but he saw further than any man in groceries before him; by 1967 he had successfully envisioned the consumer of 2017; by 1978 he had perfected a strategy for private labeling that has come to dominate the industry, even as competitors are still playing catch-up trying to understand and mimic it. He did this meticulously, through hundreds of pages of internal documents—he called them Theory Papers—whereby he forecast cultural shifts, currency fluctuations, and educational trends and drew on philosophical tracts, military planning strategy, and ecological theory to predict consumer habits and supply-side shifts during perhaps the most molten time of the twentieth century.[3]

"He leaves you," his wife, Alice, tells me. "Nowadays people think, oh, he's just an old spacy guy. But I've known him since he was eighteen years old and he's always been that way. He goes deep into a thought. Something he's read. He'll go back and reread it while you're here in front of him. Certainly when he was putting together Trader Joe's he'd go off in his brain and put all the things together. Then he'd sit down and write a Theory Paper with his findings."

---

3   The Theory Papers are obsession made literal. They are the mind of a man feverish with groceries. Pawing through them in aggregate evokes those movie montages of equations being written on glass, or crazed men in attic rooms connecting newspaper clippings with yarn. Joe will latch on to a single phrase in an article—perhaps Walter Bagehot's distinction between the "dignified" and "efficient" parts of the British government in a 1982 *Wall Street Journal* article on a new class of attack submarines—and then connect it all, the dignified, the efficient, and the attack class submarines to potential merchandising decisions. A few pages later he will have jumped into the science of semiconductors, linking the role of "impurities" in silicon to his decision to do a short-term promotion on Wishbone salad dressing. The result is delirious, with Joe leading a master associative class, weaving, say, geology, evolutionary biology, and the historiography of science to discuss investment strategies, and always—always—dead-ending these insights into retail grocery: "Cash reserves must be accompanied by a mental organizational posture which is ready with creativity," he writes in an essay comparing the medieval architecture of the Reims Cathedral with its twentieth-century replication in St. John the Divine in New York. "I always think of this when I read about Safeway trying a few experimental 'gourmet' supermarkets. Safeway's resources are so great that it doesn't have to design these stores against limits: there's Safeway steel behind the Gothic façade . . . It is fundamentally dishonest design."

His exodus—first to that cabin in Lake Arrowhead, then afterward via plane—was the product of precisely that type of deliberation. In 1965, one month after the damnation of Pronto Markets, Joe disembarked in St. Barts in the Caribbean with its white-sand beaches and lapis-blue water. The trip was the opposite of panic. It was a move into mental white space. A wealthy friend of his father-in-law had offered the family unfettered access to an isolated beachside house. It sat on a private beach at the far southern tip of the island in a region at that time completely undeveloped. Joe felt it was almost a cosmic opportunity. He had never taken an international flight before, didn't have the money for a vacation, but he knew he needed distance to see things properly. Convenience retailing was dead to him; Southland's entrance made it clear it was an opportunity simply too good for his financial resources. Instead of trying to compete with big players, he decided he needed to move sideways, to create. He had sixteen stores under his control at this point, and their physical frames, leases, and employees represented the only constraints on his reinvention. And so Joe began to study, immersing himself in the history of the industry. The house in St. Barts sat on the edge of a cliff. The veranda was lined with hanging basket chairs. Joe would sit in them all day long, floating in the trade winds, rum and soda in hand, reams of reading material piled around him, and do absolutely nothing but think about the grocery store.

From Ape to Man

In the beginning, there was the general store, center of the retail world. Selling dry goods alongside clothing and hardware, the general store has about the same relationship to the supermarket of today as a baboon does to a human. About two-thirds the size of a convenience store, it was typically staffed by two to four male clerks, working for a dollar a day, dressed in vest and tie in more urban areas—like Kansas City—or just overalls and a hat in a slightly more agricultural one—like Yonkers. The clerks would wait on customers individually from behind a counter. Everything for sale was on display but untouchable: the walls jammed with boxes of clothing, boots arranged soles out, a hanging basin or two. On the counter, big jars filled with Imperial Cookies, coffee, crackers, and tobacco. Next to them, a balance scale ready for measuring grain. Beyond that, the "drug corner," opium, rhubarb, laudanum, turpentine, in little vials. And on the floor, barrels: flour, sugar, molasses, and dried fruit. Fresh produce was scarce and exclusively seasonal.

Perishable food was available, although the specifics were highly regional. The meat market was probably the most common of these purveyors. Meat streaming down from the ceiling, sausages layered thick like beaded curtains against one wall, against another, whole birds—strung by their feet, heads off—in a wide range of sizes. Below the birds, hanging thick and rectangular like wooden shutters, pork ribs, cut in blocks. The counter here would be low and covered in pale hardwood, functional for chopping, unlike the chest-high operation at the general store, and decked out with a decisive-looking cleaver, about the width of a man's face, along with several other slender knives for deboning, trimming, and picking. Next to the knives, little steel enameled pans for the vitals: the eggplant-black kidneys and mollusk-like chicken hearts. The whole place was a mess of flies, buzzing away, always landing on the meat except where ammonia or other preservatives scared them off. And in the center of it all, the butcher: white apron over jacket over tie, probably with a mustache the size, shape, and ferocity of a shoeshine brush. Next to him but lower, the resident cat to kill the menagerie of rodents who coinhabited the place.[4]

These two pillars of grocery life were rounded out by smaller venues depending on the size of the community, perhaps a corner fruit store,

---

4 Rural areas might also have what was called a tree butcher. This gentleman would hang up his meat on the side of a tree to skin and dress it. Customers would come to his temporary location and deal direct.

or maybe a "spa" with a soda fountain and candy in glass jars. Cities often had a public market, stalls of vendors selling to different classes of citizens at different times of day. And, on the periphery in every community, a jumble of horse-and-wagon peddlers rolling around, hawking specialty items like exotic fruits (e.g., bananas), baked goods, and milk courtesy of the milkman.

Bargaining and haggling were common. Prices were typically unmarked, and clerks would almost always charge wealthy customers more for the same item, though usually by giving them access to first-cut produce or fresher meat. With every item located behind the counter, the uneven quality that marked every shipment allowed natural price tiers to develop. The indigent and poor would be allowed to buy the rot everyone else had passed over for pennies.

Once a price was settled on, transactions at the general store were handled almost exclusively on credit. This in turn created a fierce loyalty to particular stores. In rural areas, families might shop daily but settle up only once or twice a year. For farmers, this typically coincided with harvest. Obviously the massive reliance on credit put everyone in a very precarious place. One early supermarket owner remembers his father's general store going bankrupt when the boll weevil destroyed local cotton crops for three years straight. His customers simply couldn't pay him for the food they had already purchased. But this reliance on credit also fostered a natural connection to the agrarian economy. The grocer was linked to the farm by more than mere happenstance of the product he was selling; the farmer's economic success determined his own.

Our current shopping experience arose from this premodern retail soup less from a singular stroke of insight and more in the same halting fashion of biological evolution, several loosely connected shifts coming together to create a real change.

The first of these was technological. Forget the invention of the wheel. When it comes to technology that we assume was omnipresent and everlasting, what about the box? Paperboard, the handmade precursor to cardboard, only began to be used for commerce in 1817. Prior to that, cartons and vessels existed, of course; wine had been stored in amphoras since the Greeks, apples in giant wooden barrels, but these were burdens for trade to overcome: heavy, ungainly, expensive.

Then, in the 1850s, corrugated cardboard: paperboard folded vertically in arches and smooshed between two horizontal planes like a sandwich. The interior curve gives the material a disproportionate strength. And so inside every flap of cardboard is the science of the cathedral, ten thousand vaulted arches distributing compression, allowing pulp to transcend into something lightweight, rigid, and, above all, cheap. It is the stuff of revolutions.

Its first use is in giving structure to gentlemen's hats. Quickly thereafter, it is adopted for shipping boxes, though the first of these requires a clerk to meticulously fold the cardboard around a wooden frame. It is slow and cautious work, item by item, until, in 1890, Robert Gair of Brooklyn begins to manufacture precut, easy-to-fold boxes. The effect on the grocery store cannot be overstated: regular shipments of products suddenly make economic sense. Producer and retailer become connected in a far more consistent manner.

Alongside corrugated, a similar revolution occurs on the level of the individual product. The flat-bottomed paper bag matures into its own during the Civil War when cotton is in short supply. A series of advances in canning allows the preservation of food to move from fragile, expensive glass jars to cheap and hardy tin. Card stock, the thinner brethren of corrugated, used for cereal and cracker boxes, is perfected on the industrial scale. Where containers were once handmade and laborious creations, they can now be pumped from conveyor belts: separate, individuated, and eager to take on whatever identity their labels give them. By 1900, the shift is momentous: packaged food is responsible for one-fifth of all manufacturing in the United States.

Modern life does not exist without this shift. Directly from the box springs the brand.[5] From the brand the advertiser. From the advertiser, perhaps, ourselves. One of Robert Gair's first clients was the National Biscuit Company, aka Nabisco, of RITZ Crackers and Shredded Wheat fame. The impossibly perfect so probably apocryphal story about their early negotiations illustrates the power in packaging: after putting in an order for biscuit boxes, Robert Gair's son tells the befuddled company "You need a name" to put on the otherwise bare box. Nabisco takes him literally and Uneeda Biscuit is born, the name slapped against the cardboard. It becomes a blockbuster. The original packaged-food fad. By 1900, Nabisco is selling more than 100 million packages of Uneeda biscuits a year. A product previously sold only in anonymous bulk

---

5   It's not that the brand is a new thing per se but rather that the creation of the inexpensive individual container—cardboard, tin, or glass—changes its reach in such a profound way that we are forced to think about it differently. Think of how the move from card catalog to Google indexing has changed our relationship with information. The brand itself is ancient, probably blown into existence in 1500 BCE by glassmakers stamping their products with their name. By Roman times we have trademarks, such as the famous Fortis oil lamp, suggesting a container and its contents are sold as a single unit. But for the next two thousand years branding was reserved for luxury products—perfumes, silvers, and high-end liquor—rather than consumer staples. It is not until London in the seventeenth century that the concept of the brand descends to the masses. The discovery of the Welsh coal fields, and subsequent shift from wood to coal furnaces in 1611, rocks the glass industry, transforming the bottle from luxury item to commonplace good. And as soon as these new bottles are available, the brand rushes in to fill their void. It arrives in its modern form—the unique answer to a need that probably cannot be solved—but embodied in the particular historical weirdness that is patent medicines. Suddenly London is awash in a riot of odd names, brazen claims, and distinctive glass vial containers. Stoughton's Drops, Turlington's Original Balsam, potions hawked by folksy quacks on horse-drawn carts. In hindsight, we can see the actual ingredients don't matter a bit, even as they are the exact differentiation being sold. It would be an odd historical riddle, except the entire process is actually just a warm-up act. And so two centuries later, when cardboard, tin, and then plastic helm a strikingly similar, even more rabid democratization of packaging, the brand truly comes into its own, not exactly new, but newly empowered.

is differentiated by nothing more than a throwaway name. Nothing on the shelf of the grocery store will ever look the same.

All these individually wrapped products beget something even more precious to us. Choice. As synonym for control. In a world without boxes lit with insignias, colors, and slogans, there is little need for a consumer to touch anything. It's all the same. But suddenly, with cardboard boxes flying off the factory line, the greedy tentacles of customer demand are excited; they head to the general store and request particular products. They grow suspicious of the clerk behind the counter: Is he substituting, swindling, or otherwise shortchanging us? This suspicion is then weaponized by manufacturers. Suddenly America is awash in advertising lauding the package as proxy for security, as barrier against tampering or fraud. Buying Kellogg's replaces buying cereal, Crisco comes for lard, and Pepsodent captures toothpaste as consumers are urged to seek out brands they can trust.

The result, in 1916, is the next lurch toward the grocery store of today. Self-service. Clarence Saunders, a classic American eccentric self-taught businessman and loudmouth southern gentleman, alternately described as "one of the most remarkable men of his generation" and "essentially a four-year-old child playing at things," designs a store where customers can touch the merchandise themselves. Retail operators across the nation declare his experiment lunacy. But it turns out this is the type of apostasy Americans love.

Born a reedy, intense, and dirt-poor country boy in Amherst County, Virginia, Saunders spends his first few years in the tobacco fields and decides that a life there is intolerable. His salvation is groceries. At the age of fourteen, he drops out of school to begin an apprenticeship: room and board and a $1 per week salary to stock the shelves at a local general store. Soon he graduates into the role of a "drummer," something of a proto–retail consultant, calling on rural stores on behalf of wholesalers and offering them advice on how to stock their merchandise. In the process, in and out of dozens of stores, he becomes obsessed with efficiency. The general stores he sees are sluggish, backward affairs: the food is stocked haphazardly and a single clerk is often mobbed by dozens of women all trying to put in orders at once.

He decides he can improve on this.

In particular, Saunders is inspired by a new type of novelty restaurant called the "cafeteria." If we want to think about the introduction of the supermarket as a birth, the cafeteria was foreplay. During the World's Columbian Exposition in Chicago in 1893, John Kruger builds a temporary American "smorgasbord" restaurant where patrons can peruse a series of different options. In 1898, Childs Restaurant in New York riffs on this structure, giving each customer a tray and asking them to walk single file down a line selecting their food from various steaming pans. The result is a sensation that sweeps across the country. Career male waiters in their starched white uniforms are out, their job now easily done by just one or two perky young women.

In Saunders's vision, the grocery store could become an even more fully realized version of this setup. Customers would enter single file, pick up a basket, shuffle through a turnstile, and then head down a winding one-way route that would guide them past every item in the store, anticipating the hell of today's Ikea by about fifty years. The path they were forced onto would pass only heavily branded prepackaged goods—items that could speak for themselves and didn't need a clerk to recommend them—which customers could size up, fondle, select, and replace to their heart's content. Finally, after winding through the store, the line would empty out at a bank of checkout counters where the customer could choose the shortest line and pay.

It was an inverted assembly line with the customer as belt.

And like the assembly line, it would reduce labor costs, cutting overall staff, and allow the owner to hire largely unskilled workers to do little more then fill shelves. One day, watching beady-eyed piglets charge a trough, Saunders decides the piggies are laughably similar to customers charging an overwhelmed clerk. In honor of all his piggy little customers, he names his new store the Piggly Wiggly.

In 1916, just three years after Henry Ford introduces his more famous assembly line, Saunders begins to turn this vision into reality. He designs the store himself, right down to the fixtures. He writes the advertising copy in the most flamboyant style. At the grand opening, he hands roses to all the women with red hair.

At the time, loss from theft was almost 6 percent, so unlike conventional markets of the era, Saunders decides to separate entry and exit points. Pictures of the first Piggly Wiggly are filled with obtrusive steel fencing surrounding the turnstiles, evoking a prison yard rather than food mart, preventing shoppers from nabbing an item and running. The entire effect creates the modern retail dynamic. Passing through the turnstile, the customer enters an unconscious bargain: you are invited in to frolic among the abundance, but expected to pay in the end.

Shopping is suddenly a far more personal act. It is an exercise in selection, an opportunity to demonstrate the skill of choice. For the first time, customers can use all this conscious sifting as a vessel for meaning: saving money becomes an act of loyalty for family, picky acquisition a sign of concern for health, and the decision to buy your child a more expensive but longed-for item an act of love. And, of course, as reward for undertaking this new effort, we get the impulsive treat. Perhaps a plucked grape snuck on the way through produce, or a new-fangled chocolate bar studded with freeze-dried raspberries nabbed at checkout. A moment to puncture all that arduous judgment with a sneaky little delight.

By 1930, there are more than 2,500 Piggly Wigglys stretching across the land, and Saunders is a millionaire several times over. As he begins building a gargantuan pink marble mansion for himself in downtown Memphis, replete with an indoor swimming pool, ballroom, bowling alley, and pipe organ, the story of the grocery store leaves him to take one final leap. It takes everything Saunders uncovered about personal choice, and blows it out in that perfectly American fashion where bigger is better and biggest is best of all.

This is the supermarket. It comes to lifelong grocer Michael Cullen as if in a dream, and then grips his brain like an obsession. Cullen is working at the then midsized chain Kroger, managing a fleet of stores in southern Illinois. Like Clarence Saunders, Cullen is a lifer. Born in Newark, the child of Irish immigrants, he saw the general store as one of his few options and enlisted in grocery at eighteen. In 1929, after serving more than thirty years in the industry, working his way up from clerk to central manager, he is seized by a new vision.

His plan was as simple as it was inelegant. Take Clarence Saunders's self-service and expand. Cullen wanted to build stores that were "monstrous in size," locate them just off the downtown, and then use the power of volume to sell goods cheaper than customers had ever seen before—cheaper than they could even conceive as possible—to create a buying frenzy.

"I would be the 'miracle man' of the grocery business," he prophesized before opening a single store. "The public would not, and could not believe their eyes. Week days would be Saturdays—rainy days would be sunny days, and then when the great crowd of American people came to buy all those low-priced and 5% items, I would have them surrounded with 15%, 20% and in some cases, 25% items. In other words, I could afford to sell a can of Milk at cost if I could sell a can of Peas and make 2¢, and so on all through the grocery line."

This is the blueprint.

He drafts a letter to the regional vice president of Kroger, of almost fantastical specificity, laying out the cost of construction, the number, type, sex, and salary of his employees, the precise number of items the store would sell, along with projected profits and details for expansion up to a fifth store. All while displaying the deep self-righteous confidence of the messianic capitalist: "Can you imagine how the public would respond to a store of this kind?" he asks the vice president. "It would be a riot. I would have to call out the police and let the public in so many at a time. I would lead the public out of the high priced houses of bondage into the low prices of the house of the promised land."

He ended the letter with a call to action. He'd "never been so confident in my life," he crows. "This will be the biggest money maker you have ever invested yourself in. . . . What is your verdict?"

The verdict from Kroger was to reject him.

And so he did it himself. When his request for a meeting was denied, Cullen resigned his position and moved back east. In just a few months, August 1930, he opened the first King Kullen grocery store at 171st Street and Jamaica Avenue in Queens. His tagline: "King Kullen, the world's greatest price wrecker." To announce the store he took out a gargantuan advertisement—a four-sheet spread that did little more than list prices up and down the page.

His success was immediate and as monstrous as his stores. Every prediction rang true. Nobody had ever seen anything like it. Thousands lined up for the cheap prices. Newspapers covered the openings like sporting events. Housewives reported feeling faint, dizzy, and flushed from the options. Others worried aloud about getting lost inside the expanse. In just two years, Cullen had opened stores in seven more markets. By 1936, he had doubled that number, and was preparing to expand nationally, when he suddenly dropped dead at the age of fifty-two.

Imitators ensured his idea lived on. They came with names like Big Bear, Giant Tiger, Bull Market, Great Leopard, announcing their size and price-chopping ferocity with a zoological zeal that puzzles the modern ear. These stores took Cullen's insight and continued to inflate. Adding in-store mascots and costumes, parades and pullout advertisements, each trying to pile up merchandise into ever higher displays of abundance. It was the supermarket as circus, and customers drove from fifty miles away just to tour these stores like an attraction.[6]

---

6 Shopping sociologist extraordinaire Rachel Bowlby refers to the circus-like atmosphere in the early supermarkets as a "happy infantilization," where housewives are encouraged to regress. And again, as with Clarence Saunders and his turnstiles, there is something here where the first appearance contains the essential seeds. Only today in our

The notion, unchanged, would dominate the industry until the end of the century. Where there was exactly one such store in 1930, a spot-check in 1934 found ninety-four supermarket-style stores already operating. Just two years later, a similar survey found that number had skyrocketed to 1,200 supermarkets. By 1965, every grocery store was a supermarket. Michael Cullen found the essential formula, the only issue left was to see how far you could push it.

"Mass! Mass! That's the key idea and we must never lose sight of it," I. M. Baker explains in a trade magazine in 1941. "We must display more . . . Here is plenty of me take all you want now." And so mass it was. Cullen's 1930 store that housewives worried about getting lost in was just 6,000 square feet. By 1940, the average store had ballooned to 9,000 square feet. By the end of the 1950s, that average had doubled again. Today a Costco or Walmart can easily reach 200,000 square feet, a retail environment that could no doubt cause genuine physiological harm to a housewife from the 1930s suddenly transported to its looming halls.

Along the way, there were minor tweaks. Sylvan Goldman, an Oklahoma City grocer, introduced the shopping cart in 1937. He noticed that customers wanted to buy more but got physically tired holding the items in their basket. The idea was by no means a sure thing; customers ignored the carts until Goldman hired shills to push them around. Plus he had to make them foldable, lest you have a separate parking lot entirely for carts. And yet it worked. By 1952, you had the Nest Cart Junior, a miniature version, which allowed a child to push and place items inside while Momma did the real shopping above.

These changes were absorbed gradually by the American psyche,

---

gleaming superstores, all universally decked with a paradise of produce and a thousand signs trumpeting the purity of our ingredients, we don't want to regress into infants in the grocery store so much as we want to fall back even further—into a pristine Eden, a chemical-free world uncorrupted by complication and anxiety.

but their effect was positively dissociative to the outsider. At the 1956 International Food Congress in Rome—one year before Joe Coulombe would open Pronto Markets—the USDA set up an "American Way exhibit." It featured the first fully stocked supermarket outside of the United States. This was a modest staging, designed more for easy assembly and dismantling. It held a mere 2,500 brands, a few packaged meats in a lone refrigerated case, and a small selection of prepared food. When the exhibit opened, and crowds finally entered, the Italian women went berserk. One notable enthusiast began running up and down the aisles shouting, "It must be heaven . . . There are mountains of food!" Press reports describe others as standing "stunned," "goggle eyed," "bewildered," and "shrieking with surprise and envy."

This was not media hype. Pope Pius XII himself weighed in, announcing his blessing from the Holy See. A few year later, when Khrushchev toured Washington, D.C., in 1959, the supermarket brought a temporary détente to the Cold War. As the Soviet premier scanned the store, he erupted with spontaneous praise: "I want to greet the manager of this supermarket. I am truly filled with admiration over what I see."[7]

Despite the astonishment of the rest of the world, for Americans the grocery store had already become routine. It would continue reliably expanding—advances in preservation, refrigeration, and packaging al-

---

7 Later, when Boris Yeltsin made an unscheduled stop at a Randalls supermarket in Houston, Texas, during a tour of the Johnson Space Center in 1989, the experience was even more profound. "When I saw those shelves crammed with hundreds, thousands of cans, cartons and goods of every possible sort, I felt quite frankly sick with despair for the Soviet people." He told his advisors that if the Russian people ever saw this, "there would be a revolution." The raw shock in these remarks underscores the very real way that grocery—along with the World War II spending boom, unions, and the G.I. Bill—was directly causal to the rise of the American middle class. The shift in percent income from food to the other trappings of American life—from ride-on mowers to down payments on homeownership—is simply too powerful to ignore. Imagine circa 2020 and our wealth-divide populism, the authentic middle class that might develop if a sector of the economy where we spend 30 to 40 percent of our income evaporated away over a few decades. Oh, the things we'd do.

lowing ever more products to hit the shelves—but neither size nor cheap prices were novelties at this point. The hysteria had subsided and was replaced by good old-fashioned presumption. By 1965—as Joe floated in St. Barts, meditating on the future of selling food—the grocery store had settled into a plateau. It would continue to grind forth, inching ever bigger and ever cheaper each year, but by this point it was no longer a sensation, simply an institution.

Cult of the Mainstream

If you've been inside one, you know the store Joe would go on to create is not the largest, nor the cheapest. It was not the first at anything in particular, nor did it punctuate the equilibrium of the grocery world like Michael Cullen's bomb. It did not pioneer a new technology or revolutionize the buying experience in any tangible way as Clarence Saunders did. It does not have the most luxurious, sustainable, ethical, or health-conscious food out there. In all those attributes it is strictly unremarkable.

Instead it did something both more mystical and impressive. In an industry with innovations that all look and feel banal because they tinker with superficials, Joe advanced by looking deeper. In the process, he changed the fundamentals of the game. Joe interrogated the retailer–shopper relationship; he rethought what it meant to sell food—the core responsibilities of retailer, the latent desires of the customer—peeling back the surface of the buying experience like it was a scalp to reveal the substrate below. As many have remarked, he created a cult. But it is a cult that would go on to take over the mainstream. Like it or not, shop there or not, you as an American in 2020 are probably a member of that cult: either in the specific sense that you are the precise demographic Joe targeted way back then—the overeducated, underpaid, and inquisitive; the customer who understands and cares for the world foremost by understanding and caring for themselves—or in the general sense that you are a consumer who flourishes from demographic targeting, expressing yourself through your purchases, loyalties, and decisions. What Joe did—was one of the first to do, if not the first—was to create a store that provides products that reflect an identity, that exist in opposition to some generally homogenized mainstream. In the process, by necessity, he commodified individuality itself. He learned to sell you you. If you were the precise you he was after.

The results speak for themselves. As of this writing, Trader Joe's has the single highest sales per square foot of any retail grocery chain, basically doubling its nearest competitor, Whole Foods. When it comes to sales per foot for chains in San Francisco, there is the gleaming white shrine of the Apple Store, our technological pusher, selling items that cost thousands of dollars and fit in our pockets; there is Tiffany selling literal jewels to newlyweds; and then there is Trader Joe's, a grocery store. It does that business while absolutely dominating rankings for customer satisfaction and employee well-being. It is consistently listed as one of Glassdoor and *Fortune*'s 100 Best Companies to Work For. For the entire twenty-five years of Joe's term, net worth grew at 26 percent per year every year, a compound growth of baffling, almost Madoffian consistency. To say its customers are devoted is a misleading understatement. Trader Joe's customers are evangelical. The chain has inspired no fewer than three *lines* of independent, unaffiliated cookbooks with recipes that use ingredients exclusively sourced from its stores. When it declined to open a store in Vancouver, a thriving import-export business known as Pirate Joe's opened in response, sneaking "authentic Trader Joe's" products across the border to sell. Along the way, Trader Joe's invented modern consumer staples like almond butter and sold excellent Brie from France cheaper than Velveeta in America without losing money per sale. And it did all this with essentially no press outreach, shunning the mainstream media requests for access, and spending a fraction of what its competitors did on advertising.

If that reads like PR flack, I want to disclose fully that I am, and have always been, something of a Trader Joe's agnostic. I shop at the Trader Joe's near my house. Occasionally. And when I do, I am always sort of mystified and troubled by its appeal. The checkout line at the downtown Brooklyn location nearest me, a cavernous store in the frame of an old Federal Revival bank, often wraps completely around the building. That is the entire perimeter and down the frozen aisle, perhaps five hundred feet in total, its terminus swinging back around to the cash registers ouroboros-style so that when you find the end, demarcated by a cheery dude holding a pole that should say, *This Is the End*, and actually get on it, you can wave goodbye to those lucky folks exiting to pay; and while it moves fairly swiftly, there is no rational comparison to the wait time at any other grocery store in the area much less the ones I grew up with. But forget the line. The produce is hit-or-miss.[8] I have been burned by the pre-bagged onions so many times I won't consider them. And the perishables, meat and veg, are typically, defiantly, encased in the type of excessive packaging that elicited picket lines at McDonald's during the 1980s. The number of plastic clamshell containers almost feels nostalgic. Instead of fresh food, the vast majority of the baskets seem to be filled with the chain's endless frozen options—aka TV dinners—while the shoppers attached to those baskets gloat about the lack of "artificial" ingredients in said TV dinners, ignoring the evident heavy processing, gargantuan quantities of salt, or gelatinous meats. Two different food safety experts I spoke with told me the unofficial FDA nickname for the chain is Recall Joe's. And while the FDA won't comment on that specifically, it's clear from a survey of its publicly available list of food recalls that when it comes to quality assurance, the chain is anything but above average. So I shop there, yes. But I'm not here to exalt the experience.

Instead I came to focus on Trader Joe's honestly. I heard too many

---

8   For my quick take on this hit or miss produce, see the endnote on page 288.

people who worked in retail grocery tell me they admired the chain and didn't fully understand it. Too many people who told me it existed in a class by itself. Manufacturers who wished they did business with the chain but couldn't figure out how to get inside its stores. Consultants who pitched themselves almost exclusively by knowing "Trader Joe's secrets." Grocery managers who were envious of the loyalty, quality, and unabashed enthusiasm the chain elicits. And when I coupled those anecdotes with research and started digging into the history of the grocery store, Joe stood out as a natural heir to Michael Cullen. He picked up the grocery flag from merely large sizes and low prices and marched it forward, planting it back down firmly in our hearts.

A Black Sheep Founder

When Joe founded the Pronto Markets in 1957 he knew nothing about the grocery industry. He was twenty-seven years old and had never taken a course in retail, nor did he have any particular interest in food. He had never pulled a register, waited on a customer, or filled out a purchase order for a wholesaler.

Which makes this a very atypical grocery story. The majority of retail grocery chains in this country, now as then, are legacy affairs: family businesses that follow the prototypically American progression from heartwarming, bootstrapping, backstabbing founder to eager scientific expansion in the immediate offspring to a sluggish, almost hostile complacency in the third and fourth generations.[9] Joe didn't come

---

9 To dwell for a moment, because it is salient: in Joe's day, grocery was a true path for upward mobility. The vast majority of the founders of America's dominant retail chains started out as clerks themselves, working those sixteen-hour days, sweeping the floor, and chiseling dried fruit out of barrels. Similarly, in the current era, during my interviews I repeatedly talked with older employees—from store managers to central executives— who came up through the ranks without anything more than a high school diploma and a long tenure. However, simultaneously and structurally, ownership of chains through

to food from family. He came by rebellion, the black sheep son of a black sheep father in a tribe of restless inventors and engineers.

Born June 3, 1930, just a few weeks before Michael Cullen cut the ribbon on that first King Kullen, Joe Coulombe grew up in a small house in Del Mar, California, that his father built. His father, an East Coast engineer, had fled west a few years earlier to abandon the family profession and pursue his dream of being a rancher. There, in rapid succession, he fell in love with a beautiful but dirt-poor Arizona schoolteacher, failed completely as a rancher—with an unquestionable assist from the Great Depression—and used the last of his savings to buy a courtyard apartment complex in San Diego for the family to manage.

Joe came of age here. Sweeping out the garden. Fixing broken screens. Chasing down escaped cats. There were twenty-one units and so every week through high school, Joe lugged twenty-one barrels of trash to the street. In an alternate world, this could have been his life. But at

---

the fat middle of the twentieth century tended to be incredibly dynastic: tightly controlled by the founder's family, passed down from father to son. This created a situation where the last generations of men (and until recently it was almost exclusively men) have been raised on the mythos of a founder without grappling with the context of that founder's struggle. They are by almost universal acclaim arrogant, bullheaded, increasingly angry owners, slowly getting eaten alive by changing market factors that they are simply unwilling or unable to address. There are exceptions—the Wegmans, the Heinens, the H-E-Bs—but I'd posit they exist to prove this rule, not complicate it. The margins in grocery might be tight—less than 1.5 percent of gross profit in many cases—but the money generated has been so reliable, their role in the local community so prominent, and their vast number of employees per store so feudal and dependent, that flexibility, self-evaluation, and innovation simply haven't been selected for in regional chain ownership. And the reason this is salient is it (proximally) explains no small amount of Joe's success, and (distally) is a very real reason behind the massive consolidation and gobbling up of regional chains by private equity and vulture capitalists in the last fifteen years that has taken an already lean industry and thinned it to the bone.

seventeen, his grandfather died and suddenly, despite the Depression, despite the ruination of ranching, Joe is told there is money to go to college. On a whim, he heads down to the local library to take the entrance exam for Stanford University, and on that whim gets in.

And so, in 1948, Joe found himself in Palo Alto, alone for the first time in his life. It was an upsetting transition. He made a lanky, awkward freshman. His schoolteacher mother's insistence on enrolling him in kindergarten a year early ensured he would always be the youngest in every class. "Getting along with the girls, all of who were older than me, got me fed up," he tells me. Polite, shy, and ignored, Joe dropped out of Stanford as quickly and impulsively as he had enrolled. Within the month, he decided to join the air force.

"It was the best thing I ever did in my life," he says with a hush.

This was the year Truman integrated the air force. Joe arrived in San Antonio and stepped off into a new world. A bus of nervous African American men unloaded next to him. Joe introduced himself. "And then I got to know the Texas hillbillies, and the kids from West Virginia whose diet was so poor they broke their bones in basic training, and the Hispanics from back home." Lackland, just outside of San Antonio, was true cowboy country. Men wore spurs on their boots walking down the street and didn't make much eye contact with the outsiders. But on base, everyone was so new and raw, eager and afraid, that otherwise impossible friendships formed by default.

"I wouldn't call it an awakening," he says. "But there is a lot to learn in this world—and I began to understand that."

He was active duty, but after basic training got weekends off. While others would stay on base, drifting in and out of consciousness in the San Antonio heat, Joe would hitchhike. "I realized I could just step off base in uniform and I'd be picked up." He crisscrossed the country, going to Michigan to see the football games, Cincinnati to see the opera for the first time. When it came time for his two-week furlough, he made it all the way to Manhattan. "I saw every damn play in town. I went to the old Met twice to see the tenors. They'd let you in for two dollars if you were enlisted." Then he went down to Washington, D.C., to see the monuments, hitchhiking all the way.

This was an odd gestational moment for travel. Just a generation earlier, to visit his mother's family in Arizona, Joe's parents drove the Borderland Highway, part of the Old Southern Trunkline, linking Florida and San Diego. The Borderland was a single-lane gravel road built in parts by prisoners with pickaxes and shovels. The southwestern stretch in particular was marked with frequent "low spots," where mountain rains would collect with standing water, rendering them impassable at any speed faster than a stroll. In one stretch, a surveyor counted five of these low spots per mile. Winter tires didn't exist, which meant mountain snow would leave cars sliding off the road like sleds. Fuel stations were scarce, and on these trips gasoline was generally bought out of a barrel at the local hardware store. Travel by automobile at this time was an enormously exciting, often dangerous luxury that bore far more in common with the stagecoach era than our current system.

By the late 1940s, when Joe was hitchhiking out of Lackland, the roads had been paved, 100,000 gas stations had been built in just a few rushed years, but car travel was still more novelty than routine. So much has been written on the physical effect of the automobile on how we get our food—the suburbanization of the supermarket, the drive-in fast food, the ability to do a week's worth of shopping in a single day. But Joe confronted the automobile and saw something different. Alongside the remaking of our roads, towns, and markets, the automobile was remaking our minds. The great naturalist Aldo Leopold once said, "Game is a phenomenon of the edge," by which he meant that to spot wildlife you should sit at the boundary between two habitats, where the forest meets the meadow, or the mountain opens onto a stream. So it is with insights: they exist in moments of cultural contrast, and Joe traveling the country by car in the 1940s was able to see clearly one of the defining insights of his career. Travel was happening in an entirely new way, and this would fundamentally change the way people saw the world, what they expected from their lives, and of course, what they'd want for dinner.

After Lackland, Joe returns to Stanford, meets his wife, and graduates on to business school, selling Kirby vacuums door-to-door to pay his way. Soon his intellect is noticed, and upon graduation Joe is snapped up by the giant Rexall Drug Company, owner of the Owl Drug chain.

Owl was failing and Rexall wanted the young MBA to find out why. When Joe unearths 7-Eleven in Texas as his answer, Rexall's response is to ask him to start an imitation chain in California. This strikes Joe as madness—he knows nothing about retail—but nevertheless Rexall corporate selects six failing Owl drugstores and declares they will form the basis of this new chain. Joe is named president, and Pronto Markets of the red-checkered shirts is born.

His first act as president is to find what he thinks is the best-run grocer in town and apprentice himself, offering to work free on weekends in exchange for a half hour of the owner's time after each shift. The owner is giddy—a Stanford grad mopping his floors!—and so for months, Joe spends his weekends slicing boxes and stocking shelves, then heads to the back office with notebook and pen, asking every simple question that comes to mind.

Later he would call it the best way to get an education. One observer tells me, "That grocer got a smart young kid to work with him for a few months. Joe got a billion-dollar business." But Joe's own personal takeaway: he doesn't really like the grocery world. His wife, Alice, tells me, "Grocery is a very conservative culture. And Joe didn't belong. Or attempt to belong. Early on we went to a single grocery industry convention. Then we decided never to go again . . . In hindsight, we were lucky. It meant we kept our own path."

The result became a whole family adventure.

After school, everyone piled in the Ford station wagon and counted houses. Joe and Alice up front, the two kids in back. Each was assigned a quadrant of the block and impressed into service as demographers. "This was before our youngest daughter, Madeline," Alice says. "Which was really important because everybody gets a window and nobody fights. Then we would drive around and count." Did the houses have bicycles laid out on the lawn? Was there a boat in the driveway? What were the make, model, and age of the cars? Back in his home office, Joe had maps with colored pins and different zones. He would stay up late quantifying Southern California while Alice sat on the living room floor, matching invoice and delivery slips from each of the Pronto stores.

"Our kids saw so many miles," Alice continues. "We'd have them scout rival drugstores. We'd tell them they could choose one thing for themselves. Which made them agents. Nobody pays attention like a child on a mission." And every Friday, the family would time these trips to end outside of Disneyland. "That was when the fireworks went off," Joe explains. "We never went in. We didn't have the money to do that. But we always watched them anyway and it never felt like deprivation."

During this time, Joe makes two decisions that puts Pronto at odds with both 7-Eleven and the rest of the grocery world.

First, he springs for good help.

"Having seen the low-quality people in 7-Eleven, I felt life's too short," he tells me. He breaks down the local union contract for grocery workers and decides Pronto will pay employees $7,000 per year for a forty-eight-hour workweek, the precise union equivalent including overtime. It just so happens that $7,000 matches the median family income in California at the time. Joe likes the coincidence and decides to peg Pronto salary increases to median family income wherever it goes.

"What I did not foresee was that all these women would go to work," he says.

In 1957, America was overwhelmingly a country with one breadwinner per family and so median *family* income essentially was median *employee* income. But within ten years, as women poured into the workforce, that calculation is toast. Joe, stubbornly clinging to his decision to pay individual employees family income, now had access to a far higher class of worker.

The second decision is an even greater break with tradition. He decides that nothing in the actual store is essential. Rather than worry about which items his customers expected, he becomes obsessed with products that have a high value relative to size.

"Joe would measure every product with a ruler and calculate price per cubic inch," an early employee explains. "It didn't mean we wouldn't carry something big like paper towels, we'd just give them much less room." It is the advent of scientific retailing and Joe decides to follow the logic wherever it leads. The store goes heavy into items like magazines, phonographs, and hard liquor. L'eggs hosiery sold from a vertical spinning rack that occupied less than one square foot of floor space becomes his Platonic ideal. Weird items like ammo become big winners.

"We were doing 2 percent of sales in bullets each month," the same employee explains. "Little boxes, incredibly easy to handle . . . It was only when Bobby Kennedy got assassinated and they became so highly regulated that we dropped them, what with all the new forms to fill out."

In 1962, Justin Dart, the owner of Rexall, becomes infatuated with Tupperware and, over the unanimous objections of his board, decides to liquidate his entire empire so he can buy in early. This works out brilliantly for him—in part because he is forced to partner with several oil refineries needed to make all the plastic. It also gives Joe an opportunity. Amid the fire sale at Rexall, the tiny Pronto operation is an afterthought. Joe sells his house, takes the entirety of his family's modest savings, walks down to the bank, and on his personal signature borrows the rest of the money needed to buy the Pronto chain for himself. And so this odd hodgepodge of bullets, hosiery, ice cream, and booze—staffed with the most expensive employees in grocery history—plows forth, doing ever-growing business, only now with Joe alone at the helm.

Then One Day an Egg Guy Walks in the Door

As a rule, grocery stores are a mess of deliveries, and someone is always calling. Delivery trucks dropping off a half pallet, antsy reps stopping by to make sure their product is looking swell, drummers with samples trying to hook a new sale. They come at all times, always with a form or two. But in the 1960s, despite their haphazard influx, almost all these visitors are connected to the same place.

It's hard to overstate the importance of wholesalers in this era. When I speak to early employees of either Pronto Markets or Trader Joe's, they all, without exception, refer to the stores by number. That is, not by the address or cross street, or with a reference to the manager or city they are located in, but by the two-to-four-digit serial number arbitrarily assigned to them by Certified Grocers, their wholesaler at the time. Thus the first Trader Joe's is called #51, simply because its number on the Certified billing sheet was 3851.

"Certified was everything," an employee of that store tells me. And not just for Joe but for all grocers. "All our product came from Certified. Every single item. If you wanted to put in an order for Coca-Cola, Welch's, you name it, the managers would open the Certified book and place the order." In other words, you could mess with the mix of products, as Joe was beginning to do, but the origins of those products almost all came from a single choke point.

Eggs were an exception to this rule. Just as Joe had a personal relationship with Adohr dairy, he used an egg broker to source his eggs locally. And in the exception came the insight.

"So this egg guy walks in and wants to know if I'm interested in extra-large AAA eggs," Joe tells me. "He explains every grocer in Southern California is selling large AA eggs, but that he can sell me extra-large AAA eggs at an even cheaper price . . . This makes no sense!" Extra-large eggs were by state regulation required to be 12 percent bigger by weight, and thus a superior product being sold for less money. But rather than run toward them, his competitors were all staying away.

The egg broker couldn't unload them for his life. And he explains it to Joe. The reason most stores don't carry AAA eggs is there aren't enough of them. It takes a big bird to lay an extra-large egg. These are the older hens. And because they are older they die off in the summer heat. "It makes for a real discontinuous product," he said.

A real discontinuous product.

The idea hung in the air between them and then the entire grocery world opened before Joe's eyes. "This egg guy shook me awake," Joe says. A discontinuous supply might not seem like much of a knock from a consumer standpoint, but the mentality of the supermarket manager simply couldn't handle it. The supermarket was based—and still is based—on endless abundance. On mechanical regularity. On the commodity and its consistency. "Safeway wouldn't touch extra-large eggs," Joe says. "They were afraid to run an advertisement around them because they might sell out and disappoint a customer."

This meeting with the egg guy would become one of Joe's foundations. "We went with the extra-large eggs," he says. "And it set me wondering whether there weren't other discontinuities out there in the supply chain. It taught me that if you learned about an area deep enough, you could find deals someone else had overlooked."

When we first speak, he is eighty-six, and it is the morning after the election of Donald J. Trump.[10] Joe has stayed up until three a.m. the

---

10 Joe voted for Gary Johnson, the third-party Libertarian candidate, a fact he volunteers freely. This was not, I think, a protest vote. Joe's politics were forged over four decades of close study and then exploitation of government regulations. He took glee in understanding the laws better than anyone else and then using them to get systematic advantages over his competitors. To call it a cat and mouse game would be correct, though I think the usual quip of government regulator cats chasing gamely after nimble mice they rarely catch is inverted here; the more accurate, realistic, and morbid one is where Joe is the curious, intent eyes of the cat, standing over a mouse he is batting around. There was an asymmetry in intelligence. And Joe took pleasure in picking apart regulations to

night before watching the returns, and is shuffling around his living room in the brightest sea-blue pants I have ever seen, so chromatically saturated they almost glow. There is a balcony behind him, and the Southern California morning light pours in, washing over us. I'm worried about his recall, of events, people, and decisions thirty to forty years in the past. But this fear is quickly dismissed. His memory is startling and incantatory: demonstrating the quirks and physical fidgets of former employees, describing their wives and mistresses, the makes and models of the cars those wives and mistresses drove, all these odd personal details presented without judgment or complaint. "Change is always happening," he says when I ask him about the election. "It is happening now." And instead of sounding cliché or simplistic, it echoes his presentation of those odd personal details: a detachment that is the very opposite of disconnection, the active choice of a man who takes great pleasure in pure observation.

"When I was founding Trader Joe's," he tells me, "I watched everything. I'd steal from anyone . . . The supermarket became my window to understand our world." And with that we begin discussing what he saw and how it shaped the chain he built.

Grocery as Divination

Sitting on that veranda in St. Barts, thinking about how to pivot his Pronto Markets to survive Southland, Joe saw three big things.

---

create opportunities his competitors couldn't understand or follow. Food, beverage, and agricultural laws—especially on the state level—are so unrelentingly perverse, so transparently the result of specific lobbying interests, that they are one of the few areas of law that routinely unite big-government liberals and fiscal conservatives in mutual outrage. Joe's political consciousness was raised on his study of these laws. "We found a loophole, and by god, we drove a truck through it," he told me about California liquor licenses once, and indeed his greatest pleasure seems to come from finding these "loopholes" and then pulling the proverbial pants down on the entrenched interests who have been benefiting from their artificially raised prices.

The first came from an article in the *Wall Street Journal*. He cannot remember when he first read it, but in St. Barts the idea would not leave him alone: "In 1932, only 2 percent of the people qualified to go to college actually went. In 1964 that number had jumped to 60 percent," he tells me. This was change. The extreme growth in college enrollment was largely the work of the G.I. Bill of Rights, guaranteeing returning veterans—first from the Second World War, then Korea—a college education. And Joe realized the reason he kept coming back to the article was the wave hadn't crested. The war in Vietnam meant the G.I. Bill was about to hit a third generation.

"All these college graduates," he says. "I just thought they might want something different to eat."

When I ask him to elaborate, his wife, shuffling around in the background, pipes in, "When I went to college, I learned where to look things up. I learned how to talk about the world. It opens you." Beyond additional income or the specific details in a course of study, college broadened people in the same way Joe got stretched at Lackland: an awareness of just how much was out there. "Trader Joe's was designed for people who had grown up simply like we had, but who had been exposed to new things. Who could speak a new lingo," Alice says. "People who had gotten an awareness of their intelligence."

"Better educated, not more intelligent," Joe grunts. "They weren't any smarter, but college gave them a different vocabulary." And he decided he was going to give them a chance to flex it while they shopped.

The second thing Joe saw was in the air. Pan Am had just placed an order for twenty-five airplanes of a radically new design. The Boeing 747, the first "jumbo" jet, would take four years and the labor of fifty thousand mechanics to get off the ground. And while much of the world followed its progress, marveling at the engineering required to get a tube of steel the size of Lady Liberty aloft, Joe read about the 747's development and saw the future of grocery.

In 1937, the average airplane carried only 6.5 passengers. The 747 could hold nearly 500. That was two and half times more than its immediate predecessor, the 707, but requiring only a slight increase in crew. To Joe all of this was revolutionary.

The first insight Joe had was about the balance sheet. By keeping the number of crew stable relative to the expense of the new plane, the airline had figured out how to increase investment per employee while expanding their service. The more Joe thought about this, the more he saw it as a better articulation of his current strategy. At Pronto, he already had the highest-paid employees; rather than grow his business by diluting that talent pool by, say, increasing floor space or opening tons of new sites, he decided he wanted to grow in a way that maximized that investment. Things like liquor licenses—which at the time cost almost as much individually as the start-up cost for an entire store—were perfect. Each one he snapped up would increase his investment per employee. It would be a grocery store that operated on the financial principles of the airplane.

But that epiphany obscured a greater profundity. The 747 would finally pay off the promise of air travel. In 1937, a flight from New York to Los Angeles took over eighteen hours and included three stops midway. This occurred in a cabin with no pressurization, no climate control, and that accordingly could not travel at altitude to avoid turbulence. And for the pleasure you would pay almost $4,000 in today's dollars, more than most people earned in a month. Air travel was uncomfortable, arduous, and for the elite.

And then, in a blink, it wasn't.

In St. Barts, Joe realized the 747 would be the turning point. And he was right. At that time, in 1965, over 80 percent of Americans had still not set foot on a plane. Within a year, the 747 had cut the cost of flying in half and the skies were democratized. The real cost of flying to

Europe fell to one-fifteenth of what it had been a decade earlier. Like the G.I. Bill, Joe saw this new era of frequent low-cost air travel as a crucible forming a new consumer. Not a smarter one but one whose mind had been awakened to new experiences. Who would come back from those trips wanting to purchase new items. After all, true to the cliché, travel was another form of education.

His final observation was self-expression. In his period of study, Joe had become engrossed in the history of television, radio, and advertising. "In 1966, I guessed that network television with its 95 percent–plus audience share just couldn't go any further," he explains. "America at that time was frighteningly homogenous and I didn't see it lasting." Ever since the advent of mass broadcast, the grocery store had relied on manufacturers to advertise their products. The process was extremely effective, with major shows—from radio's *Amos 'n' Andy* to television's *I Love Lucy*—creating a dominant market share for whatever sponsor graced their intro. But this setup placed the retailer in a passive place. The store itself was brand organized rather than product organized— little more than a landlord leasing shelving space—all of which made it absolutely unnecessary for anyone in the store to develop knowledge about the food they were selling. Instead they had to maintain relationships with manufacturers and negotiate—like landlords—around the twin gods of price and space. This was fine with obedient shoppers— people Joe would call consumers, not customers—who dutifully followed the script laid out by national advertisers. But with the homogeny crumbling—the single dominant media voice fragmenting into individualized channels—those obedient shoppers began ceding space to a new breed. The traditional grocery store wouldn't just overlook this new breed, it was built to fail them: oriented toward national brands in such a way that it was almost incapable of adapting to serve anyone who wanted anything else.

The genius of Joe is, of course, that he made these observations before the 747 ever got airborne, before the war in Vietnam escalated the G.I. Bill, and before network TV viewership had begun to sag. This was grocery as soothsaying, peering into the hazy present, and laying wagers about where the world would turn.

Tap the Admiral

The next step was to build a house for these observations, a conceptual frame for the store itself. The knot that tied all his observations together was booze. "The correlation between education and alcohol consumption is about as perfect as one can find in marketing," he tells me. And so hard liquor, the ultimate high-price-per-cubic-inch product, becomes a cornerstone for his store.[11] From booze and travel, it was just a small leap to tiki. All around Joe, men and women were meeting for drinks, pink-and-white leis slung around their necks like frothy Elizabethan collars, their plastic coconuts of flaming rum threading a weird cultural needle between escape and irony, refuge and sincerity.

It's hard to imagine tiki as sincere. But there was a time. It swept in with the high arts gone low, Gauguin, Picasso, and Miró and their fascination with the remote and un-Westernized Pacific. Then came the cocktails, early-1930s rhum rhapsodies, using ostentation as authority, insisting through sheer force of garnish that you goddamn better be relaxing. By the early 1960s, James Michener's best seller *Tales of the South Pacific* had won the Pulitzer, been adapted into a movie, then a musical, and fully collided with real wounded, angry soldiers coming back from two confusing wars. It is here that tiki loses its sincerity but gains its cultural force.

---

11 The first TJ's would open with one hundred brands of scotch, seventy brands of bourbon, fifty brands of rum, and fourteen tequilas, along with the "greatest assortment of California wines ever assembled," an assortment that petered out at just seventeen labels and was valued most of all for the slogan it produced.

Joe credits the Jungle Cruise at Disneyland for making him see the connection. The ride opened alongside the first Pronto markets in the 1950s and, in its original incarnation, was done completely in earnest, no puns or jokes, just a stilted, geographically incoherent fantasy cruise through Southeast Asia, Africa, and Amazonia. It featured plastic elephants spouting water, unmoving stuffed zebras, and scared animatronic Africans in little red hats scaling a tree to get away from lions. In short, a ride whose capacity to open minds despite its crude and vaguely idiotic execution demonstrated just how shuttered people's understandings really were. Its 1965 version was only slightly more evolved, swinging back and forth between exoticism, like the piles of shrunken plastic skulls, sarcasm at how cheesy it all was, and attempts to produce actual, sincere awe.

Which was tiki. Or at least the tiki Joe wanted to channel. Square pegs playing dress-up in what they imagined were round clothes. White dudes with severely parted hair hunched over with nervous smiles loosening up. The perfect refuge from the encroaching, very real threats of a complex multicultural society. A space where the nerd could feel empowered, even sophisticated.

It also had the benefit of being extremely cheap. Discarded marine artifacts were in abundant supply and Joe could go down to the salvage yards near the harbor and pick up the flotsam for pennies per pound. And so the first store was "a riot of marine artifacts including a ship's bell, oars, netting, and half a row boat." The checkout stands had their own thatched roof, the counters were made of old hatch covers in which seashells had been sanded down and fiberglassed over. Employees wore Polynesian shirts and Bermuda shorts. The manager was called Captain, the assistant manager, First Mate, and the stock boys, the wince-worthy Native Bearers. Joe had read an article in the *New Yorker* that Hawaiian music played in stores slowed customers down. So he pumped Don Ho and the cheesiest slide guitar he could find through the loudspeakers until his employees snapped and smashed the records. "Which was fine with me. Only so many days you can listen to that stuff on repeat without going mad," Joe says with no humor expressed or intended.

The location of his first store was the payoff of all those family weekends in the station wagon. Late one night, he popped a pin down at the intersection of Pico Street and Arroyo Parkway in Pasadena. At that time, the region was basically an extended campus with Caltech, Pasadena City College, Fuller Theological Seminary, Ambassador College, and Cal State Los Angeles all located nearby. It was his epicenter, ground zero for advanced degrees, a mecca of dorky people with knowledge to prove.[12]

The rest—the inventory, the employee schedules and practices—he just pulled in from Pronto. Advertising was almost nonexistent. He sponsored music on the local classical station, reasoning that was a cheap and easy way of hitting his overeducated demographic. And to save money, he just snipped his design aesthetic directly from used books. The Victorian sketches that have come to define Trader Joe's merchandizing were cost control: books published before 1906 were pre-copyright and so free for Joe to repurpose with a funny caption. He spent hours cutting them out himself at his home easel.

And so there it was. The first iteration of the first grocery store of the twenty-first century: a convenience store dressed up in a slightly too-large Bermuda suit, with a giant liquor section, and a genuinely bizarre assortment of high-density items designed to appeal to the educated traveler: *Playboy* magazine, upmarket ladies' hosiery, and a photo finishing station. "Most people driving by thought we were a restaurant," Joe says. "Which didn't bother me at all."

---

12 Note the shocking demographic similarity with Boston, the location of the first TJ's on the East Coast, when it finally leapt out of California in the 1990s.

———

Luckily for the fledgling chain, the manager of that first store was a semi-functional alcoholic. His strong sell methods, boosted by his authentic, cellular interest in the product, made the wine program a huge hit. The fact that he routinely left for three-hour lunches before eleven a.m. was more worrisome. With sales booming but coworkers annoyed, Joe, who knew nothing about wine—who drank Paul Masson cooking sherry to relax—decided that, for the sake of his business, he needed to loosen his dependency on that manager and study wine seriously himself.

And so he taught himself the basics from the ground up. It was the most consequential decision he would make as a grocer.

Lesson one: there was no such thing as wine, only wines. Even product from the same grape, grown on the same soil, in the same climate, crushed by the same vintner, varied so much year to year that price in wine was never set by brand but by vintage. Wines were the opposite of Cola-Cola and just about everything else he was selling. When you sold out of a vintage, it was gone forever.

The second lesson was that wine was a deliriously complex business—and that no one, including the experts, seemed to have a grasp on the whole thing. This included the wines as food—the different varietals and tasting notes—but even more, the legal apparatus surrounding them.

At the time, California liquor law was dominated by a series of Depression-era regulations called Fair Trade, which were designed to limit competition and help smaller independent stores. In theory, Fair Trade was simple: all retailers must set the same price for alcohol. Meaning grocers were legally prevented from going Michael Cullen and cutting price to drive volume. But in practice Fair Trade was a byzantine maze: competing regulations overlaid on top of one another year after year in response to lobbying interests, court cases, and various regulatory agencies. And by and large, rather than wading into that regulatory swamp, Joe watched as retailers and wholesalers alike simply took their cues from one another; instead of studying the source material, they studied the competition.

Joe, on the other hand, decided to embrace the tangle. He traveled to Napa, then France, attending lot auctions and learning production. He studied the Fair Trade regulations like it was midrash, digesting the thousands of pages of law, case law, and legal commentary until he could quote regulatory subclauses like chapter and verse.

Above all he asked a lot of obnoxious questions.

And in one particular question, he hit pay dirt. It would perhaps not be worth getting into, except it defines a pattern. In 1970, Joe noticed an anomaly with the price of a Marques de Olivar wine. None of his buyers could explain it. When he started tracking Marques de Olivar as it snaked to market, he realized bottles that came through Monsieur Henri, the wine arm of Pepsi, had slightly different prices than those coming through smaller wholesalers. The longer he studied the issue, the more convinced he was that he had stumbled onto something astounding: imported wines that did not have an exclusive distributor could be posted at different prices, depending on the wholesaler. Now, I realize this is dry. But it is also Joe. At his finest. Here, buried in the weird phase boundary that is the interface of regulation and practice, he had figured out something nobody else in the entire industry had seen: there were no Fair Trade pricing controls on imported wine. The fact that everyone acted differently was nothing more than received wisdom, inflected slightly by laziness. All Joe needed to do to take advantage was to find a wholesaler willing to post his personal prices, and he could sell imported wine at whatever price he pleased.

So Joe tracked down Ezra Webb, a man he refers to as a "great gentleman and veteran importer," who confirmed Joe's analysis and agreed to buy whatever wines he asked. The first sales were glorious. The price of wine shattered. "Thirty years later people still come up to me and talk about how they bought Latour for $5.99 or Pichon Longueville

Lalande for $3.69," Joe explains. "As I learned time and time again, success in business often rests on a minute reading of regulations."

In three years, TJ's was the leading retailer of imported wine in California.

At which point, Joe turned his attention toward domestics, where he learned his third lesson about wine. With domestics, actual wine knowledge proved much more important than regulations. The ability to discriminate between a wine that would sell and a wine that would cause his customers to sneer was not something you could learn by reading case law. It required a physical depth of knowledge.

"And so we sat down and pulled sixty corks every afternoon," Joe tells me.

This was knowledge acquisition with maniacal glee. In the courtyard outside Trader Joe's small central office in Pasadena, Joe installed a tasting table. He had it built chest-high so nobody could sit, lest his entire operation pickle up. And next to it, against the wall, he installed a sleek porcelain urinal where people could spit. Then he began sampling.[13] "Neighbors came. Friends came. Buyers came. Everyone came and did a tasting," an early employee tells me. "Sometimes we'd do them blind. Sometimes we'd make a presentation. The only thing we asked was that they answer a few questions and tell us how it ranked."

And this was lesson three: people were stunningly clueless about value. Wealthy friends would instantly vote down wines priced less than three dollars. Joe's enthusiasm introducing a bottle would sway the entire room, derailing any chance at an authentic response. Wines from highly regarded producers often stunk in the blind. Other bottles, regarded as swill by their producers, went over big. And so, slowly, after

---

13 When I ask whether any of this was personal curiosity, a chance to explore something he was interested in outside of business, he slams his hand against the table. "No! This was business. I didn't drink a drop of wine until I was thirty-seven. I saw this would be big and knew I had to learn."

uncorking, sniffing, and spitting tens of thousands of bottles, they learned enough to trust themselves.

"Our first real product knowledge came from wine," he says. "That indoctrination flavored everything we subsequently did in foods." Supermarkets revel in the continuous product. It makes everything easy for them—if you promote Coca-Cola you don't have to explain it, don't have to worry about it; all you have to do is advertise Coca-Cola and note the size and price in the copy.

Wines resist this. They change too often. They reflect an authentic variability. Owners pride themselves on their scarcity. They require judgment and knowledge and a tolerance for risk during acquisition. And for whatever reason, as consumers we have been trained to understand this in a way we haven't been trained for, say, jam or ice cream or any other branded product in our lives. So, for wines, we typically make products of their retailer. You find a good wine shop and then trust the owner to point you in the right direction. The more Joe thought about this, the more he realized it could be true of grocery as well.

Quote Health Foods

The first chance to really put this idea to the test came the following year. The September 1970 issue of *Scientific American* was dedicated to the "biosphere," a word Joe had never heard before. "I converted on the road to Damascus," he says. "Right there, I looked at the evidence and turned green." This was not a business decision. Within weeks, he had subscribed to the *Whole Earth Catalog* and *Mother Earth News*. He turned his front lawn into an organic garden and retrofitted his car with diesel. And from that Christmas on, the family only had "living trees" that got replanted in the backyard come the New Year.

Which is to say, Joe was a true green. But he never made the jump to health food. "How eating healthy would save the biosphere was never clear to me," he says. To Joe, the whole "health food" scene felt fraught with fad,[14] full of quacks each with their own small take, all trying to play on a mix of altruism and fear. But when green friend after green friend began begging him to try to eat more consciously, he sensed a business opportunity.

Within a year he traveled up to San Francisco, paid a young woman to teach him the hippie lingo, and started packing TJ's with raw milk and granola. And the more he looked into it with his grocery eyes, the more wonderfully weird it all became. It turned out the health food fanatics were the exact same demographic as his wine connoisseurs. "The concept was obviously founded in schizophrenia," he explains. "The people who really thought about what they ingest—wine connoisseurs or health food nuts—were basically on the same radar beam." Both were rejecting the masses contented with Folgers coffee, both had an internal need to assert their individuality. Both were seekers who craved information, shoppers for whom buying was a material expression of that craving.

Perfectly emblematic of his ambivalence was the riddle of bran. Here was a real health food that could actually help people. His doctor was emphatic about its benefits, and the more Joe read, the more he bought in. But bran was bran—you could fill the whole room with it for a few hundred bucks. It absolutely violated his high-price, low-cubic-inch commandment. So Joe scoped the scene, and asked his bran supplier to bring in nuts and dried fruit. "It turns out nuts are regarded as healthy now, but that's not how we got into them," he says. "We got into them to pay for bran." Cashews, almonds, these were the type of high-density, high-price products he wanted to build his chain around. And the more Joe looked into nuts, the more he saw what a lazy job most grocers did with them. So TJ's dropped bran, dropped the nut

14 One of the most endearing things about Joe, both in its consistency and precision, is that he never once can bring himself to just say "health" food out loud, instead referring to "quote health food" every single time.

suppliers, and went in hard on their own, learning about nuts the way they learned about wine. The buyer involved in the negotiations tells me: "We reworked the whole supply chain. No one was doing anything like it at the time . . . And all of a sudden we were selling nuts so cheap people lost their minds."

From nuts, Joe moved to vitamins. Another "quote health food." Another perfect high-value-per-cubic-inch product. Another space in the grocery store where the intricacies of production had led to a cartel of suppliers accustomed to setting whatever price they wanted. Within a year, TJ's had mastered the regulations, created an alternate supply chain, and was doing 3 percent of total sales in vitamin C alone.

But the biggest thing Joe discovered as he peered into the supply chains of health foods was that he had been right. Almost every product in the grocery store could be sold like wine. Continuity is in the eye of the beholder. Commodity is a matter of perception. Coffee can be Folgers or it can be terroir: the regions where beans are grown span continents and microclimates, lumping them together under a single label is as silly as lumping together Ethiopia and Brazil, or jungle and mountains. To anyone who bothered to look, the idea of a unified commodity coffee called Folgers was an invention based on simplifying trade.

But, just like with wine, most grocers couldn't be bothered to look. They didn't want to look. It was actually antithetical to their business models to look. And so Joe filled their blind spot. He went deep into Walla Walla onions exclusively sourced from Walla Walla, Washington. He carted in fifty-gallon drums of maple syrup from Vermont and sold it based on location. He was given the best-tasting corn of his life, and created "Trader Joe's Vintage Dated Canned Corn." This was corn grown in a specific field in Idaho, isolated so it wouldn't be cross-pollinated, and each year TJ's would have to outbid the Japanese to buy the entire supply. And the most important thing about it? Those last few sentences were things Joe could tell his customers. He was wine merchandizing corn, and the unthinkable happened. His customers recognized it. They beat down the doors for *canned corn*; it flew off the shelves and another window opened in Joe's mind.

"Our most important decision was to become a genuine retailer," he explains. The word "retail" comes to us from the Middle French word *retailler*, meaning "to cut into pieces," more etymologically related to the English word "tailor" than anything having to do with sales. The original French retailers were oriented around precision, buying only a few key goods in bulk and carefully apportioning them for their customers. They added value through product selection, negotiating routes of supply, and expertise in handling. And yet, by going Michael Cullen, American supermarkets had abandoned these basic duties, forced by the volume of their offerings to outsource these decisions to wholesalers, distributors, and manufacturers respectively. It left them without much expertise of their own, forced to accept whatever their partners gave them.

It would take another twenty years for this passivity to wash through the system, but eventually it did. And in the process a great winnowing occurred; the vast majority of America's supermarkets shuttered or consolidated, battered by market forces they neither understood nor controlled.

Joe saw this very clearly a decade early in the mid-1970s, and began frantically theorizing how to avoid it. In a company-wide memo, he rejected several hundred years of cliché and announced, "The Customer Is Not Always Right." Trader Joe's would no longer try to honor them at all costs. Instead it would flip the narrative, empowering buyers. He reasoned he already had the most expensive and intelligent buyers in the industry. Rather than use them as cogs in charge of replenishment, why not let them run free? His buyers actually engaged in the nuance of manufacturing, regulation, distribution, and nutrition. Customers on the other hand were amateurs who, aside from actually being the demographic he was after, had little to recommend themselves in terms of judgment and understanding about how to serve that demographic.

In rapid succession, he banned all outside salesmen from the store as distraction and then drastically cut back his offerings. If buyers were going to be making decisions, they couldn't be overwhelmed with paperwork or juggling the logistics of every possible food option on the planet.[15] At the start of this transition, his managers selected from about 15,000 SKUs to stock their stores. By the time Joe was finished, a single store carried less than 1,500 SKUs.

The heuristic driving this tightening was *outstanding*. "Outstanding" meant something very particular to Joe. It meant a product that was the lowest price in town by a clear, consistent margin. It meant having a superior flavor profile in an unmistakable manner. It meant a product with a point of view that differentiated itself from all others. Most important, it meant that each product added to the bottom line of the store all by itself. "No loss leaders are permitted," he boomed in an internal memo.

Then Joe decided these rules would be absolute. If TJ's buyers determined the chain couldn't be outstanding for a product, Joe decided the store just wouldn't sell it. Even a tiny slip—a beer found crosstown for cheaper, a mayo not noticeably more tangy and delicious than Hellmann's—would not be tolerated. Those inconsistencies were as ugly as "a pimple on our image," he said. They ruined the whole presentation.

---

15 Trader Joe's in-store promotional copy is famous for explaining the store's deals as occurring from "eliminating the middleman." But that's just marketing copy. "Joe was never against the middleman," a buyer explains. "He loved the honest middleman. He recognized the value they added. He thought it was our job as buyers to know the value of the items in front of us. And so it was our responsibility as buyers to know which middlemen were gaming us and which were helping us."

This was crazy talk. Like Clarence Saunders letting customers touch merchandise crazy.

There was simply no way to be that type of outstanding with most products they sold. The national brands were definitionally resistant. From Coca-Cola to Bounty paper towels, these were products bombed out in unlimited quantities at identical levels of quality. The only way for Joe to post the lowest price for Coca-Cola was to grow to be the biggest chain in the land and negotiate, or to take a loss on the product. The former was a race to an unstable top in his view. The latter directly contradicted what Joe meant by being outstanding.

And so, following his logic, Coca-Cola had to go. And then Bounty. And then every single other mainstream brand both he and his customers had ever heard of. Worse, there were whole categories where, no matter how hard his buyers tried, they couldn't get an edge: plastic silverware, tampons, tinfoil. Rarely food, but products people still expected to find on a trip to the supermarket.

His managers rioted. They had to deal with this on the ground. Almost to a man, they predicted failure.

"The hardest work selling is always to your own employees," Joe explains. "For every one of these ideas, I had to convince them first of all. And for almost all of them, they've resisted the hardest."

"Of course the rhetoric is nice," one buyer tells me. "But how the heck are we going to actually do this? We had less than twenty stores at the time. We could never negotiate even a generic mayo for less than Safeway . . . You can't just go to a manufacturer and say, 'Hi! Give me a special deal, please.' Cause that ain't going to happen."

The answer was Trader Joe's private label program, the embodiment of an entire approach to retail.

Almost as old as the grocery chain itself, private label is simply an item sold under the retailer's name. Synonymous with "generic," it is typically just a copy of a heavily branded product. In principle, the retailer can strip out advertising costs, slap on a plain label, and pass on the savings to the customer. In practice, especially at that time, the private label was drab, associated with inferior quality and only grudgingly placed in the basket.

Trader Joe's private labels would become the exact opposite. And it is no overstatement to say that the line of products that resulted transformed the entire industry for better and worse. When Whole Foods launched its 365 brand, they simply hired away the Trader Joe's team. Kroger, Safeway, Wegmans, Costco—all have programs built on the same essential DNA Joe pioneered in the mid-1970s.

For Joe, private label needed to be an extension of the store's identity. It would allow him to create a parallel stock of items that appeared to exist outside the national homogeny, simultaneously, continuously produced, but more precisely targeting his demographic. A line of products that captured the knowledge his buyers brought to bear.

In a series of internal memos, he exhorted his troops: "Any fool with cash has 'buying power' . . . What distinguishes our products from those sold by the supers is the INTENSITY of the effort put into finding, developing, packaging or distributing them . . . [We bring] information to bear on customer problems every bit as real as the creation of electricity from coal."

That is, the new barriers in retail were intellectual. But not in the sense of being merchandising inventions or relying on differentiation that was gimmicky or exotic. "German instant coffee may be intriguing in the short run," he wrote, "but if it doesn't have depth, if it doesn't provide customers reasons to buy beyond novelty, it is no better than its American counterpart." Instead, the path to a meaningful private label was "deep product knowledge" and "intensive study" that would require buyers to innovate—in the manner of electricity from coal—to create real value.

In the words of a buyer from the time, "It was guerrilla warfare on the whole supply chain." It began with deconstructing existing products and ended with inventing new ones. And it would go on to shift the balance in grocery decisively. Retailers would grow dominant, dictating the terms of production to manufacturers, persistently driving down price through competition.

The actual work spanned from the superficial—"Every private label product must meet the current shibboleths of the health food movement: no MSG, no added sugar, no artificial coloring," Joe proclaimed early on—but extended to far more complex undertakings. Often it meant moving sideways, solving intractable problems by abandoning them. For instance, being outstanding in peanut butter is extremely difficult. There are only so many costs you can drop. So instead of competing with other chains, the nut buyer decided to pivot. TJ's was already doing a big volume in almonds, what about grinding them? The technology was completely different, but after a search, he found a religious sect in Oregon who was willing to try. And so Trader Joe's invented almond butter as a consumer product, something infinitely more intriguing to that overeducated, underpaid demographic. And then this mentality moved down the line, taking the time saved by not competing on vegetable oil to, say, corner price on the best avocado oil, trading Utz potato chips for those made from parsnips, or by working with wine producers to make a thoroughly drinkable Two Buck Chuck.[16]

---

16 The story of Charles Shaw—the notorious red wine Trader Joe's rolled out at the mind-blowing price of $2 a bottle and sold into essentially unquenchable demand (up to 6,000 bottles a day per store, coming to represent a solid 12 percent of the total California wine market all by itself)—is almost a perfect embodiment of Joe's entire ethos. It was built on the knowledge acquired by their wine program, and stares with a bull's-eye back at their target audience—so devoid of character it achieves an almost frictionless drinkability, yet neither too sweet nor thin to inspire scorn. The buyer involved in the deal presented it to me as one deal among many, a longtime distributor pitching them an idea and TJ's refining it to better hit their customers' perception of value. And that seems exactly right: this was not some freakish stab in the dark that got proven right. Whole

There were failures innumerable. Low-salt TV dinners that tasted like cardboard. A "peel in" applesauce that almost caused an industrial explosion. Bottled raw carrot juice that kept fermenting to shatter in terrible pops right on the shelf. Which is to say, these were easy ideas to articulate, but required a lot of tenacity for a store to actually implement.

Or, as one employee from the time remembers, "I can't tell you how many executives came in over the years, traveling our stores in their suits, trying to figure out what Trader Joe's is doing that they couldn't duplicate—it was the extra work."

Finally, Joe married merchandising to this work. In a world of design firms, advertising agencies, and retail consultants, he did it all by himself: clipping the art from old books, writing the copy for the *Fearless Flyer* at his easel, coming up with sly witticisms with Alice around the kitchen table. It was a master class in understatement. "I wanted to create a silent conspiracy among all the over-educated, underpaid people in town, so as they moved down the aisles they would read secret messages on the products, get a chuckle," he writes in an unpublished autobiography. Hence, the Sir Isaac Newtons, the Heisenberg's Uncertain Blend of coffee made up of the different roasts that had fallen off the conveyor belt and mixed together in unknown quantities, or the Trader Darwin's and Next to Godliness brands, for the chain's vitamins and cleaning products, respectively.

He wanted to flatter his customers' vocabulary and tickle their minds, not tell them what to buy or convince them his products were the best. "We want to be a chain that requires explanation," he explains

Foods, Walgreens, or Kroger all could have put out a $2 bottle of wine; none would have had the success of TJ's.

in a Theory Paper from the mid-1970s. "I aver that Tide and Folgers don't need that human intervention—they can be sold by machines and probably will be someday . . . We want a private label that requires people. We want to cultivate judgment."

In this way, Joe made me believe in the idea of business. Or rather he made me see what business could be. Our society is awash with founders, all listening to the same leadership podcasts, doing the same kettlebell lunges to improve grip and leg strength at the same time, then dissolving identical Tim Ferriss–approved muscle-building complexes into their post-workout shakes to transform their previously similar mesomorph bodies into something even more metabolically equivalent. All while making parallel grandiose-style projections about their own app, disruption, or innovation whereby their personal self-interest miraculously aligns with the interest of society writ large and places them as CEO/founder/servant-leader on the very prow of the vessel of civilization. It is lunacy. But somehow it is *our* lunacy, the ascendant lunacy of my generation, which has put IPO-chasing founders in the same category we once reserved for poets, statesmen, and philosophers.

So it is with wariness that I bring up the cliché about business being a creative act. But, hey, that's what Joe made me see. He has the empath's ability to toggle back and forth between different perspectives, to be able to obsess over detail and zoom out to the bigger picture, as well as a world-class comfort with intuition and nonlinear process. "The most important thing to know about a man is whether he is right- or left-handed," he tells me. "Dyslexia lurks in the brain of every lefthander, which means we see the world differently, sometimes profitably!" He shunned the limelight and never strove for fame, not personally, nor for his brand. Joe was a student. And understanding his career in grocery as humanism, a man trying to learn as much as he can about people, life, and cultural shifts, is one of the more helpful ways to think about the reason for his success and what grocery has to offer.

To embody his vision, he surrounded himself with the self-taught. For a store serving the overeducated and underpaid, Joe brought in the undereducated, and offered to overpay them; this allowed him to carefully select a certain type of employee for central management: extremely intelligent but never clever; generalists who liked hard labor; strivers who wore their enthusiasm the way Joe wore his Hussong's Cantina T-shirt, just under cover, but blaring out. Joe cultivated an office full of these human golden retrievers, and he groomed them first into astute foodies, then into retailers in that etymological sense. Turnover was virtually nonexistent during his reign.[17] He valued their sense of wonder at the world as it expanded before them and relied on their fresh takes to cut through received wisdom.

This tactical egalitarianism extended into social areas. The Southern California of his youth was a hotbed of xenophobia and racism. His mother was an elementary school teacher at both the white school and the segregated Mexican school, and so Joe was raised under the separate but equal paradigm but with a clear sense from his mother that everyone was equally deserving of education, and the separation only made her life more difficult. Two of the five highest-ranking employees in his organization were Japanese men who had been interned by FDR during World War II. He repeatedly emphasized how the racism and sexism of his competitors represented their stupidity as businessmen, a

---

17 At one point, tenure under Joe almost became a liability, the company bottling up far more human capacity than it had stores to place them. This surplus of qualified employees goes a long way toward explaining the success of TJ's rapid expansion from 1990 to 2001, where it moved from a small-to-midsized highly regional chain of 30 to 40 stores to an aggressively growing national brand of 485 stores today. An expansion like that often kills a grocery chain, yet here it was a balm as hundreds of assistant managers found a route to advancement in a company they loved and would never leave but which had kept their talents confined. These were golden retrievers straining at the leash and when the reins were loosened it allowed the chain to go nationwide in a relative blink.

laziness of imagination that carried over to how they ran their stores. He believed having female secretaries was sexist, and instead employed women in his most esteemed position as buyers. He not only ensured that these women would be paid equally to their male counterparts but wrote a company-wide memo detailing everyone's pay in a transparent fashion, particularly calling out the fact that he was giving a female employee a raise because it was likely he had underpaid her.

Like most things about Joe, this egalitarianism existed less as a separate aspirational/noble quality, more just as plain common sense. Useful, intelligent people existed in all colors, ages, and came with or without fancy degrees. And so Trader Joe's true believers, who shop those aisles, smile at the hokey puns, relish the quality food with wholesome ingredients, and imagine an organization run along those lines, take pleasure in knowing that was exactly the case in 1979 when Joe was firmly at the helm.

Every Beginning Is an End

At this time, across the globe, a drab, ruthlessly efficient version of Trader Joe's was on the rise. If you subscribe to Jungian ideals, this store was Joe's shadow: a firm of almost eerie similarity, but all opposite, drained of Joe's wit, cheer, and curiosity, completely uninterested in new products or expansive taste, indifferent to travel, leisure, or wine, but, like a Janus, somehow grown out of a common spine.

Karl and Theo Albrecht were born into the industry of Essen. A vast wooded mining town in the northwest corner of Germany, Essen was built between the coking plants, industrial rail lines, and piles of pit waste that follow coal. Their father was a miner who dreamed of baking, and in 1913 he provided their mother, Anna, with enough savings to buy a general store on credit. It was a tiny thing, located in the workers' quarters, and she began selling very basic goods to other miners at extremely low prices. By the time the boys were in high school, their father was dying of emphysema, and their mother was struggling to pay the loans on the store. The boys, blond and lean, came of age selling baked bread around Essen on a wooden cart, yelling for sales until their throats burned. Then Weimar inflation hit, and in quick succession their mother's debt was wiped out, their father died, the store became theirs, and the entire country descended into World War II.

Beyond coal, the other anchor for Essen was Krupp Ironworks. An ancient German weapons manufacturer, the Krupp family supplied weaponry to every German conflict since the Thirty Years' War in 1618. By 1937, the firm was an enthusiastic supporter of Hitler. Known as the Armory of the Reich, Allied forces designated it a "primary" target when the war broke, and for six years it rained bombs. Block by block, Essen was reduced. Buildings became a tangle of stone and splintered wood. Cobbled streets were blown into concavities. The factory itself persisted, although by the end, it operated almost exclusively from enslaved POW labor: 1,200 workers sleeping in a space with only ten toilets, a mess of human excrement, starvation, and fleas.

When peace was declared, the Albrecht brothers found themselves in this new non-Essen. Miraculously, their store had survived. It stood a lonely box on the corner of a destroyed street. They named it Albrecht Discount, or ALDI for short. And then they went to work rebuilding. The result would be a grocery store every bit as revolutionary as anything conceived by Michael Cullen but uniquely suited to postwar Germany. Where American grocery achieved low prices by circus and frenzy, supersizing the physical footprint to increase sales volume, the Albrechts took an equally effective if opposite approach. They kept store size the same but shrunk their offerings to a tight core. Rather than leverage the new advances in manufacturing to fill out their store with products—creating that American paradise of choice—the Albrechts rode their manufacturers hard, pushing them to transform those same advances into simpler but cheaper products. It was low prices through stubborn practicality.

The model was simple. A typical ALDI was 6,000 square feet but held only 280 SKUs. These SKUs were the most basic groceries—largely canned goods and shelf-stable milk; no fresh, refrigerated, or frozen products. They targeted only products with high turnover, allowing them to further cut costs on warehousing and storage. To stock, the Albrechts would put out a formula for a generic product, say mayo, oil, or ketchup, and ask manufacturers to bid to their spec, taking the lowest offer. They then sold that product to the public at a gross profit just under one-third of the typical grocery store. There were no decorations in stores and advertising amounted to less than 0.1 percent of sales. It was a very difficult model to beat. By the end of the 1940s, they had expanded to more than fifty stores, each additional store increasing their effectiveness, creating more pressure on their manufacturers, locking them into a race to lower prices. Their eventual success would be titanic—spreading over almost every inch of Europe—directly credited by economists with spurring the postwar German recovery. In the process, the brothers would become folk heroes, "billionaires who taught a poor country to save," elites who continued living lives as spare and simple as their stores.

In 1970, after a heated discussion about carrying cigarettes, the brothers split their empire. Karl, the elder, took Germany south of Essen, Austria, Spain, and the UK. Theo took northern Germany, the Netherlands, and France. It wasn't a feud. They continued to live in Essen, fifteen minutes apart in two modest houses, and saw each other regularly. They had simply decided they would fight less if they divided things up.

Which leads us back to Joe. In 1975, Karl came to the United States and staked a claim, buying the Benner Tea Co., a dying regional grocer in Iowa. He saw Benner as sort of an insurance policy. This was the height of the Cold War. The idea the Russians might come over the border through East Germany was real. America was neutral territory for the Albrechts: neither allocated in their division of the planet nor under immediate threat from the Russians. Sibling rivalry kicked in and Theo decided he wanted an American grocery store too.

And so one day in late 1977, Germans started showing up in Pasadena. Then Theo Albrecht himself. He had spent the last two years scouring America for a grocery store to acquire. Unlike Karl and Benner Tea, he wanted something with potential, and after sizing up the American grocery world, he zeroed in on Joe.

A courtship began. Theo and his family came to Los Angeles to spend time with Joe. Joe flew back to Essen with Alice to meet Theo, his wife, Cilly, and their two sons. Theo had the aloof disposition of an architect; Joe calls him "impressive, handsome, quick, intelligent," but the Albrechts' cold intensity gave him the creeps. He didn't like the way ALDI treated their employees. The store violated his ecological bent. It had no whimsy whatsoever. In the middle of negotiations, he snuck to Essen's downtown train station and fled to Paris.

But Theo allowed himself to be neither offended nor deterred. He made the offer sweeter. He flew back to Los Angeles.

"They were ten years older, but very vigorous," Alice remembers. "They had done it themselves. They were immensely rich, but practical. Men who built an empire one store at a time."

When Joe made up his mind to sell, it happened very quickly. The final deal was a one-page contract and a handshake. The Albrechts were to "neither put a penny in, nor take a penny out." Joe would stay on as CEO. No changes would be made to the way TJ's was run.

But Joe, the benign dictator, man of ten thousand ideas, was not capable of being someone else's employee. Tension built slowly. It started with a series of small disagreements over the issue of growth. Theo wanted the chain to expand more rapidly than Joe believed sensible. Then a major disagreement. Joe wanted to bring on someone from the outside to help manage the expansion. At first the issue was argued with logic. Then with heat. Then abruptly Joe faxed his resignation.

He was out.

"You have to understand, Theo is immensely wealthy," Alice explains. "Stunningly so. But also living very simply. The way he exercised his wealth was by getting precisely what he wanted. And he wanted Joe to stay. But he also wanted Joe to do exactly as told."

Or as Joe says, "The Germans started acting German, and I acted like myself."

When Joe talks about selling there is a nervous sadness. It is a decision that he has rationally resolved a thousand times, moved past, justified, and benefited from tremendously, but that is still coupled with an emptiness he does not fully engage. At the time, he was weighed down by what would happen if something happened to him. One of his executives, a close friend who had been with him since the Pronto days, had just died of a heart attack. The chain was big at that point but still vulnerable to changes in laws. The family had no savings. But to sell was to walk away from an existence. "I experienced life through Trader Joe's," he writes. "I knew I would be selling my shadow."

He did not think much about the money. "I was guided by the Hellenistic ideal of sophrosyne," he explains. "Nothing too much." The amount the Albrechts offered was plenty by that standard. It would secure his family and his reputation within the business community.

But does he regret it?

It is something he can't even bear to talk about when we meet. I bring it up and he ducks and dodges. He refers to it as an amputation. He says:

"Let me put it this way, when I left Trader Joe's, it was the best place in the world to buy a bottle of wine for two bucks, a pound of cheese for two bucks, and a loaf of bread for two bucks . . . My wife was a schoolteacher, my mother was a schoolteacher. This was about helping the schoolteacher."

Which is noticeably not answering the question. A few moments later, we are talking about an early employee when he lurches back.

"I feel sorry for Trader Joe's now," he starts. "First the stores are so much bigger. The SKU count has had to rise. This burdens the whole system. Then the volume of the stores has changed. It's not so easy to find suppliers that will meet the needs for bigger deals."

The conversation pauses for a moment. Then we return.

"I remember we worked with a pizza operation. They made very good frozen pizzas. Delicious. But we simply got too big."

And compared to even the wildest, most aggressive visions of Trader Joe's expansion, ALDI was an actual monster: its ten thousand tentacles orchestrating the food supply for almost all of western Europe. If Joe saw deals become harder to find when he jumped from a small Southern California chain to one that spanned the entire state, what happens to a chain when it spreads across the planet? At ALDI, this size was increasingly coupled with claustrophobic secrecy. In 1971, Theo was kidnapped and held prisoner for weeks for ransom. The experience would take his natural introversion and warp it to an extreme of privacy and seclusion. He stopped making public appearances. His photo was never knowingly taken again.

Alice remembers the two of them leaving for a private dinner in Essen with Theo and his wife a few days before the sale. "It was the first time I was ever in a car with automatic locks," she tells me. "I got picked up, settled in the back, and then they all clicked at once." The small, creative chain she and Joe had built from scratch, the one where she packed produce while her children played in grocery carts, where they scouted housing demographics as a family in their station wagon, was changing.

"And when you left Theo's house, for instance, there was a button," she continues. "And once it was pressed, you could see the grills coming down over all the windows." They lowered slowly, sheets of bulletproof steel rolling down in front of the glass. And as Joe and Alice walked toward the private car waiting for them, their backs to that descending steel, it was a new era: their entire life in groceries was now contained inside the machine it takes to source, stock, and fuel an international empire like ALDI.

PART II

Distribution of Responsibility

Emerson, in his spare stony New England, a few miles from Walden, could write: "Things are in the saddle / And ride mankind." He could say more now ...

—Randall Jarrell, *A Sad Heart at the Supermarket*

Three A.M. Outside the Aldi Distribution Center in Oak Creek, Wisconsin

I'm balled up shivering. Fists clenched beneath armpits, knees clenched to chest, in some sort of woke rigor mortis, blinking aware in the three a.m. darkness, listening to the first sounds of this new day, a quiet whisper of a trickle as the trucker in the bunk below me slides to the edge of her bed and begins softly pissing into a plastic garbage bag. We are parked here in a rumbling cab not twenty-five feet from a truck stop and its bank of well-lit, regularly cleaned bathroom stalls. But this bag pissing, this dedication to efficiency even at the cost of common sense and common smells is the way of the trucker. Or so I've been told. There is a moan of relief like a back massage. Then a long pause.

"Well fuck me, tomorrow came today. We got fifteen minutes."

There is fit of coughing at this. The cough of a woman who smokes two packs of cigarettes a day and drinks a six-pack of Pepsi every morning before noon. A disgusting cough to listen to, wet and moldy, a tumbling of moss and rotten sponge.

"Rise and shine, sunshine," she growls. "I'm getting coffee. You want any?"

She slides through the seats, cracks open the door. The yellow overheads pop on in the cabin and the roar and heat from the 250 trucks idling around us pour in from the outside. And Lynne Ryles, this coughing, sputtering, stumbling trucker, clicks leashes on her two beagles and clambers down the five-foot drop from the driver-side door to walk them in the parking lot below.

Fourteen minutes later, twin coffees steaming in the front seat, we're rolling out to an ALDI distribution center on a mission to deliver a load of groceries.

I didn't seek out this most elemental point in distribution so much as sink into it. Reportorially gravitating to Lynne Ryles, no different from water when it settles to the lowest point after all other outlets are sealed. And make no mistake, all other outlets were sealed. In general, as has been well reported by others, industrial food is a paranoid business. Big, fat, pushy corporations all clinging to their tiny edge, well burned by bad press, convinced that their customers are skittish and insane, best treated like children, to be protected for their own good from information that they can neither assess nor understand. It's a self-serving parochialism, but not completely unfounded. People *are* skittish and insane when it comes to their food. They not only want, they demand, through buying power, completely impossible, unsustainable opposites—low price and high quality, immediate availability and customized differentiation—and then react apoplectically to the often ingenious, if Frankensteinian, solutions industrial food creates to bridge the gap.[18] The result is our current mess of Ag secrecy laws, rotten third-party certification, and no-comment press releases, perfectly symbolized by those windowless, sealed concrete bunkers that make up our nation's slaughterhouses.

But even within that backdrop, the secrecy in retail grocery is staggering. The 1.5 percent gross margin and microscopic points of differentiation create conditions where trade secrets are very real. When push came to shove, it took me two days to line up an undercover visit to a cage-free chicken facility to fact-check ethical claims about animal treatment. It took me two *years* to find a retail food broker who would let me shadow him on his rounds. A consultant I speak with estimates that 50 percent of his meetings are "single blind," where he doesn't even know the identity of the brand he is consulting on, or the specifics of the product they are paying him to comment on, because the people hiring him are too afraid he might share details with a competitor. Every single grocery executive I reached out to either demanded an off-record conversation or spoke in such vagaries as to render our conversation imbecilic. They were happy to outline a vision of the grocery store available to every second grader willing to open a Richard Scarry book. But details, forget about it.

Which is to say, when I decided I needed to visit the warehouses and distribution centers that form the hubs of the food world, the type of behind the scenes access I was looking for was uniformly denied. Instead, I was left with either applying for a job in a warehouse, which

---

18 In terms of the ingenious, if Frankensteinian, solutions, I'm thinking in particular of "pink slime," i.e., the use of high-powered centrifuges to upcycle otherwise discarded beef trimmings and inject them into ground meat, a process that slurps the protein matrix right off the bone and compresses it into a rosy goo. It was a process greeted with universal outrage when revealed—not just because of that rosy goo but because of the ammonia gassing required to smother any pathogens in it—yet also clearly, even endearingly to my weird eyes, an attempt by a sociopathic industry to find a win-win: giving customers the lower fat, higher protein meat they wanted at an ever lower price.

I thought long and hard about, but rejected as impractical, or smuggling myself in with a trucker, which sounded kind of fun until I did it.

I met Lynne a week earlier in an empty parking lot. She's talking on a Bluetooth headpiece, stomping around the asphalt, her rig gleaming behind her. I didn't know what to expect, but not this. Standing a solid six feet, two inches, large in all proportions, overweight in none, Lynne looks like she walked off some Cro-Magnon shot put team. Her hair hangs straight down like a stringy curtain over her face. She wears cowboy boots, a T-shirt, and jeans with a strategic rip up by the hip-butt, a mushroom-white patch of flesh peeking through and winking when she takes long strides. She brushes back that hair to a take a cigarette from her mouth. Then she says "He's here" to no one but me, her phone call definitely over, the Bluetooth off her face, and suddenly a giant hand is stuck out to greet me, attached to a very skeptical glance.

We stand there in handshake for a moment.

"I recommend you get yourself a Gatorade bottle." She looks me up and down. "Wide mouth for you."

I don't believe that I react to this.

"Stop looking pale. I'm just fucking with you. Nothing in those pants looks like you're a wide mouth anything." She turns back toward the truck. "I'm saying we'll be doing a lot of driving. Hope you know what you're getting into."

I didn't.

As soon as we get on the highway, a whole new landscape pops into view. The four-wheelers—Lynne's terminology, which I helplessly adopt—shrink, zipping around like annoying gnats. There are ubiquitous signs that I've never noticed: height restrictions, axle restrictions, prohibited bridges, each vital points of information that cannot be ignored.

The vigilance required is exhausting and lonesome. The four-wheelers below, Lynne tells me, are completely unaware of the dangers lurking above them and must be managed like children. The trucker is constantly on edge, recalculating braking distance based on the load, expecting and then reacting to major equipment failure, tensing up at the slightest precipitation in a manner that simply has no analogue in the modern car. Runaway ramps are meaningful lifelines. Shifting into the wrong lane, merging onto any and every off-ramp, a momentary lack of caution, or just for a half second treating your truck like a regular car, will lead to a death. "In a car, your blind spot might be a few feet. Mine is fifty-three feet," Lynne explains, slowly shifting lanes. And nobody out there—except your fellow fraternity of truck drivers—gives you any credit. Safety is a baseline we all take for granted, as we should. But it is alternately unnerving and impressive to sit in the passenger seat of an eighteen-wheeler and see how much effort and focus go into maintaining that baseline.

The interior of the cab is snug. Directly behind Lynne sits a giant blue Rubbermaid cooler packed with ice and Pepsis. Lynne estimates she drinks about twelve cans a day. Buried in the ice, I also find a gallon-sized ziplock bag of hard-boiled quail eggs, a present from a retired trucker friend now farming. Lynne tells me she's trying to get into them. She wants to go Paleo. Next to her, at all times, cigarettes. They get lit end to end, marking the drive in ten-minute increments.

Her steering wheel is comically big, just over a large pizza in diameter, and covered in a custom pink leather casing for grip. It is an awful pink—all flesh and innards. To her right, suctioned to the dash, there is a pink iPhone case, in a somewhat more reassuring shade. A pink Trapper Keeper serves as her logbook. In the back is the bunk area, pink blankets tucked in military tight with pink pillows atop them. By the pillows, a cold steel revolver wedged into a pink holster. And when she gives me spare keys to get into the passenger-side door, the ring is a little pink penis with pink balls to serve as chain.

From our vantage, now humming along the highway, ten feet aloft, the four-wheelers below are transparent. It's like a nature show: humans in their habitat, completely unaware they can be observed. I see couples fighting, a man drinking a beer, countless drivers texting, their micro-swerves as they tap and look up and tap away again, obvious as they are oblivious. One of the great comforts of a car is the sense of containment and privacy; it's a little pod of refuge in a life harried by other people. But whatever you think you are getting away with, the trucker can see it all.

"People whip their dicks out," Lynne exclaims. "You'd be shocked at how many men are driving around in the cars with dicks out. What the fuck are you guys doing down there?"

She says this with a straw in her mouth, one hand on the wheel, one hand reaching back into the cooler to grab a fresh Pepsi, a zombie motion of habit.

"I've called in so many DUIs. So cocky, malt liquor in the cup holder. Yoo-hooo . . . I can see you . . ."

Lynne narrates the world to herself with the intensity of someone who has known absolutely awesome amounts of alone time. It is a diatribe against loneliness, as if she must re-create the world as she sees it verbally lest it disappear and her own existence get negated.

At first this seems like an interviewer's dream. A subject overflowing with commentary, dripping with color. The curse words fly, the anecdotes hum. I learn about her mother who had her at sixteen, that bitch Clarissa who stole her car, the daughter she had at twenty-two, her teeth, her lack of teeth, giving her daughter up for adoption, a husband she didn't see for twenty-two years. But then we move from anecdote to commentary. Commentary to random observation.

For a while, I thought she did this for my benefit, almost performance art, and I often wanted to let her know she didn't have to speak on my accord. But early on our third day, I realize that is all wrong. We had parked for the afternoon, to nap in preparation for a two a.m. wake-up. Lynne had gone to let the dogs pee, and I crawled into the upper bunk desperate for some alone time. I hear her approach across the lot with the same laughing, swearing, coughing, sighing monologue as always, talking to no one and everyone at once. Listening to it, knowing it wasn't for my benefit, was both curious and exhausting.

By the end of the fifth day, it is assaultive. Lynne will have four-to-five-hour conversations with me that consist of continuous monologue, where I am reduced to cowering "yeps," "uh-huhs," or the occasionally completely flat, tonally non-ascending "really." I start to wonder whether her conversation with me is obtuse/oblivious—i.e., she simply doesn't recognize or care about the social cues I am sending out—or actually combative, using words as a weapon. I know things have taken a dark turn when I consider getting earplugs for hanging around a woman I am ostensibly here to interview.

Bunking in the cab of an eighteen-wheeler is a little like sleeping inside a refrigerator, which is, of course, close to what you are doing. The reefer unit behind you blasts air at thirty-four degrees to keep the carcasses or broccoli cold. There is a perpetual hum from the motor, and you are living inside the rumble on a bunk shelf, not unlike a condiment, up there next to the eggs. If you're driving team and sleeping back there on your own, there is often no light until the door is cracked and the overheads come on. The vents gush A/C. So you're shivering in this rumbling, humming box. Looking around in the darkness, everything feels held over from the nautical world, the eighteen dials on the dash each registering something different and essential about, say, the pressure in your landing gear, or the temperature of your brake lines. Their presence is deceptive, of course. The real metrics, the ones you are judged on and paid for, are automated and digitized, beamed direct from your cab to your controller back at dispatch. But all the little dials and meters are reassuring and human scale, giving the illusion of individual control. In all, from bunk to dash, it's a refrigerator about the size of a midtown elevator, maybe seven feet across, seven feet to the wheel, height sloping upward with the windshield. The cold of the A/C makes huddling under heaps of blankets an obvious choice, the decision to get up and move a painful one. But as the week progresses, I realize there is something more paralyzing going on, something enervating about the truck itself, a draining dependence on machine. It is a complacency not unlike feeling yourself glued to your couch, disgusted with the TV but also somehow unable to get up to click it off. The truck itself, by its very confinement, in the way all possessions and comforts are just an arm's length away, by its foreclosing of the outside world, creating a little pod of convenience—submarine- or shuttle-like—weans you from a desire to connect or exert. It then gradually increases this stasis through a feedback loop: the more you stay in the truck, the more it acts on you; the more it acts on you, the more you stay in the truck, the inaction itself growing like a depressive mold. I see it everywhere at the truck stops we pass through: the unwillingness to get out of the cab to stroll around, that insistence of urinating in a bag rather than in a bathroom, the lonely men eating behind the same wheel they sat driving at for the previous eight hours, the feeling of isolation despite the presence of a sizable population. And after a few days I can feel it happening to me. I start to stay seated at rest stops alongside Lynne. We both get up and move around, but don't crack that door. The landscape outside involves just enough marginal effort that I'll find myself deciding to stay put and send a few emails from my phone rather than walk around, while next to me, Lynne stares into her cell phone and narrates a game of Farm Town.

The roar of the truck stop itself is a more monstrous groan of the refrigerator hum inside each individual cab. It is a sonic blanket, muffling all other sounds in the dark, a silence at sixty decibels. I walk through one night. It's earth-moving. Dinosaurs at slumber. Each shivering in their lane, each with a little human inside. The smell is of urine and fuel, the asphalt hot and wet, water from air conditioners puddling between the lanes. Looking in, I see a true multiethnic family of truckers, all isolated in their cabs. A man preparing ramen in his underwear, an obese woman doing seated stretches, arms above head. Then there are those outside the family of truckers: the dealers alternately offering to sell me "twisters" and just begging for a dollar, the gaunt prostitutes rapping on windows for work. As I walk, I count the trucks, but give up around 180 cabs. I have just begun and row after row remains ahead in the dark.

When I go inside the truck stop, the smell is of dryer sheets. It's twelve thirty a.m., the floors bright and gleaming and crowded with drivers. Some just waking groggy, about to leave for a delivery. Others wandering aimless, trying to process a landscape not moving at fifty-seven miles per hour. I realize every reader has been to these types of rest stops before—the Flying J, Love's, or Petros—many of which overlap with the type of truck stop I'm describing. But where you and I walk in from the front and exit with a Styrofoam cup of coffee, the trucker enters from the rear. It is an alternate side, far bigger and stranger. I walk past a tattoo parlor, a barbershop, then a laundromat. Up the stairs, I find a gym and locker room. Every few minutes there is a crackle over the loudspeaker, "Attention professional driver number 153, shower number 7 is now available." It breaks over the Christian rock with a sad functionality similar to the way dancers are called up to the stage at a strip club.

Off to the side, past an empty blinkering arcade, past a separate room of creepy coin-operated kiddie rides that look profoundly unridden, I find the driver's lounge. It is a dismal place, darkly lit, full of men sleeping chin to sternum, hands clasped over belly, belly barely moving. The TV is on the Weather Channel, but nobody is speaking or watching it. Some sit with guts out and proud, others with guts bound by suspenders like they're there to frame the guts' magnificence. Mesh hats on the fat white guys, du-rags on the fat black ones, cowboy boots all around. These are the loneliest parts of the grocery world. All these silent men, coming and coming into these rest stops off the conveyor of the road, quietly stocking themselves like items on a shelf, in these faux leather chairs, in front of this TV that nobody is watching, hands crossed over their bodies in a hug, palm on arm, flesh reassuring flesh even if it is their own flesh.

Let's pause to locate Lynne within the trucking ecosystem. First of all, understand that everything—*everything*—in your life comes to you on a truck. This is a favorite, self-affirming aphorism truckers love to repeat—I hear it constantly—but it has the benefit of being true. From the big appliances of our lives to the smallest bite of food, every single staple, butter knife, copper wire, or ceramic mug comes via truck. This is true whether you order online next-day delivery for your milk or opt to live off-grid and self-sufficient. If you build it yourself, the parts you use for building arrived on a truck. If you grow it, the seeds, organic fertilizer, and baling wire for your compost bin arrived that way too. Trucking as an industry is gargantuan: 10.7 billion tons of freight per year get moved around this great land on trucks, which breaks down to 54 million tons a day, or 350 pounds per man, woman, and child. Per day. It is the most common form of employment in the majority of

American states, with more than 12.6 million commercial drivers circulating our highways. And at the same time, it is one of the most dangerous jobs, right up there with deep-sea fishermen and timber cutters, boasting the highest total number of deaths per year of any job. It is also an industry uniquely connected to life. In a literal sense, trucking is the circulatory system through which GDP flows, and truckers are particularly keen to its kinks and expansions, their routes reflecting the strength of Christmas giving or a sudden recessionary anxiety. Some items see only a few trucks in their lives. Most see dozens. Some hundreds. Trucks backing into manufacturing centers, unloading items themselves manufactured, themselves brought in on different trucks, from different manufacturing centers, down down down to eventual raw material extraction, a supposed zero point but, upon closer inspection, itself a mess of lugging and unloading choked with trucks, a process of input as much as extraction, for feeding the workers, for delivering the pesticides, for maintaining the machinery, so that you can almost fractally descend at any part of the chain until it feels like the only constant beyond carbon when it comes to our possessions is truck, a fabric, and glue. And within every truck, a trucker, snuffing down Pepsis, coughing phlegm, butt bouncing high on the seat, invisibly but unrelentingly attached to consumption itself.

Within that ecosystem, Lynne is just a tiny node:

Driver, Lynne. Long haul or OTR (over the road), the unhelpful acronym used by the trucking industry to define her work as someone who runs an inconsistent (termed "non-dedicated") route, picking up commercial loads in one place, dropping them off in another, going wherever she is told.

Load planner, Kirk, overseer of Lynne's load board. The load board is a stock exchange of need and availability. Kirk surveys a region, connects dots of demand, and programs a route the driver will take. To do this, he sits in front of a Google Maps–like display with every driver in the area pinned there. He can see driver stats—miles per week, on-time percent, load refusal, complaints about attitude—and, like a teenager at the Risk board, he can push the pieces around with surprising caprice, rewarding favorites, penalizing anyone who makes his life more difficult.

Dispatcher, Jim. He just had a heart attack. Jim is a messenger between the driver and the load planner. He is tasked with managing the human being. He checks in and cajoles, bullshits and answers questions. Lynne loves him. She notes, however, that Jim gets paid when she is sitting on the dock waiting, trapped and unpaid and unable to leave. But then, so does basically everyone else in the system, so it's hard to hold it against Jim too long.

Dog, Lynne has two, Katie and Bella, both beautiful beagles. They are there for sanity and to provide connection. Truckers cling to dogs with an intensity that rivals the mother–child bond. Trucking without them would be a cruelty that might not be tolerated by the driver as opposed to a cruelty that is.

Receiver. I'm using this loosely to cover everyone from the smart-ass at the guard station to the workers zipping around on motorized pallet jacks like they are in *The Jetsons*. The receiver is where the load gets delivered, generally a giant warehouse or distribution center, but often, especially with bigger grocers, the back of the store directly.

Lumper. This is the person who physically unloads the truck. Lumping is brutal work, injuries are common, and so employing someone who is neither an employee of the shipper, the trucking company, nor the receiver allows the larger companies to avoid liability. Lynne is invited to "lump her own"—often for as much as $200 a load—but she refers to that as "insanity," by which she means the route to a quick injury that would lay her up for weeks. Instead she pays the lumper with money supplemented in her paycheck for that purpose.

Producer. These are the great food manufacturers of America. Industrial vats full of boiling marinara, canisters of vanilla extract taller than a ten-year-old boy, the blur of assembly lines and robotics that package, box, and stack our food so it is ready to be picked up by

Driver, Lynne.

From the highway, the ALDI distribution center is a white box of light in the four a.m. darkness. As we drift up the exit ramp toward it, we slowly queue behind other trucks, then we stop completely, idling in a long line waiting at a guard station. Despite the early hour, the activity isn't surprising. The drive from our overnight spot was among a caravan of truckers, cab to trailer, all plodding forth, this mechanical herd taking over the road while the world it serves sleeps.

Lynne flips her pink logbook open as we sit, making handwritten notes against the steering wheel, carrying on a conversation with a trucker two states away trapped in the middle of a similar delivery. They cackle over Bluetooth about the best places to sleep in Gary, Indiana, while we inch forward. Finally we arrive and Lynne rolls down her window to announce her load.

The man clicks around on his console station. Swivels to the side, speaks into a headset microphone, then swivels back to us.

"You're early."

"Yes, sir. About fifteen minutes, I'd reckon," Lynne says, shifting into a register of respect and concern I haven't yet seen.

There is silence on the other side. Some non-obvious power dynamic is going down.

"Okay, then." A long pause hangs here. "Head in."

We rumble through the barbed-wire fencing into a gargantuan parking lot capable of swallowing our eighteen-wheeler, rendering it Matchbox-sized all of a sudden. The distribution center, so banal from the highway, is mammoth now, wide enough to accommodate at least eighty trailers on its four sides. We roll around the building slowly, Lynne looking for her assigned gate. Each of the eighty spots is filled: every truck plugged into its own loading dock, the trailers sticking out perpendicular like USB drives snug into some central processor. Their lanes are tight, just enough space to walk single file between the trailers. As we roll past, we see drivers at the wheel, each filling out paperwork, scrolling on their cell phones, or staring lonely into the night as their trucks' innards are pulled out behind them.

Once Lynne backs into her lane and inserts her trailer into the assigned gate, for all practical purposes, her work is done. She has delivered her product safe and on time. But she isn't free to leave. Instead, Lynne enters one of the many gray portions of her labor market. She's at the mercy of her receiver's schedule. It can take thirty minutes. Or five hours. The last several loads we delivered went seamlessly. Lynne pulled up at her appointment time, and within an hour, the truck was emptied or filled respectively. Lynne set down her cell phone, ambled out of the cab to swap paperwork, and we rolled on our way.

This morning we wait. First, there is someone in her lane. So we pull to the edge of the parking lot until they leave. This takes about an hour. The sky begins bluing with impending dawn. Then, after backing in, nobody is ready to unload her. This adds another forty-five minutes. Finally, when the lumpers are ready, we have about an hour and fifteen of waiting for her paperwork to clear. That's a third of a day of unpaid, unrecognized labor at the ungodly hour of four a.m.

And the entire time is spent in the truck.

"Anything that happens out of this truck, I'm not insured," Lynne explains to me. "If I get hurt on the dock, I'm screwed. So, yeah, I feel better in here. I just play Farm Town."

I nod.

"And let's be honest, what's going on out there that I'm missing?

"You know I've been playing Farm Town for six years. I used to have DVDs and videos, but then I found Farm Town.

"I thank God for Farm Town."

Another Hundred-Dollar Workweek

While we wait, we try to calculate what she might make for the load. We started at Alamance Foods, outside of Charlotte, North Carolina, as spare a cement loading dock as exists in America. Two Mexican lumpers scooted pallets of something labeled DAIRY into our depths. From there, Lynne scrawled her signature on a clipboard, the lumpers pulled down the back door, slapped us goodbye on the proverbial rump, and Lynne drove off. We had 1,050 miles to go and three stops to make at different distribution centers.

For this Lynne gets $1,231 gross or $1.16 per mile, which Lynne tells me is pretty decent for a brokered load. On top of this, the shipper Alamance adds in a $368.50 fuel surcharge, a dollop extra to pay for fuel, her single greatest cost by a wide margin. It all sounds fairly good for two to three days of work. But that is the lure. Now comes the hook. First, a blizzard of deductions: 28 percent of the gross and 10 percent of the fuel is snatched off the top by Cargill for the privilege of driving in their fleet. Then there is a $300 weekly payment for leasing the truck she drives. There is the $300 she has to pay for the week prior, when work was slow but her truck payment was still due. Then there are the lumper fees, heavy-usage taxes, costs for various federally mandated fuel additives, and a mandatory cleaning service after every load, where a dude with a jetpack-like device sprays down the inside of her trailer no matter how clean or dirty it is.

So without any other expenses we are below $500 for the entire trip.

From there reality continues to intercede. The fuel surcharge almost never covers her actual expense. The truck is supposed to be able to make 6.0 miles per gallon when fully loaded. But we never break 4.5 miles per gallon the entire time I'm riding. This 4.5 mpg is also exclusively driving time. It doesn't count the quarter tank Lynne estimates she loses when we idle overnight. That quarter tank, by the way, is not the quarter tank of your Honda sedan. Lynne's Peterbilt has two tanks on each side, both massive: 120 gallons on the driver's side, 150 gallons on the passenger side. Not to mention a 50-gallon refrigerator tank that keeps our veggies crisp and that lasts only twenty-four hours when Lynne is hauling a load.[19]

Then there are the fixed costs that aren't taken out of this particular load, but need to be accounted for somehow. Lynne pays taxes per mile, per state, and needs an accountant to handle the complexity of that, or at least the trucking company who issues her check demands that she use one. They also demand that she retain their lawyer to handle billing disputes. Then there is insurance, also demanded by the carrier without the opportunity to shop around. Then maintenance on her truck, which when you drive twelve thousand miles a month is a whole different ball of wax than regular car maintenance. Then an escrow account called her "security," to which—again—she is contractually obligated to contribute, which is maintained by the trucking company, held entirely at their discretion, and that serves as a backstop should she ever throw up her arms and decide she wants to walk away from her lease-to-own agreement. Finally there are a host of tiny fees for administrative work, for mapping devices, "mobile communication terminals,"

---

19 This is where you can do some greenhouse gas calculations in your head and realize that even if you are driving the most virtuous Prius-Tesla-Volt in the world, your lifestyle is still burning through hydrocarbons like the dickens. Our trucking fleet consumes gasoline in an unimaginable manner. Rivers burned every night across America.

some of which she can't completely explain even as they bleed her paycheck.

Finally there are the inherent risks. Which as an owner-operator Lynne has assumed entirely on behalf of her trucking company. The week before I joined her, while she dozed at a truck stop, the driver next to her crunched into her. Lynne awoke to the jolt and scrambled out of her bunk only to watch as the driver fled the lot. She guesses he was a rookie and his whole career was on the line—one early crash and you're out. But regardless of his identity, she was stuck with an insurance claim.

I bring this up because that ever-diminishing sum we calculated Lynne would make for the load consisted of her earnings before beginning the trip. The open road is unpredictable in almost every way except one: the longer you are on it, the more certain something costly will happen. It takes a shift in mind-set, one the rookie driver almost never makes, but this is not about bad luck. A hit-and-run might be rare, but it is just one risk among thousands—trailer brakes failing, tires blowing, reefer line freezing—that collectively become inevitable.

In this case, the damage was exclusively to her fairing—the plastic paneling around the undercarriage—the best possible outcome. It was both superficial and inexpensive. And yet, despite her insurance coverage, the thousand-dollar deductible on her policy left her liable for the entire amount. "If I need a repair done, and I actually have the money, I just pay for it," she says. "But that is never the case. Instead I gotta get approval, then I gotta get a loan, then they charge extra fees for the loan, and then I have to use their garage to get it fixed." Worst of all, every time there is a repair, Lynne sits. No loads, no money coming in. And suddenly a tiny incident takes her from a marginal place to ruin.

To drill in to one small but telling detail of these deductions: Lynne currently rides for Cargill because she lacks what is known as an authority.[20] If she had one, she could deal with a broker on her own. She could negotiate rates that are higher, and she wouldn't have to sacrifice almost a third of her pay off the top.

But Lynne can't get one. It isn't the cost of the authority, which at the current registration fee of $1,200 is not outrageous, although probably unattainable for someone who chooses to skip meals to save money. It is the structural requirements behind the authority.

As she tells it, even if she were given $1,200 for an authority today, she would be no closer to getting one. "If I was on my own, I'd pull a load tomorrow and not get paid for six months," she tells me. Like a lot of contract labor, pay comes slowly and irregularly, and operating as a true independent would require a minimum of six months of fuel out of pocket, six months of grocery bills, and six months of fees to her accountant and attorney. So even though Cargill—like all carriers—takes a healthy percent for allowing her use of their authority, she stays put.

"I'd need an office too," she says after some thought. "Which could be in your house, but I don't really have a house. I have an RV right now." She pauses. "But that's in storage." There is a long pause here. "What I'm saying is I'd need an address."

Lynne estimates she grossed $200,000 last year—that is a rough calculation based on miles driven—but that she took home less than $17,000. This for a fourteen-year veteran trucker who knows her industry inside and out. Who participates on trucking blogs, mentors younger truckers about the snares and scams. Who lives in her truck and stays out on the

---

20 I also cannot stress how over-the-top enthralled with Cargill Lynne is. She repeatedly tells me they are the best employer she has ever had, that they treat her with a respect that she hasn't found with any other trucking company, that they are reliable and friendly, and give her quality loads. This seems important to note, as her outsized, almost manic gratitude for basic decency is probably one of the best second-order indicators about what her life was like with prior carriers.

road three weeks at a time. Who works more than seventy hours the week I am with her, much of it spent in a state of a constant vigilance, where she sleeps in four to five hour bursts, and wakes up for three thirty a.m. appointments that are make-or-break for her career, but ignored by the distribution center on the other side. Who didn't see her mother for two years because she didn't have the time off and couldn't get loads that lined up with her mother's location. The $17,000 also—based on my experience with her—is a number likely inflated by pride. The week I'm with her, Lynne receives a weekly paycheck for just $100. Which is what she received the week before. And the week before that.

"It's in my contract," she tells me. "No matter how many expenses I have, I always have the right to a check for one hundred dollars. So that is what I usually get . . . I've gotten pretty good at knowing how to stretch it."

And in reality, the week I am with her that $100 represents nothing. When going over our time together, I estimate she nets something closer to negative $150 after factoring in extravagances like cell phone bills and an unanticipated repair. So it is no surprise that when sleeping in the bunk one afternoon, I overhear her ask for a cash advance from her future $100 paychecks, so she can afford to eat dinner that night.

The next morning, Lynne turns to me and says, "I think I can get back in the black. Maybe another three or four weeks of this . . ." And it is completely unclear what she means. She is losing money. Another three or four weeks like this and she will be even deeper in debt, further beholden to Cargill.

"Or I could run into a ladder on the interstate that tears my brake lines," she says to complete both our thoughts.

To recap: Lynne is homeless, sleeping exclusively in the cab of a truck she does not yet own and almost certainly will eventually lose when she can no longer make payments on it. Her credit is shot. She has outstanding vet bills for her two dogs, the closest and most beloved members of her family. Her personal health is so wrecked, it's hard to even discuss. Suffice to say, she cannot eat most food because she lost every one of her teeth and her new dentures are not properly fitted so it pains her to chew. Her obsession with Pepsi for calories shifts in my brain into absolute sadness when I learn this. She is also very good at her job. Hypervigilant on the road and extremely hardworking, a team player, who never in my presence complains about a task given to her or her lot in life.

These things are not unrelated.

Debt and Hope

There are some jobs where it is almost impossible to succeed because they are very difficult. Then there are jobs where you are designed to fail. Lease-to-own programs in OTR trucking seem like both to me. During my time with the reefer trucks, talking to the men and women who constitute the circulatory system of our economic lives, who touch each and every can of beans we touch twice, I come to see the trucking industry as structurally vampiric. I don't say this to be dramatic. It is an industry that creeps along the margins of society and seduces the vulnerable, feeding itself on their aspirations, coaxing them to lend a little bit of their lives and credit in exchange for a promise that is almost never delivered: a stable job and control over their own destiny. Debt is the financial instrument that best expresses hope. Industrial trucking is brilliant at this precise exchange. I hear repeatedly about trucking recruiters[21] who cruise for drivers from homeless shelters, soup kitchens, recovery wards, prison work-release programs. Many more come from minimum wage retail, from construction, from several tours of duty overseas. These men and women are promised "Guaranteed jobs!" "No experience? No problem!" "Get paid while training" "Fantastic money!"; salary quotes range from the reasonable and enticing ("Earn

---

21 Recruiters typically must bring in three drivers per week to keep their jobs and naturally work on commission, earning extra if they bring in more.

up to $60,000") to the patently absurd ("$100K per year and freedom!"). They are offered free one-way bus tickets directly to training centers if they quit their old life. They are housed in company motels with all costs paid for up front by the company, and assured they can pay back everything from future earnings.[22] Meals are provided. And with just a quick signature on the third or fourth day, suddenly they are students, who have taken on real-live student debt to prove it, training to earn a commercial driver's license. Once in the classroom, they are pounded with further praise for seizing this chance to control their own destiny. The job they were initially offered vaporizes, and an even better offer appears. Now they can become owner-operators, and by signing just a few more papers, they will get their own truck without having to pay a cent. Once they accept, they will then be run ragged, desperately trying to make good on their end of the bargain, spending their next six months deciphering pay stubs, trying to understand why running tens of thousands of miles at $0.30 to $0.90 a mile never gets them more than $100 a week, not realizing until far too late how difficult it is, at which point drained of the motivation that initially made them useful to the carrier, they are bounced out of the industry, financially crippled, embittered, and often too proud to admit it.

For this opportunity, all that is required is they have a clear driving record for the last three years. Smaller hurdles like a minor drug or alcohol problem can be smoothed over.

"They told me to ease up on the honesty speech. Quit doing it," Tom Hansen, trainer at one of the larger companies, told Dan Rather when describing his attempts to weed out substance abusers.

---

22 The stories from these training center motels will loosen the jaw a solid thirty degrees. Junkies wandering the hallways looking for a fix—and finding it from another recruit—fistfights, armed robbery, self-harm from obvious mental illness, and if you are one of the 5 percent of recruits who are women, sexual harassment from a fellow recruit, senior driver, trainer, or all three.

And, if at any point in the process, you wake up in your motel bed, shivering because it lacks insulation, squinting at your third roommate who has been leaving a cheap nine millimeter out on his duffel, and decide this whole experience is not precisely what you thought it was going to be: you are on the hook for the cost of the entire training, somewhere between $3,000 and $8,000, depending on the carrier. And you still have to buy that one-way bus ticket back to whatever life you quit to come out here.

Trucking used to be a middle-class job. This was during the long golden stretch from 1935 to 1980, when transportation was a tightly regulated, almost cartel-like industry. Federal law, as applied through the Interstate Commerce Commission, restricted the number of carriers, allowed overt price collusion between those that remained, and exempted the entire industry from antitrust laws. This was not a good thing, nor a sign of a healthy industry, but it allowed a small cohort of carriers to grow extremely powerful, and correspondingly provided the perfect conditions for collective bargaining. Jimmy Hoffa was a teamster first and foremost, and the strong, if corrupt, union he led was able to wrest a middle-class salary with benefits from that cohort. By the 1970s, trucking became the favorite scruffy but loveable blue-collar profession. Hence the slew of corny hit movies—from *Smokey and the Bandit*, *Convoy*, and *Breaker! Breaker!*—that would flop instantly today if released in any format except for horror. This golden era was anticompetitive, inefficient, and opposed across the political spectrum from Ralph Nader to Ronald Reagan, but it provided a stable, respectable income for the individual trucker.

Then, literally overnight, with the scrawl of President Carter's pen, everything shifted. Trucking underwent a radical course correction, deregulating in extremis if you were a driver. Carriers multiplied, authorities fell from the regulatory sky, nonunionized workers flooded the market, and the price of transport dropped by 20 percent in just the first few years. From the golden '70s, the trucker suddenly found himself in the red and green '80s, the colors of the now essential methamphetamines drivers gobbled by the handful—were given by the handful by their dispatch—to carry out the marathon runs they were now asked to complete so the carrier could survive. The success of that initial phase of deregulation under the 1980 Motor Carrier Act led to a frenzy of further deregulation under the Reagan administration. Soon the sheer volume of carriers resulted in precisely the conditions the deregulators intended. Trucking became a commodity, and control over prices swung to shippers who could float a bid confident they would always find someone willing to run their freight cheaper or quicker or both.[23]

This is our current system. A machine being asked to run at ever faster rates in the name of competition, with leaner oversight, less routine maintenance, less long-term investment, with everyone involved knowing this means the belts will start to smoke and the smaller, cheaper parts get replaced as they fail. It is the payoff of deregulation and perceived as pretty much a good thing, since it certainly benefits the consumer. Margins are tight and everyone from broker to receiver to carrier CEO is sweating, jockeying for position. This is what is meant by "running a lean operation," "cutting cost to the bone," and "shaving inefficiencies," terms I hear repeated like sacred incantations by carriers explaining how they are scrambling to compete. There are real savings. Freight is cheaper. Groceries are cheaper. It turns out, however, that in trucking, along with the tire tread, brake pad, and transmission, the trucker himself is another one of those parts structurally designed to be worn to failure. I think everyone involved agrees that this isn't quite ideal, that in a perfect world, the problem of the human driver would

23 Or to concretize: "Long-haul truckers are producing twice the amount of measurable output, compared with the late 1970s, for wages that are 40% lower," author Steve Viscelli notes in his excellent 2016 ethnography, *The Big Rig: Trucking and the Decline of the American Dream.*

be tidied up and eliminated by drone, automation, or some other insentient mute machine. But in the meantime, the long meantime, the customer and the lowest price prevail, the belt smokes, and the ingenious ways to render a man or woman disposable continue.

To put this in perspective, over the last ten years industry turnover in trucking has ranged between 95 to 112 percent. Which is, upon reflection, a range of percentages that barely makes sense. The turnover at a top law firm is 17 percent and that has been deemed a crisis for the profession. The turnover at Starbucks is around 65 percent. One hundred percent turnover in the trucking industry means that every single member of a fleet either retired or quit or was fired and was successfully replaced that year. One hundred twelve percent turnover for a given fleet means that cycle repeated more than once. This might make sense if trucking were a declining industry, unable to pay its employees, but it has been growing aggressively over those same years.

So what is going on?

What appears to be happening is that the industry has figured out not only how to make humans replaceable but also how to make money off their replacement. The labor shortage is profitable. Recruiting rapaciously and dishonestly, convincing recruits to take out lines of credit for the opportunity, and then paying those new recruits the lowest possible wages for the labor—they call these "training rates"—all work synergistically. I am told by various industry observers that the trucking industry earns its highest profits on student drivers. They then use the accrued debt as a tool to force the driver to work at these rates far longer than they would otherwise. When I described trucking as structurally vampiric, turnover is the force that creates the suction.

Churn and Burn

The latest and greatest scheme in this department is team driving. When a driver emerges from even the best CDL school—much less the recruitment mills previously discussed—they are simply not equipped to drive an eighty-thousand-pound rig. Trucking may be blue-collar, but it is not unskilled.

So the driver is paired with a trainer. The first month of this partnership is called running "solo." The new driver must be observed full-time: when the driver drives, the trainer sits in the passenger seat and trains. By the second month, with the new driver getting his trucking legs beneath him, the team shifts to "solo and a half." Now, half the time the new recruit is driving, the trainer is in the back resting up to drive himself. Finally, after the eighth week, they shift to "team driving." One man drives, the other sleeps. Then they swap. Then they swap again and again and again.

Running team doubles the amount of road a truck can legally cover and is a godsend for the carrier and the shipper.[24] Moving freight from California to D.C. takes seven to ten days on the rails; a truck driving team can shrink that to 2.5 days while offering door-to-door precision.

---

24 The federally mandated work rules around trucking are both aggressively dry and yet vital to truly understanding how all this works in practice. If you drive there are strict rules designed to limit the number of consecutive hours you can spend working in your truck—but because truckers work, live, and are forced during odd loading times to spend ungodly hours in their trucks, these regulations have significant unintended impacts into how free you are to structure your own time. For those interested in the details, here is my best take at distilling these regulations into bite-sized comprehensibility. Basically, every day, once you move your truck, a clock starts ticking and you have fourteen hours to park it again. No more than eleven of those fourteen hours can be spent driving. And you can do that day after day until you hit seventy hours of truck time within a given eight-day period. At which point you need to take a thirty-four-hour restart. If that makes sense to you on a first read, god bless, I am sure you aced the LSAT. The entire thing is the subject of endless debates and strident all-caps posts on trucking blogs, and seems to fail most significantly when a driver is stuck at one of those loading docks—as Lynne got stuck at ALDI—where the stolen time hurts triple: you are not being paid, can't pick up new work, and yet chewing away at your availability for the rest of that day/week, forcing you to rush future loads that you might otherwise have been able to rest on. It is also, for this particular footnote, what makes driving team such a godsend to shippers and carriers, solving all of those problems at once.

It is also a grueling life. Team drivers live inside that 7′ x 7′ box. They don't really come out much. The box is always on the move somewhere. This actually can work tolerably for teams of brothers, sisters, and married couples, all of whom I met on the road, all of whom had mixed emotions about the dizzying life of team but who thought they could tough it out a few more years because the money was better.

But if you are a new recruit, you are partnered with a stranger. Often a stranger who is undergoing the same stressful, debt-filled realization about the life they just stepped into that you are going through too. Your possessions are on top of each other, your needs are on top of each other, your sexual desires and rage and annoying quirks are on top of each other.

It is hard.

But it's efficient! And the efficiency of team driving coupled with the extremely low training rates carriers pay new recruits have combined to heavily incentivize turnover.

"There is so much money in students," Desiree Wood, a trucker and trucking advocate, tells me. "They work so cheap. Twelve to thirteen cents a mile. It pays for the entire system . . . And a lot of these trainers have been driving less than six months themselves. It's that extreme turnover. What other industry is it common to go from a student to a trainer in six months?

"Half the time there is a blowout, a fistfight, a brawl in the cab in the middle of the second month, and they leave that freight in the middle of nowhere," Desiree continues. "That team is shucked. But there is always some other team just starting out that is willing to come get the load and drive it to its destination." And the process continues.

Large trucking companies have one hundred new recruits coming in every week.

They have that 112 percent turnover.

And so we have cheap freight.

"These companies don't have enough independent contractors willing to do that type of work. Especially not if they have a contract with a company the size of Amazon," Desiree explains. "What they do have are students driving team."

CRST, which runs one of the larger training programs, brings in approximately ten thousand new drivers each year alone. Each of the major trucking companies—C.R. England, Swift, Covenant, Prime, J.B. Hunt—offers a similar program of their own.

When I talk to a recruiter at Covenant about the possibility of a job, she tells me, "Think long and hard. They own you for ten months."

When I ask her about one of her competitors, one recommended to me by Desiree as "one of the best of the dirty bunch," the recruiter gasps. "Oh, I'd avoid them like a disease."

Then she gets riled up. "They'll dirty pool you. They'll take money right out of your check. And the trainers—I'm sure there are some good ones—but, oh, there are a lot of slime."

Of course, all of those are things I've been told about her company.

But she's rolling now. "You gotta be careful with any training program. My first trainer was a jerk-off. He threw me off in a dirt lot. He called me a lying SOB . . . Look, sweetheart, basically you are brand-new and paired with whoever they can wrangle. Do you want to take that chance?

"I'd check out a program from a community college . . . There are better options . . ."

This from the recruiter.

They Own You

The structures that allow carriers to pressure drivers into team are essentially the same as the structures that keep drivers trapped across the system. "This is not far from sharecropping," Desiree says. "It's debt bondage. It's sharecropping where instead of the field they are tenants on wheels." And any decision point—from the signing of a lease-purchase agreement to agreeing to drive team to installing a new "voluntary" monitoring device—provides the carrier with another opportunity to mold wayward drivers back into "team players."

Students, fresh with debt, ignorant about industry norms and legal rights, are the easiest to manipulate. If you resist signing an owner-operator lease agreement or decide you would rather train solo when there is a burning need for team drivers, they will simply stall. A recent class action suit certified against trucking giant C.R. England in 2017 alleges that when new recruits demanded the jobs they were recruited for—as opposed to the owner-operator "opportunities" they were presented with—they were systematically told "trucks aren't available" and they would have to wait indefinitely for them. However, if they agreed to lease a truck or drive team, they could get out on the road immediately. This while the driver was accruing more debt by staying on company property, accruing interest on that debt, and unable to work to pay it all back. Recruits who waited this threat out were eventually given a truck. But then the stalling continued. Actual loads didn't materialize. Or they came slow and erratic. Or with too few miles to make a living. This is called "starving you out," and because the student is contractually bound to that carrier thanks to the contract they signed at training, and since they owe the carrier money, again, thanks to that training, the student is completely at the mercy of the carrier and almost always "plays ball" and "becomes a team player."

"They cut your miles," a trucker tells me at a truck stop. "You get the message."

Or as Lynne tells me about her own lease-purchase agreement, "I know there is a light at the end of the tunnel. Because I am locked into this contract and I can't afford to believe anything else."

Beyond financial strangulation, the industry also has the DAC report. DAC is the catchy abbreviation for the nongrammatical, non-sensical Drive-A-Check report, a document that serves as sort of a credit report for drivers, listing their driving history (record of accidents, traffic violations) alongside an employment history (reasons for leaving a job, reports of damage to equipment). Like a bad credit report, a bad DAC report has major consequences, typically preventing a driver from being hired by a new company. Unlike a bad credit report, the DAC report relies on information provided by your current employer. And in practice that means it is wielded like a threat.

Drivers who report on-the-job injuries might find a no-fault accident suddenly shifted into 50 percent fault on their DAC. A driver who pulls to the side of the road, reporting a problem on the brake lines, might be told to complete the run. If he fails, an abandonment of equipment might appear on his DAC. A driver who refuses an overweight load—perhaps a pallet or two higher than the eighty-thousand-pound federal limit that makes him liable at a weigh station—might be reported for not making their appointment with the shipper.

It's hard to explain just how vulnerable you are as a trucker. It reorients my understanding of the bravado in the profession. You are beholden to the carrier. They control your wages. They own your home and source of livelihood in fact, if not in "owner-operator" name. They determine when you get to see your family and when you get the opportunity to work. You are beholden to the economy as a whole in a way that is far more intimate than for most of us. You are locked in a culture that venerates self-reliance and individual persistence and is hostile to displays of weakness or need: a profession where being tossed off a truck is a common and noncontroversial practice: where death and life-threatening accidents are never far from the mind. You are also inherently isolated, lonely, and physically vulnerable by the very nature of the job. The only thing more frightening than being alone on the side of a highway hundreds of miles away from help or cell phone reception is being isolated on the side of that same empty highway with someone you are driving team with who is mentally unstable, who may or may not be about to hurt you.

"With my height and my demeanor, I intimidate most men, but at night you won't catch me dead walking around a truck stop," Lynne tells me. "I want to walk my dogs, but it just isn't right at night.

"I would never wear shorts," Lynne tells me. "The idea of wearing shorts around a truck stop if you are a woman . . ." She just pauses and trails off.

"Walking through trucks," she tells me. "That's probably the most dangerous thing you could do as a woman. I will never, ever walk through two trucks. Don't care how much time it might save me.

"If there is a group of guys standing around," Lynne tells me, "I walk the dogs the other way."

Lynne also tells me that at a truck stop she never makes eye contact with a man. That she doesn't like taking showers at truck stops after a certain hour. That just talking to a man over a meal might get her labeled as a truck stop whore.

"Sometimes I just dress up like a guy at night if I have to go out," she says, cracking up with laughter at the notion. "Tuck my hair under a ball cap. Wear a big leather jacket to hide my tits. Oh, that's common. My friend Alison does the exact same thing. We were just laughing about it."

Women make up about 5 percent of truckers. Every vulnerability that male truckers suffer is amplified.

During my time with Lynne, I talk with the women we bump into at distribution centers. Elaine, a trucker I met at the ALDI warehouse, tells me the one piece of advice she would give to a younger woman considering a job in trucking: "Stay out." Saneria, young and heavily tattooed from Chicago, tells me most nights she refuses to get out of her cab at truck stops, especially if she sees big groups of men. Another woman I met at a Dairy Fresh distribution center tells me about getting out of her cab for dinner and being noticed by a man who proceeds to jump on her running board and knock on her window several times that night.

Every woman I spoke with had a story of an abusive trainer, either one who assaulted them, harassed them, threatened to rape them, or did one of those things to a friend. The single exception is a woman who was trained by her husband and drove team with him exclusively.

Lynne tells me, "If a female trucker told me she had two trainers and said she wasn't sexually harassed, I'd be shocked." Indeed, Lynne's first trainer would sit behind her while she drove and watch porn on his computer with the volume turned up. This continued for weeks. She complained, but he denied it. It was his word against hers, and she was stuck with him. Later he grabbed her chest hard enough to leave a bruise, which she reported to the police. Finally, she was given a new trainer. "And the company was like 'Maybe you misconstrued it,'" she says. "And it's like 'His hand was on my chest, what the fuck did I misconstrue?'"

While we are driving down a tiny two-lane highway in West Virginia, Lynne starts to tell me about Amy. It is the first time I ask her about being a woman in trucking. We are cruising through a narrow valley, bright green forest on both sides, the occasional collapsed farmhouse. She met Amy at orientation for her CDL. Amy was the only other woman at the training, so they bunked together.

"My first impression of her was 'Damn she's short,'" Lynne says as the valley opens wide around us. "She was five foot nothing. A lot of other women see me as competition, but I think because of our size difference we could talk. To be honest, we weren't close at all. I do remember she was neat and tidy. This tiny little thing."

One night about nine months after their training, Lynne got a phone call from a number she didn't recognize. Lynne answered, and it was Amy and she was crying.

"They raped her underneath the trailer," Lynne tells me, staring straight ahead at the road. "There is four feet of clearance there. Nobody heard her scream.

"She crawled back to her truck and I was the first person she called. I was two hundred miles away. We talked all night long." Then Lynne explained to her dispatcher that she had an emergency to attend, did not wait for his response, unhitched her trailer and drove to Amy. "I took her to the hospital . . . While they did the rape kit, she kept telling me she was screaming at the top of her lungs and nobody came to help.

"I didn't know what to say. I just cried with her. She didn't have anyone else. I only knew her from training . . . But I didn't really know her at all."

Then "Oh, damn," and for the first time in a thousand miles Lynne goes completely silent and we continue driving through the West Virginia valley.

Here again, in her fear, her experience, and her friendships, Lynne appears representative of the entire industry. I simply do not have the hard statistics to make an empirical case about the trucking industry's treatment of women. But I do know that any time official resources scratch the surface, the stories come flooding out. A massive 270-person civil discrimination case brought in 2012 against trucking giant CRST by the Equal Employment Opportunity Commission was filled with agonizing depictions of harassment, abuse, assault, and rape. Woman after woman came forward to detail her treatment. The case ultimately hinged not on the veracity of the allegations but on whether the EEOC had properly honored a statutory obligation before filing the lawsuit.

Both in district court and on appeal, the court found they had not. The actual substance of the women's claims—from assault to rape to merely spending days in a cab with a man obsessively masturbating behind them while they were teaching them how to drive—were never even considered.

"Every woman I've ever talked to in trucking has this type of story," Desiree Wood tells me. "The problem is the culture. When incidents get reported, they cost money. So the attitude is 'We'll make the person who reported it go away. We'll make it seem like they are crazy or a problem'—and there are enough crazy people in trucking that this works. The carrier can do that because they know most drivers aren't smart enough or connected enough to sue them or do anything about it . . . The attitude is they'll slink back right where we got them.

"The problem is this just empowers the predators," she continues. "There is no accountability. Instead they get recirculated around the industry."

And the shipper and receiver?

"They don't have a clue about the drama out there. They don't want to look. They just love the results."

The Results

While Lynne is waiting in her truck, that dawn sky bluing around us, I head inside. The receiving area at the ALDI distribution center is just about what you would imagine: an endless warehouse space, spare and cold and buzzing with forklifts. We're unloading into refrigerated, so it's maybe thirty-five degrees. All around, sweating men with big white Mickey Mouse–style gloves dart in and out of the trailers pulling pallets. Everyone everywhere is on the move and on top of each other, except the truckers who stand against a far wall, waiting for paperwork, bleary-eyed and bored.

For the first time all trip I see the product we have been carrying.

Out it comes on pallets piled chest-high: canisters of whipped cream, row after row, red plastic nose cones straight up like little missiles. The receivers swarm. The whipped cream gets barely a glance—classic continuous product off an assembly line—but this being the refrigerated area, most other arrivals are produce. These get scrutinized, receivers patting down the sides of boxes for indentations, rifling through flats to pluck out individual strawberries. This forty-five-second inspection is perhaps the most important stage of quality control along the entire chain. Up until this point, there has been no sale. Now the retailer needs to fish or cut bait. Many loads never make it any farther. To my right sit the rejects. Moldering boxes of lettuce, leaking jugs of juice, a leaning tower of eggs—18" x 36" across—stove in from some collision, the yolks dripping down. Other loads are placed in holding. A glass-paneled lab sits in the corner, where this potential food can be sliced open, probed with calipers for firmness, or blended into a slurry to test for sugar content. If it passes, it is popped on a forklift and whizzed deeper in the warehouse along with our whipped cream.

The probes and lab evals hint at something more. The big lie here is that the warehouse is just a location for passive storage, where items are slotted in, sit around, and then get retrieved as needed. The truth for perishable grocery is closer to an NICU ward at the hospital: blazing technology furiously working to sustain premature life. The fruit and veg of our lives are alive and need to stay that way until we bite into them. Unlike the NICU, however, the distribution center has no interest in survivability per se. Instead all this technology serves to control. The teenage ambition to stop-start time, pause, and then unfreeze life at the perfect moment is steadily being achieved for many forms of produce. At the various distribution centers I visit, I walk into sauna-sized rooms full of butter-yellow bananas, ceiling to floor, jammed with a network of probes and wires. A few doors down, I'll find wall-to-wall racks of rock-hard avocados or red unripe tomatoes, tomatoes so firm they fall to the floor and bounce with the thud of a baseball. All of which can be kept in suspension or fast-forwarded toward a ripe, salable version depending on need.

That fresh apple you bite into has typically been sitting in dormancy for close to a year. Red cherries, that epitome of summer freshness, might have been stuck stabilized for two and half months. Bananas, avocados, tomatoes, and limes land somewhere in between. There are exceptions. Even in perfect conditions, most leafy greens deteriorate in just under three weeks, but even that would be thought of as a miracle when earlier grocers had three to four days to get them from field to fridge. My beloved blueberries have probably sat around for forty-five days on their journey up from Chile or down from Maine.

The core of this control comes from regulating ethylene, a gaseous plant hormone that causes ripening and color development. Within the right conditions, suppressing ethylene keeps fruit in a suspended state of development. And if the right conditions can't be created, the product can be sprayed or waxed with ethylene antagonists, coating them during production with chemicals that bind to the fruit's natural receptors. These modified atmospherics are complemented with an array of antibacterials and preservatives, perhaps a rinse with molecular iodine or a dusting with bioflavonoids. Nothing is simple; the needs of a tropical papaya are radically different from a Bartlett pear, but ultimately our nation's storage facilities can build for that, creating an eerie array of these chemo-cryogenic chambers, all evoking some madman's humidor, little pods keeping each type of immature produce in dreamless stasis until the market leans over and kisses it awake.

I watch a few more loads come in and get inspected. And then, everyone busy, I slip through a giant plastic curtain into the rest of the warehouse. This is the dry-goods area. The pallets here are stacked high so they tower above, and gridded out in narrow lanes. The air is still, the vista endless. In the distance, a jack stretches off its base, extending maybe fifteen feet upward, some combination of the mechanical and prehistoric—megafauna foraging on the high leaves—before forking into a load, shrinking back down, and zipping off with its catch. Watching it move, I realize I'm probably the first person in weeks to venture here on just two legs. This section of the warehouse is a deathless space. The precursor to the center aisle, a reservoir of food structurally unable to spoil, the boxes bound in thick layers of translucent, almost amniotic wrap, an industrial Guf where all the souls of our cereal, cookies, and crackers wait to be delivered onto shelf. Seeing almost any product in bulk is debasing. And it is no different here. Walking around the warehouse, studying the towers of familiar brands, I'm reminded of being eight years old in McDonald's pumping ketchup into little paper cups for my fries. And, curious, lifting the entire cover off the pump to peer down into the reservoir, coming face-to-face with a dark, plump slurry. Ketchup as molten grainy mass, nothing like the cute dollops I'd been squeezing for my fries. Commodity is contempt all the way down, and wandering the ALDI distribution center I realize just how much materialism depends on individuality, on our ability to inject meaning into *things*.

The longer I spend with Lynne, the more context she provides on her life and decisions, the more important meaning becomes here too. I come to see her as dedicated to a dream. Lynne is vigilant on the road, her attention thousand-eyed and all-seeing behind the wheel. I see her save lives when totally unaware sedans try to beat her to a merge lane. Off the road, I see a remarkable persistence. What she calls her ability to "take it"—do her duty and withstand—a sense of obligation that also rhymes with an ability to shut down, swallow pride, and self-contain. In our time together, I watch as she gets pelted with petty aggravations, canceled loads, endless hours of unpaid labor, impossible deadlines, outright lies, and none of that—from the most unfair to the most aggravating—is greeted with anything more than a chin-tucked, head-down, plow-forth attitude.

The truckers I travel with are angry, conspiratorial, overtly paranoid, unclean, but also undeniably sharp, often wise. They are quick studies, typically self-taught, with that mix of insight and brash insecurity that marks the autodidact. The ability to hum down America's highways under the moon, to watch it rise into blackness and eventually disappear into dawn, is privileged stuff. These are men and women who have slipped the nine-to-five grind, shook the ritual obligations and routines that deaden most of us. And they fill that time with a type of quiet, nonjudgmental observation that would make most yoga instructors jealous.

It is a lifestyle that pounds home the reality that liberty and freedom are deeply related to loneliness and isolation.

The most satisfied truckers I meet are the ones who have explicitly recognized and chosen that trade-off. Who understand that on some level what they are asked to do isn't economically rational, but is instead an act of devotion to a certain myth of the American road.

For those few truckers, it is a beautiful thing. But there are far too many who didn't make this choice, who were not warned about it, and for whom the job ends up crushing them. In my time with Lynne, with all her words, I see her occupy all these spaces at different times. "You know"—she turns to me on our last day together—"if I ever lost my CDL for anything, they'd have to put me in the ground. This job is misery, but it's the only thing in the world for me."

At nine thirty a.m., now the morning after ALDI, we finally crash at a rest stop a few miles down the road. I feel soggy, puffed, and swollen, my mouth raw from the nondairy creamer and beef jerky dinner the night before. It's hard to imagine the type of bacteria that would colonize such a palate, but whatever species of microbe, they feel fuzzy on my gums.

We nap for four hours, me crawling onto the top bunk, Lynne

flopped with the dogs on the bottom. For the first time all trip, the truck is turned off. Is this an accident? An oversight? I don't know. But when we wake at one thirty p.m., both of us staggering around like drunks, the cab has heated into a death box and I understand the A/C all of a sudden.

I plunge for the side door and gasp at the light. All around us, two hundred, three hundred trucks are vibrating in their lanes. I almost run to the strip of grass on the side. Behind me Lynne is coughing like an avalanche: phlegm tumbling over phlegm. It is a new cough, containing echoes of chunky soup, a wheeze, and someone weeping. The day has begun. In another thirty minutes, we'll both be buckled in, heading to a new shipper to pick up a load.

PART III

Self-Realization Through Snack

Men who Achieve—with hands or brain—
  Who Rise, who Lead, who Win, who Act—
They fight on simple grain—
  On Quaker Oats—to be exact.

—Quaker Oats campaign, 1903

Gradually I began to realize that modern advertising could be seen less as an agent of materialism than as one of the cultural forces working to disconnect human beings from the material world.

—T. J. Jackson Lears, *Fables of Abundance*

When Did We All Get So Fucking Bored?

At eight a.m., it doesn't smell like a specialty food show. It smells like new car, the off-gassing of five straight miles of newly laid fuzzy gray carpet blanketing this convention center. By noon, the carpet will be speckled with salsa like bird droppings, a walkway of crushed nuts, crumpled cups, and an endless litter of discarded toothpicks covering the ground like industrial pine needles. But at eight a.m., it is clean and vast and filled with entrepreneurs assembling booths. The sound is the crickets of the marketplace, thousands of boxes being slit open, the crinkling of thick plastic being unwrapped, the sighs of stiff men bending over to lug out product to display, pausing every once in a while to stand back and take a long nasal inhale. It's the smell of raw capitalism, that off-gassing, and the men savor it before pulling out their phones to take a photo of the pristine booth before it gets ruined by the crush.

This is the Fancy Food Show. Three hundred thousand square feet of demonstration space, eighty thousand products, forty-seven thousand food professionals gathered in a shrine to specialty food. In grocery, "specialty" has many meanings. Perhaps most expansively, it refers to volume. Specialty retailers focus on goods that don't have large distribution networks: food desired but only selectively, hidden gems meant for sampling. It includes imports—cheeses, chocolates, and preserves—that get their distinction by being alien to the domestic market. But in its restless heart, specialty exists for the new. Those products more refined, more absurd, or more tantalizing than what's already offered. To me it is resonant with discontentment, the repetitive opening and closing of the suburban refrigerator door to check to see if anything has changed. Specialty food was our mango salsa. Then it was sriracha everything. Now it has moved on. This year's show is bursting with high-end popcorns and great globs of Greek yogurt (coated over nuts and raisins, slathered on beef jerky; Greek yogurt as magic elixir that enhances anything it touches). By the time this book is out both of those trends will be dated. We'll be on to something new, perhaps birch water (essentially the tapped phloem of birch trees, naturally filtered and sweetened by the tree itself), activated charcoal, or freeze-dried elk. Whatever it is it will sound vaguely alluring but require a slight explanation, the twin attributes of successful specialty: mystery and superiority. Above all, it will solve something. Specialty answers those questions you didn't know you were asking. Its value forever related to how unaware you were of the particular problem until the moment you made its acquaintance.

In many ways we are living in the age of specialty. The entire category gesturing toward an authenticity the rest of the food system left behind. The fact that the authenticity itself is so splintered, contradictory, and chaotic is almost incidental to our craving for it. It is personal: one man's specialty is another man's scorn. But like many things personal, the effect of seeing it all smashed side by side in a convention center is vaguely debasing. There are vomitous streams of comfort and nostalgia—every trope of Americana, Mason jars and aprons, bonnets and barns—colliding with equally vomitous visions of the techno-future—a sphere of gelato pulled by tongs from a cauldron of liquid nitrogen, marshmallows cut so aggressively square, as if by laser, their form is basically a middle finger to the whole concept of the s'more. And then there are hot sauces. Ten thousand little bottles at ten thousand little booths. Each with a howling mouth stretched open on the label. Browsing them, sampling in little dots of red and brown, I start to see all these sauces as a stand-in for the whole show. We aren't at a food conference. This is the hive mind of my condiment drawer, a gibbering id of anxiety and acquisition, responsible for all those decaying bottles in my fridge.

The act of "doing" the Fancy Food Show is a little like a yuppie Halloween. Each booth has its wares out front and center. You snoot up, make a little chitchat, and sample: quinoa crunch bars here, goat's milk caramels there. All around, big stumbling adults romp along beside you, each with several different branded tote bags looped over their shoulder, asking questions about production, all in continuous nibble.

It's gloriously fun at first.

Many of the booths are staffed by Food Tempts, my mental term for the particular class of demonstrator-for-hire ubiquitous here; usually they hold out little trays for sampling; occasionally they are involved in something more degrading, like the Perky Jerky creature, who stands confused and swaying at the end of one particular aisle, a few thousand chipotle-mango-lime sample bags stapled to his uniform, this anxious, sweating mummy in dried-beef fringe. Most booths, however, are staffed by the proprietors themselves. Their reality is still too small to outsource, even as their dreams include selling big to one of the food giants. These small operators are the spiritual center of the Fancy Food Show, looking to monetize the family onion dip recipe, or corner the market on some new tropical plant they stumbled on during their two years in the Peace Corps, all certain they've cracked whatever code America's snack obsession is conveyed in. I can talk to them forever. The former graphic designer turned chocolatier. The aging mountain man from Oregon whose home, a mountainside ranch settled by his great-great-grandfather, has a freshwater spring he is certain Walmart will want to bottle. The lunatic eyes of a Southern California farmer with an exclusive contract on an aberrant varietal of miniature avocados: "Dinosaur eggs," he tells me, holding two in his hand, "a true game changer for the way we eat the fruit."

My game remains unfazed. But I see something very similar at Trader Joe's a few years later, four to a bag, so perhaps he was onto something.

These small-time dreams intersecting with big-time production also provide my first taste of the grocery industry, up-front and personal. In between the booths, the floor is crawling with grocerymen. They are big, chunky midwesterners, squares in attitude as well as in body composition, so overwhelmingly white and male that there is a slightly nostalgic vibe, like we're in a movie about 1950s NASA. They possess the power of acquisition, ask questions about size and scale, taste quickly, perfunctorily, or not at all. I watch them as they patrol the room in clusters wielding this power, rugby shirt after rugby shirt stuffed into slacks and cinched up with a tan belt. These men typically have hair that blurs the line between crew cuts and balding, and walk with multiple electronic devices clipped to their waists, a collective style that basically serves to broadcast I'd rather be riding my mower and/or cracking jokes about murdering the guy trying to date my daughter to that guy's face. An industry consultant I meet calls them "a dying species, real live dinosaurs of retail, out of touch with themselves only slightly more than they are out of touch with America in general." But as living dinosaurs they still are a dominant force in this particular epoch and cannot be ignored. They are men who attend lectures on "snack-tivation" without irony and who, once there, take dutiful notes, underlining the phrase, as the person in front of me does at one such lecture, "Our ultimate goal is to fill the basket with snacks, healthy and delicious," or who stand up in sudden inspiration to snap a photo of a PowerPoint slide with nothing more on it than the phrase "Eyes are the window to the soul. The phone is the window to the wallet." What insight did that man gain from that aphorism? And where does that photo go? Is it sent off to some corporate overlord? Right clicked and set as wallpaper? Mulled like a koan when designing a new customer loyalty program? Listening to these men, their way of masking all decisions with good intentions, their confidence in a retail world they view as a natural physical state rather than a moment in time about to be upended by Amazon, Jet, and Peapod—teaches me more about the underpinnings of our food system than any amount of prior research.

Eventually I tire of the floor and these grocerymen, and decide to head off to the nearby education seminars. The seminars are one of the many side activities to break up the trick-or-treating. They offer industry savants the opportunity to engage the critical issues of the day, say, whether Paleo is a "trend" or a "fad," or where precisely you should place an endcap for maximum impact. These are issues you and I might never have considered, but here at the Fancy Food Show they are weighed with a fair amount of rigor and an extreme amount of self-importance, inspiring entire lecture halls packed with the type of visibly enthusiastic note-scribbling student usually found just in the very front row.

Peeking my head into one, I listen as bibimbap is described as very likely to "pop" in the next few months. This is in 2015, by the way, and the insight is presented via a seven-point evidentiary chain by two presenters in horn-rimmed glasses who suffer no fools or questions. They explain the combination of Asian demographics (point 1), the economic recession, food trucks, and impoverished Twitter-loving millennials (points 2 through 5), the "value of release," apparently a temporal thing, very 2014–15 (point 6), along with celebrity chef David Chang (point 7 all by himself), whose endorsement of the power of bibimbap is plunked in the mix like a mic drop, and who is later described as defining my generation, "not only around the United States, but across the world," all ensure that bibimbap will triumph in the marketplace, and that all of us snack-tivators in the audience will be head-in-sand fools if we ignore it when concocting our chocolate bars and popcorn flavors for the coming year. I decide I'm more impressed with David Chang's publicist than any of the particulars of the argument, but what do I know? Bibimbap.

I cheer for Korean grandmothers everywhere.

By this point, I am relieved to see most of my fellow audience has checked the fuck out and is pawing at phones and/or drawing intricate hash-mark schemes on their notepaper. I stand up as a man on the mic intones, "You will see sriracha on eighty different products down the center aisle, because it has big flavor, because you can pronounce it, because you recognize it, and because of all those things everyone is going to latch on to it and make money out of it." Which prompts the woman in front of me to write on her pad in purple ink: "Get $$$. Make it rain."

Is she joking? Does she know?

It all speaks to a restless culture, where every sharp-tasting, semi-exotic flavor that is not outright nauseating will get squeezed until it produces fifteen minutes of culinary fame. Seeing it up close, seeing it being channeled by the pros, their hunger behind our hunger, leaves me exhausted. And after fleeing the educational seminars and trawling the main floor for another few hours, popping flaxseed biscuits, rose-hip truffles, and the like, I leave the Fancy Food Show into daylight, strapped down by tote bags filled with other tote bags, taste buds burnt, dopamine depleted, slightly bloated, and swearing off everything but plain white rice and non-Greek yogurt for the rest of the week.

The Condiment That Will Change Your Life

But not before I meet Julie. She's standing at a lone bare brown table in the farthest back corner of the convention center. Behind her, splayed across a red banner in a powerfully awful font: SLAWSA. There upon a low-res photo of three jars of something. Something yellow and mealy. Something with the tagline: "A bold new flavor not out to win accolades but to make the world *more delicious*." I'm on my final tour, sampling purely out of obligation at this point, trying to meet as many food entrepreneurs as possible, convinced that their journey to populate our shelves is a critical part of this whole shebang. Julie is standing there in front of her table, apron on, hair pinned tight, and hands me a paper cup with a little nugget of sausage topped with a clump of this Slawsa.

I pop the cup like a shot of whiskey. Yummy. Then I reach out to shake a hand already extended.

There is just something about the angle of that handshake (down and sharp), the firmness of her grip (like she's trying to choke a fish), and the compact turbocharged introduction that follows, "Hi, I'm Julie Busha of Slawsa, a woman-owned business that makes the condiment that will change your life," that makes me think this woman is on a holy mission for a goddamn relish; that's batshit and beautiful and I need to learn as much from her as I can.

As a product, Slawsa is as intuitive as it is baffling. It is a coleslaw plus a salsa, jammed together in a single bottle, as well as in proprietary neologism. It is an odd, slightly off-putting yellow; a yellow that is brethren to the gaudy emerald of ballpark relish, although Julie assures me, almost before I finish asking, that it is an "all natural" color, the result of mustard and beta-carotene. In constitution, Slawsa is largely cabbage chopped finely so that on the spoon it looks like grits, but in the mouth it has a satisfying crunch. It is cold and sweet and doesn't really have much kick, just a slight tang from the turmeric and vinegar. But this lack of punch actually makes it more appealing as a partner, not less. It is a condiment that knows its place, that doesn't overwhelm. A midwestern friend, a guy with true tailgate prowess, holds the jar right up to a squinting eye and pronounces it "beguiling." A friend from Tennessee requests a jar for himself, and says, "Oh, this I can do." But as much as I like Slawsa, I can't really visualize it on the shelf. It feels like a lost puppy of a product. Especially at this show full of market-researched trends and cutting-edge design. The bottle has the tagline: "The Gourmet Topping for Everything!" And if I didn't know better I could see Slawsa as consciously edging into that so-earnest-it's-ironic space LaCroix sparkling water seems to have found. But I've met Julie. There is no irony in Slawsa. It is clumsy and sincere and evinces zero cool: just an awkward slaw trying every bit as hard as it can.

This also describes Julie.

In person she is a burst of energy, mouth racing forward, dense with information, brown hair in center part, always geared up for a meeting, nothing loose or sashaying in looks or personality or mental outlook. Whenever I ask a question, Julie takes a deep breath. She then takes two big steps back to line it up. It is the kindness of context, but also, I realize, a scrambling to make sure she has it all correct for herself, almost like the OCD ritual of touching ten things before turning the tap. But then, after setting her stage, after arranging all her grocery facts in order, Julie just goes: spraying information like a rotating lawn sprinkler—sales figures, trend lines, price points, sources of data, hedges against those sources, hedges against the hedges. She is liable to burst into laughter at her own inside jokes during all this. But it is an odd laughter. Despite all our time together, I never totally crack the code of Julie's humor. Perhaps she is good-natured without being good-humored. Perhaps she is good-humored without having a good sense of humor. Regardless, the woman loves to laugh, but not always in a way that allows you to laugh along with her. It is a laughter at her own foibles, where you are kind of worried for her, or a laughter at her own effort levels and accomplishments, where you are impressed but not in any funny way, or a laughter at her own sense of surprise that things are working out, as if any other form of acknowledgment would be a jinx.

Julie came to food from NASCAR. She knew nothing about the sport, but after taking a marketing course on a college lark and getting nominated for an internship, she found herself immersed, on the road twenty weeks a year selling the NASCAR brand. This led to consulting work with General Mills, which wanted to get their food into those NASCAR stadiums, and a growing reputation as someone who would do whatever it took to get something done.

She likes to say she has always been a woman in a man's world. Which makes navigating both the macho world of NASCAR and the male merchants of grocery easier. "When I was born, I already had an older sister, so my dad treated me like a son. He taught me to throw a baseball. But not throw like a girl. I can pitch."

"We weren't poor. Well, we weren't dirt-poor," she continues. "We were frugal." Her mother worked in a bakery part-time. Her father worked for U.S. Steel, and later in a second career as a swimming pool contractor in Florida. "My parents didn't save for college. It was always on me. It wasn't really something they expected."

In high school, Julie spent most of her free time raising livestock for competition. It was part hobby, part business, buying the swine for fifty or sixty bucks a piglet and raising them for sale at $600–700 at full weight. One day after school, before going to feed her pigs, a teacher came up to her. The school needed cross-country runners. It was under-registered, and it seemed like Julie always had extra energy.

"I had never run before," Julie says. "I was the worst girl on the team. But I had this mentality, I might not be a star, but I am going to work as hard as I can." And sure enough, after the season ended, Julie added cross-country training to her list of chores.

The first race of the next season featured Liz Lepackie: current state champion, undefeated, and already the recipient of a full scholarship to the University of Alabama. Julie lined up next to her, trying to learn something about form.

"When the gun went off, I stayed with her. I had never been in the lead pack before, so I think, this is cool, let me stay here as long as I can. Then the pack dwindles. Then I notice she is lagging. And suddenly I just . . . I just beat her."

And here Julie bursts into tears.

"I knew the very moment I crossed the finish line, 'This is going to pay for college.'"

When she tells me this, crying into her hoagie at a small cafe in North Carolina, she starts apologizing immediately. After wiping the tears away, she says, "There would be no Slawsa if I had not won that race."

And this is essential Julie. A woman who is willing to work hard and who has a gut-level certainty her hard work will pay off. In high school, she sewed her own prom dress, and then sewed a second for a friend. She became chapter president of the local 4-H and made enough money raising pigs to buy her first car. When she sold her first house, she was annoyed by the idea of paying agent fees, so she studied up, acted as her own broker, and says she negotiated the highest price per square foot in the area to date. She gets two haircuts a year because she thinks there are better uses for her money. When I ask where the savings go, the answer is always the same. Slawsa. Later, she will call a hot chocolate I buy her when we meet for coffee a frivolous expenditure she wouldn't allow herself. "My last vacation was in 2006," she tells me. "But it's not the type of thing I keep track of. I'm not the type of person who needs an annual vacation. I enjoy working."

Geographically, her home in North Carolina is only about fifty miles from where I first met Lynne Ryles the trucker, and it is hard not to think of these two women both working eighty-hour weeks, their twin beads of faith and the different ways they are both perceived and rewarded.

"Oh, I know, I just know, that in five years, someone will say, 'She had an overnight success,'" Julie tells me months later. "Uh-uh. No way. I've been working my ass off at this."

Then she looks up.

"My husband and I see the long term. The short term is just more sacrifice. That's why we haven't started a family . . . Any money I might make from Slawsa is getting reinvested in it. This is my baby right now."

Of course, Slawsa wasn't always Julie's baby.

It isn't her family recipe. There were no picnics where her grand-mother doled it out next to Fourth of July ribs. No stories of thousands of hours in the home kitchen perfecting the recipe through obsessive tasting and ad hoc focus groups of friends after dinner. In fact, she had no role creating it at all.

Like so much in retail food, Slawsa features an estranged partner-ship. These are ubiquitous at the Fancy Food Show, eerie in-room ab-sences hovering around origin conversations like phantom limbs, early investors, first believers, or culinary creators, rent off by the confusion and financial reality of bringing a product to market.

Slawsa as a food was the creation of a gentleman I'll call Jerome Odell, an electrician from Chattanooga, Tennessee. It really was doled out at his family picnics, the pride of his mother, who really did perfect it in the home kitchen, working to get the balance of crunch and sweet and tang that makes Slawsa so "beguiling." Slawsa was her riff on chow chow, an almost vanished southern relish that borrows from Chinese rail workers, Indian chutneys, and French Canadian slaws, all of which you start to notice in Slawsa once you know to look. As an adult, Jerome took the mantle. And when he brought the stuff out for friends, their eyes opened in surprise, gobbling it down, their kindness, polite flattery, or honest-to-god excitement pushing him to make a business out of it.

Sometime in 2010, Jerome got in touch with Julie through NASCAR contacts. He hoped she could get his Slawsa into Bristol Motor Speedway. At the time, he was leveraging every contact he had trying to get his baby out into the world. This was the classic food hustle, going store to store trying to get bottles on shelves, pleading with buyers to take a taste. But it all led to fairly dismal results. He got a few articles in a few regional papers, but with a full-time job and family, he was hitting the limits of passion without strategy.

Julie came down to Chattanooga on his invite. She tried the slaw, thought it tasted pretty good, and sized up the label as terrible: apparently the universal Slawsa first experience.

But she didn't know what she could do to help. It wasn't being sold in stores and wasn't being demoed at farmers markets. The nutrition information wasn't FDA compliant. So she gave Jerome generic marketing advice and assumed she had tasted her last Slawsa.

But he kept calling. And she kept answering. Soon Jerome invited her back to tour his "production facility." Julie, who had been inside behemoth assembly lines during her time with General Mills, who had watched in hard hat the ten thousand pounds of peanuts *per hour* being roasted in the big daddy roaster at Planters, wasn't sure if he was joking. This was a tiny commercial kitchen. It almost exclusively produced batches of nutrient broth for horses. Jerome talked about it like it was destiny itself. Then he sketched his plan to get Slawsa into restaurants. Slowly Julie got more involved, her curiosity changing into something much more addictive for her. Challenge. Then she was acting as broker, calling stores, harassing buyers, driving hundreds of miles around the state to different retailers. She says, "I'd never sold anything in grocery before, but I just felt like I could sell this." When they ran out of samples, she fronted the money for the next production run.

Julie won't talk to me about Jerome on or off record. In fact she refuses to even tell me his name during any of our three years of interviews, saying only it's not something she wants to revisit. And Jerome won't even answer the phone when he finds out I am calling about Julie. Neither will say a bad word about the other, because they won't even say a single word.

When I do bring him up on my own during our last interview, her face fades with exhaustion. There are huge sighs, not performative, but just old-fashioned heartbreak, where Julie looks away, slides her hands along the table, and generally deflates. She'll only say one thing before stopping our conversation:

"At some point, I realized I had put a lot of money in. Tens of thousands of dollars . . . I presented him with a fifty-fifty contract, but then he backed out of it. And I don't know what to do. If I walk away, I lose everything. So I used all my savings, almost fifty thousand dollars, everything I had saved and worked for my entire life, and bought him out."

Julie is staring straight down at the table when she says this, and I realize I'm not watching heartbreak but terror. All of a sudden, she had a product that she didn't have a personal connection to, a terrible label, and a partner who was not interested in investing further. And after putting in enough money so that she felt like she didn't have a choice, she put in everything else she had. And then, after reaching that point, she didn't even have that partner anymore; she was about to fail all alone.

The Long Odds of Even a Slow Failure

The rate of failure in food is stunning. Graveyards of product buried so deeply under other products there is no light or air down there. Typically the failure is a quick financial strangulation, maybe only six months to a year, before there are any real statistics to document them. Ideas flare up, commercial kitchen space gets rented, a few thousand dollars is sunk into packaging and design. Then lights out. These make up the vast majority of the lucky. They got out before they were allowed to lose big.

The reasons for these lucky failures are too numerous to fully excavate, like Tolstoy's families each unhappy in their unique way. Often they are made up of ideas that seem special to their creators, but that the market yawns at. Another salsa, you say? Why? Oh, yours is the best, is it? Best how? Can it last on the shelf better than Old El Paso? No? Save it for some hidden-gem taqueria, then. Or ideas that never really click along all the dimensions needed. Roasted vegetables sound great on paper. They taste like candy, hit all the new trend lines for healthy and Paleo. They are an idea that would tantalize a grocery buyer. What harried mom—and even today it is still the harried mom grocery thinks of first—wouldn't snatch a few off the shelves as a quick way to fill out her son's lunch? But look again. Is the packaging there? What about the manufacturing process? How do you prevent it from becoming fibrous mush when shipped and handled? The answer is you don't and roasted vegetables are destined to stay behind the glass of prepared foods with the 40 to 50 percent markup that entails. Then there are the quick failures that manage to hit everything— differentiated, maybe even innovative, trending, producible—but that stumble when their owners confront the complexity of logistics. Do you know your gross margins and your COGS (cost of goods sold)? Do you know what a responsible wholesale price is versus a responsible direct sales price? How quickly can you make product in response to an order? Without effortless answers to these, you are doomed before you even approach a buyer. And so the vast majority of food businesses rip through a few thousand dollars before expiring without a trace. It is money spent like a moderately fancy vacation, which is perfect since that is exactly what these ideas are, a trip sans jet plane from real life into the fantasy land of entrepreneurship.

From this sea of lucky failure, a slender percent will hatch and grow to the point they can become unlucky. I'm defining this as actually coming face-to-face with a buyer in a buyer meeting, and it is here that the real struggle of grocery begins.

Journey to Shelf

Julie's initial burst of energy was focused on transforming Slawsa from a recipe into a mass producible product. In her mind, this began with the label. The content wasn't FDA compliant, and the design looked like some nightmare wrapping paper, the logo itself holding about ten different colors swirling around a busy background. Julie hired a local firm to redo it. The result, still amateurish to my eyes, was at least an amateurishness of simplicity. Label in hand, she began work on a website. She decided she couldn't even approach a buyer until she had built a social media presence for them to google behind her back.

Then she turned to the product itself. This began with going to her local university to get a "schedule process" certification. This is a legally mandated review necessary for shelf-stable food. Once she ironed that out, she could begin pricing out production runs, determining her cost of goods, and factoring in the margin added by different distribution channels. Looking at the ingredients, she decided that an artificial yellow dye used in Jerome's product would be a turnoff. Going all the way organic seemed unnecessary; hot dog eaters, obviously comfortable with their nitrates, probably wouldn't care. But getting to all natural seemed like a helpful advertising hook to hang on the label. Although the term "all natural" isn't FDA regulated, to my surprise it isn't meaningless either. Retailers regulate it on their own, and for Julie to sell Slawsa as all natural she needed to get the yellow dye out.

This turned out to be her first decision in a much longer process: deciding exactly where to target Slawsa.

The customer experience from one retailer to the next is so similar, so standardized with the same basic aisles and shelves, that it is tempting to think of the back end as similar as well.

But as a food manufacturer you learn quickly that this is nonsense.

Kroger, ALDI, Whole Foods, Costco, your local food co-op, and Walmart do not exist on some grocery continuum—whether from big to small, or fancy to bare-bones. Instead, each occupies an entirely different niche in the retail ecosystem, offering a whole distribution world unto itself. As a customer it is hard to fully understand. But if you try to sell to them, get your baby in their stores, you'll find each runs on its own DNA—uses a different network of wholesalers and truckers, employs different types of buyers, in different buying configurations, with different mandates, takes different margins, and above all earns their profit through different means. Imagine stepping into a series of different kingdoms, each with its own rituals, beliefs, and customs.[25]

---

25 These niches include convenience (like 7-Eleven), traditional supermarkets (like Kroger/Safeway), specialty (like Fairway), natural (like Sprouts), gourmet (like Dean & DeLuca), club (like Costco), discount (like ALDI), e-commerce (like Thrive/Amazon). Some, like Whole Foods or Trader Joe's, are explicit mash-ups (specialty/natural and specialty/discount), respectively. To a manufacturer like Julie these differences mean the world. For instance, a specialty store loves trends, employs a relatively large number of buyers to find them, and goes out of their way to make themselves accessible to that hustling food entrepreneur who is rolling around a suitcase full of product. But they also put in small orders, tend to be independent, and do relatively slow business, which means that it's often more helpful to see them as a marketing channel, giving you exposure, rather than a bona fide way of making money. Convenience, on the other hand, might employ a single buyer for ten thousand stores, and cares not for trends. They put in massive orders that require extremely scalable operations, a network of brokers to keep individual stores in check, and a product that ships incredibly fast and far. This will often crush a young supplier who scores a miracle PO and then suddenly realizes they cannot

Thus your first job, as per the ancient Greeks, is to know thyself, and thy product, and determine where in the industry you belong.

"I could put my product in a fancier jar," Julie tells me. "I could spend more money on a label. And if I did that I could probably charge several bucks more per unit for it. But then my market would be those specialty guys." We are driving to her production facility and Julie is explaining her thinking around the Slawsa label, which I finally admitted I still didn't find too compelling.

"But specialty distribution marks up 25 to 30 percent on top of the store. I wanted to avoid those guys at all cost. Also, the high-end market is great, but personally I want the truck driver who drives Slawsa to the market to be able to afford it.

"Also, I like my label! That yellow script catches the eye. It's a re-searched fact."

And so Slawsa seized on this "all natural" identity—a slight upsell on relish to appeal to her customers, but without gourmet aspirations, or any overt pitch to health. It is a strategically modest place on the shelf that might make a shopper feel slightly better about picking it up without alienating them with any pretensions.

Shaping this identity took about six months of around-the-clock work where nothing visible was accomplished. Just day after day of continuous small decisions to get the brand ready. There was a learning curve everywhere: "It can be the simplest thing, like if you are going to sample at a festival, knowing you need to put a custom ten-by-ten tent on the to-do list," Julie says. "All the details that seem obvious after you actually do them."

---

keep up with demand. The footnote to the footnote is that, just like the ecological world, this all occasionally gets punctuated Stephen Jay Gould–cum–Michael Cullen–style by asteroid-meets-dinosaur-level shifts in the industry. Which of course is exactly what is happening in our current decade with Amazon, Big Data, and e-commerce, causing upheaval in just about every niche at once and making traditional distinctions less important.

By 2011, with her label street legal and her product certified for mass production, Slawsa was standing on somewhat firmer ground. And so Julie decided it was time to set up a meeting with a buyer.

The Buyer Meeting

"Take your notion of good items, and throw that out," Ian Kelleher, cofounder of Peeled Snacks, tells me. "These aren't food items. These are packaged goods . . . Not food. Food products." Ian is not saying this in the holier-than-thou, Velveeta-is-not-cheese sense. After all, his brand, Peeled, offers a line of organic, non-GMO, no-sugar-added fruits and veggies, a blitz of descriptors that make it appear almost comically conceived to answer the current call for "real" food on shelves.

"Buyers are looking for something simple," he continues. "It's not that they don't want good products. It's that they have other priorities. And what you think of as 'good' might as well be last on the list." Buyers, after all, are middlemen. They have forces above them breathing heavy on their back hair, yearly sales goals, revenue they need to make to keep their jobs. They want products that will get them there and make them feel safe. In practice this means consistency *über alles*: consistent shelf life, consistent production facilities, and consistent commodity prices that underpin the ingredients list. If your sustainable line-caught honey-chili salmon jerky jumps in price $2 per unit each time there is a shortage of line-caught salmon, you're probably not going to make it as an impulse buy.[26]

That is the background to these meetings. But what actually occurs within them once the door is closed? What should Julie expect?

---

26 Worse, if you haven't done your homework and feature an exciting new ingredient— the goji berry, acerola fruit, moringa leaf—without locking down your supply chain, it's a safe bet you'll be out of business, watching from the sidelines as an agribusiness giant gobbles your sources of supply and thus market share the exact moment that exciting ingredient starts to prove itself and actually sell.

Here is the nervous-pitch meeting, old as bartered exchange, updated with the cheap animation of PowerPoint, and set in the drab back offices of a grocery store. Those rooms you find after pushing past the bakery into the dirty non-retail space. You enter. The buyer is harried. If it is an independent, it is probably just the two of you hunched around a laptop. If you are pitching in the corporate offices, for a chain, you'll get the glory of a projector. Regardless, the presentation gives a concise explanation of your product, highlighting its eight to twelve "sell points," those factors that distinguish it from all others, explaining why it deserves space on the shelf, why it is priced to make the buyer money, and why it upsells, outsells, or outshines the current competition.

But this presentation is perfunctory. The follow-up questions are where deals get made and lost. And here it gets awkward.

"The merchant–supplier negotiation is one of the great bastions of subtextual conversation," Ian says. "People are saying words, but nobody really knows what those words mean or why those precise ones are being spoken." It is a subtle probing for information, of half steps. "A giant butt-sniffing," a buyer tells me. "Like two dogs in the park, circling each other, trying to figure out if they each have what the other wants."

"There are always two levels of conversation," Ian explains. "You can try to be as frank as you want, but there is an industry-wide attitude that if you give up information you lose something. So nobody wants to be perceived as giving up anything, even though obviously you have to for the conversation to make sense at all."

Most of the questions are about sussing out needs. A buyer asking "What type of lead time do you need?" might translate to an acknowledgment that he is being pushed by corporate for a rapid change, while also giving him plenty of space to politely decline an answer unless it hits his price. A supplier asking "What do you see happening in the category?" might be trying to figure out the weak brands that are being replaced, allowing her to reposition her pitch on the fly and target those cubic inches. Or the questions might be bananas and come from a place of total ignorance. "These guys live in grocery stores," another entrepreneur tells me. "You think they'd have their finger on the pulse, but for a lot of the older guys it is just the opposite . . . Half the time it's vertical pressure from their boss who just finally heard about coconut water and wants them to get on it. Or maybe they just took the meeting to get intel on a competing chain, and they are poking around to see what other places you are stocked and what margin that guy takes."

"The first time I went into a buyer meeting, I was sweating, I was nervous," Julie says. "Do I just sit and go through a PowerPoint presentation with them? Instead, I'm running around serving food. I want them to try it, but that feels awkward. Am I really feeding these guys who speak in numbers? Nowadays I just think, be passionate. You're selling yourself and what you can do as marketer."

These subtextual conversations can go on for months. A supplier for Trader Joe's talked about agreeing to a price with the chain within ten minutes, but then, entering a six-month extended negotiation on the specifics of the product itself—replacing a sugar-alcohol sweetener with real sugar, coming up with a slightly more rustic look for the box—and only then, once all the details were worked out—at his expense—did Trader Joe's come in with an order.

Or not.

A corporate buyer for Safeway asked Julie to send samples to every single one of his category managers and every single grocery manager at every single division. He loved Slawsa, swore he had a jar in his home fridge, and told her he was going to introduce it at one of his conference calls. Julie wrote an entire presentation for him to introduce the product there.

When I see her more than two years later, she is still waiting. No movement. No word. No new product in stores.

To make sense of these delays, both the hesitations and outright disappearances, understand how overwhelmed buyers are. A single buyer might oversee fifty categories, each with thousands of SKUs within it. At almost every major chain, that buyer is also rotated into a new category every year or two, an intentional destabilizing strategy to keep them from making personal relationships with multi-billion-dollar ag companies that historically start to offer outright bribes as soon as a personal relationship is formed.[27] This might make for a good business move, preventing a glut of overpriced Conagra products, but it also prevents the buyer from ever getting any deep knowledge about the categories they are covering. "I keep running into these buyers that are just bewildered," an old-school food manufacturer tells me. "They don't know competing items in their category. They don't know the supply chain. They don't even know price. All good people, but completely overwhelmed and confused by the volume they are now responsible for." A buyer for Roche Bros. Supermarkets, a small twenty-store chain in the Northeast, tells me he averages thirty to forty cold calls per day, this on top of six to eight hours of scheduled meetings. Buyers at Whole Foods national are sent five hundred new products per month. There is very little time for considering details or nuance, or investigating the product beyond the superficials of the pitch meeting.

And when they do consider details, flavor and quality are not first- or even third-level considerations.

"I see a lot of young entrepreneurs too locked into recipe, the name of the product, the packaging. That should not be on the radar screen in the beginning," Annette Dunlap, an agribusiness consultant who helps launch new food companies, explains. "You need to understand your costs. You need to understand the needs of your store."

"Stop thinking about food," Ian says. "Think like a buyer. Then problem-solve based on a buyer's needs . . . And if you are lucky, and everything goes right, at the end of the meeting they'll throw you a bone and let you give them free product."

27 Of course, as one buyer said when I mentioned this aside, "You think it is only the big guys offering bribes? Payoffs are everywhere, and the little guys are often the worst!"

The Crack, a Crack, Just Crack

Once you agree to ship that free product, we have statistics. Just over twenty thousand new products hit the shelf each year. Eighty-nine percent of those fail within eighteen months. It is a reaping. To understand this rate of failure, the failure of the products that got their act together enough to succeed, you have to understand one big thing that most starting food entrepreneurs do not. Grocery does not just make its money off people buying things in its stores. It makes its money off its vendors.

To make sense of this, let's return to our buyer. He is charged with a small fiefdom to administer. This is his category, a strip of shelving or fridge or freezer space he can manipulate as he sees fit. Maybe it is that twelve to twenty-four feet of yogurt almost every grocery store in America features. A buyer does not see cultured milk when he looks at this territory. He does not taste test samples side by side looking for the richest and creamiest product to stock there. Instead he sees and tastes reams of data—the performance of each subcategory: Greek, nondairy, liquid, multipack, singles—broken down into discrete metrics according to basket share, seasonality, volume per price per promotion, or just the plain old vanilla UPSPW, units per store per week. He scans all that data on the printout his analyst gives him, but then puts one big hairy eyeball on the two numbers at the end: total sales dollars and gross profit. Those matter fifty times more than everything else. They are the metrics that keep his boss happy. And what matters most of all is that he can grow those numbers year to year.[28]

28 Every buyer I spoke with talked about "the passion" of the entrepreneur as being an extremely important factor in their decision-making. But how they qualified this passion is telling, allowing us to see the precise and slightly skewed manner buyers relate to food and new product trends. When buyers talked about "passionate suppliers," it wasn't because they believed in their passion per se (though that certainly helps; buyers are not machines, at least not yet), it is because they see it as a leading indicator. Two different buyers I talked to brought up the passion around GMO-free products, that is, food

Here he has options. He can look for new, exciting products, or at least ones with longer shelf life and higher gross margins, that he can use to replace the weaker, scrawnier SKUs in his herd. Or he can try to change his mix, creating offerings that nudge consumers in certain profitable directions by, say, eliminating a high-quality private label line that might be stealing sales from more expensive traditional options. Or he can lean hard on his existing suppliers, relying on their increasing efficiency—for example, the miraculous ability of their trucking carriers to reduce cost, whatever the means, it's not his concern as long as they agree to shave off a few pennies per hundred pounds—to inch up his margins.

But all those options are time intensive. The first are risky, the last interpersonally demanding and conflict heavy.

And so he takes a third path. An almost effortless, inexhaustible way to grow his gross profit, which requires no time or risk on his part. He simply demands a payment from the young entrepreneurs who come to his office in exchange for putting their items on his shelf. The entrepreneurs are desperate. They are probably already leveraged, and so what is a little more debt to them? They also have no hope of a return if their item is not on a shelf. And if every buyer in the industry begins to do the same thing, they really have no choice.

"It's crack," Errol Schweizer, the former head of grocery for Whole Foods, tells me. "Every buyer is addicted. You charge a fee and it gets added to the budget. Every year, you are expected to bring in more. This

---

without any genetically modified ingredients. They talked about their attraction to these passionate founders, who would light up pitch meetings with their drive for change and genuine commitment to transparency in the supply chain. But both these buyers noted that they didn't believe in the specific controversy around GMOs—one buyer calling it "climate change for the left." But this buyer felt the passion in his GMO-free suppliers was a conduit to the desires in his customers. That as makers and designers, suppliers were sensitive to trends before they came to his attention. So he valued their passion, but in a special, almost sociopathic sense: passion was a marker he didn't want to ignore even if he remained completely detached from its substance.

is serious money. It can bail you out if you are in a mess. Often there is no return for the supplier. It is essentially extractive."

The euphemism is "trade spend" and it is an area of the industry nobody wants to talk about too loudly because it is so murky and backward. The idea that the best products are on the shelf—rather than, say, the producers who ponied up the biggest bucks—benefits the supplier and the store. And what the customer doesn't know can't hurt them.

"At heart, it is a pay-to-play system. Don't have money, you don't get to play," Lisa Curtis, CEO of Kuli Kuli Foods, tells me. "Life on the shelf is ruthless, you are fighting fighting fighting, but not just your competitors—you are fighting to survive the store itself."

In its simplest form, this trade spend comes as a "slotting fee," which is a pure cash-for-placement exchange. The buyer asks for money; in return you get inches on the shelf. Not a special endcap display, not a center spot right at eye level, just inches, somewhere. These payments amount to $9 billion a year in industry profit. To get a sense of how lucrative these can be for an individual store, in January 2017, one national retailer was charging $55,000 for 22 x 12 inches of shelf space. For a single month. This is a retailer likely operating with those industry-wide 1.5 to 3 percent gross margins, so we are talking rocket fuel to their bottom line.

But slotting fees are nothing. They are so transparent and obvious that many retailers have moved away from them. In their place, a mad, inventive spree of different taxes and extractive demands has emerged.

There are "promotional fees" (subsidizing the cost of two-for-one deals, tag sales, and other discounts). There is "free-fill" (a free case or ten in each flavor for the retailer to sell at 100 percent profit). There are "advertising fees" for unwanted but mandatory placement in the company's internal newsletter (a promotion that almost no one will read and will produce no benefits), or fees for receiving the privilege of being broadcast on their "radio network" (a network that consists of interrupting whatever Muzak is bopping from their in-store speakers to announce your product). There are negotiations around the length of credit. There are payments for waste, spoilage, or just because your product—that they bought—doesn't sell. There are mandatory "requests" that you use their specific overpriced proprietary supply chain "solutions" ("You must pay for our style of bar code, despite the fact that it costs two times the normal amount and the difference disappears into our pocket," a consultant tells me), and fees for package redesign or store-mandated market research. There are fees on top of fees. And every movement or change offers new opportunities: money is demanded when the retailer opens a new store or refurbishes an existing one, when a competitor opens up nearby, when the category gets its annual overhaul.

To be clear, as a supplier you would never be hit with all of these fees at once. Just bitten slyly, occasionally. The precise charges will vary year to year and retailer to retailer, but in each case you as a supplier are directly contributing to the store's gross profit.

"People don't realize Costco isn't providing those demos. Whole Foods isn't paying for the second one you get free," an entrepreneur tells me. "It's mandated. Companies are spending thousands and thousands of dollars to get their foot in the door. The retailer loves it because it makes the shopping experience more fun, but the young supplier is often bleeding."

Ian Kelleher, co-founder of Peeled, tells me, "It is a huge initial start-up cost. I entered in several stupid deals. We paid about one thousand dollars per store for eighteen stores out west. They slotted us on the top shelf, which means nobody sees you, and they put us in the wrong category. This was Peeled—a vegetable snack!—and they put us in *baking*. Then we spent another $2K to sample in their stores. And in less than six months they pulled us. We were out. With no relationship. They kept everything.

"At this point I am over it," he continues. "The only bone I have to pick is with myself for ignorance. But it could have destroyed us. And I have seen it destroy other companies. They were cynically exploiting our desperation to get on shelf."

In 2015, trade spend added up to about $76 billion taken in by retailers. It was the number two cost for an entrepreneur, below only the cost of raw goods, far above more traditional costs like packaging, production, distribution, or advertising. And a 2011 Nielsen study suggests that 55 percent of this spending is extractive, failing to grow the brand.

All these loans from aunts and uncles dribbled away.

I don't bring this up to bash retailers. In many ways, they have simply, quietly reinvented their business model. At this point trade spend has become so pervasive that every responsible vendor includes it in their budget, so it is only when retailers exceed the 12 to 18 percent standard that it really becomes destructive. Further, when used responsibly—in a joint effort with the supplier to grow sales—there are extremely productive forms of trade spend. Promotions, discounts, and demos are tools that can get new products into minds and carts. Endcaps, which almost always require a promotional fee, have been shown to increase sales more than 500 percent. But the wrong type of trade spend—especially when targeted at the rookie food entrepreneur who is most vulnerable—is destructive. It also has long-term effects on the food we buy and who is able to sell it. It creates conditions where innovation doesn't break in or spread easily. It pushes retailers away from the Joe Coulombe model of building food expertise into the more abstract position of seeing food as a financial instrument. And in general it makes the entire system far riskier for the entrepreneur. *Frozen & Refrigerated Buyer,* an industry trade, estimates the cost of national rollout for even a single frozen SKU at $1.5 million. It all combines to create a squeeze play: you take out massive loans to play with the big boys, usually selling major portions of control to venture capital, or you stay tiny, unable to break in.[29]

---

29 This risk factor is compounded quite significantly by the distributor. If by hook, crook, and slotting fee, your new product ends up on the shelf at Target—woohoo!—but then it doesn't sell, and the distributor *charges* you to take it off the shelf. This is called

"The longer you are with a buyer, the more they are going to come to you for money," Ian tells me. "If you are making money, they are going to ask for a piece of it . . . It's not how the consumer thinks about the grocery store, but it's how the manufacturer needs to think about it."

Ian is wound up at this point. "The founder of Chobani was not the first person to introduce Greek yogurt to the American market. He had the financial backing from his family, and wow, was that crucial . . . Every year there is a category with a pioneer entering—someone with a great vision and a great product—who just gets wiped out. It makes the entire industry a gamble, and the last few years with venture capital flooding in, the price of the gamble has gone so far up I'm afraid we are going to lose an entire generation of our most creative entrepreneurs."

In the winter of 2012, Julie makes her first sale. Ingles Markets, a local chain, just a short hundred-mile drive from her home, takes a flyer after she repeatedly drives over to pitch them. From Ingles, she gets the cred to approach a number of small independents. At each one, when she is asked for slotting fees, Julie responds with the honest truth that she simply cannot afford them. "A lot of retailers said, 'If you don't put the money up, or you don't give us free cases, then we can't put you in,'" she tells me. "Hey, I accept that. But my response is, 'I am going to grow my business at your competitor's location' . . . I tell them, 'Let me be your partner. Let me give you something more meaningful than money.'"

And Julie is certainly ready to give in alternative ways. The more time I spend with her, the more I realize she runs on generosity. It is

---

"charge back," and a standard part of most distribution contracts. You now not only have a ton of unsold product, inventory that was supposed to be out there selling; you have to pay the cost of getting it back. There is no opportunity to grow slowly; instead, each part of the system compounds risk, escalating a small mistake into a bankruptcy.

energizing and anxiety producing, this benevolence as fuel. Watching someone give and give right up to the point where you wonder about nullification, wonder whether she is literalizing selflessness and/or giving until there is absolutely nothing left. It also is remarkable to receive. I will send Julie a short email with a question about distribution channels, and Julie will bang out a four-page reply, complete with references, personal asides, and a list of contacts who might know more. She will get back to me that night. She will follow up a few days later to see if I had questions now that I've digested. This is not special treatment. I see her do it repeatedly for others, strangers she meets through Facebook, a woman who comes up after an entrepreneurship panel. At one trade show in New York, a woman who drove down from New England to volunteer for Julie grips my shoulder so her fingers push toward bone and whispers, "She is amazing." Message received! But what's incredible is that I understand the intensity of that woman's awe.

And it is all channeled into a single product. Slawsa is the fulcrum from which her generosity swings. The universal donor to conversations with strangers ("Where is that? Long Island? Oh, Slawsa's at a Stop & Shop there!"), the gateway to physical strength (Julie's shoulders are ripped in the way of the fitness model, but not from endless side planks, rather, from lugging her shoulder strap bag full of sample product), and the source of endless if questionable cocktail trivia ("Did you know Polish people consume three times as much cabbage as Americans? It's a real shame, because back in the 1920s we consumed twenty-two pounds per person"). Her day starts with Slawsa at six a.m., when she flips open her laptop in the dark, before the dogs are awake, and begins jamming out emails. It ends with Julie a few feet from where she started, at a tiny desk in an alcove in her suburban living room, a quarter pallet of Slawsa stacked beside her, her dogs back asleep again, pushing the laptop down to get some rest.

Very little of this work involves food, or food production, or flavor. The work of the food entrepreneur is marketing. If a popular family blogger writes about her breast cancer, Julie will ping her with a medical journal article that might interest her readers linking lower cancer rates to cruciferous vegetable consumption. If the blogger responds, Julie might send a jar of Slawsa with that one particular cruciferous vegetable, cabbage, highlighted on the ingredients list. If a morning TV host anywhere in America mentions they like to grill, Julie will have a sample of Slawsa en route by midafternoon. Always with a handwritten note, always ending with the scrawled sign-off "Stay Slawsome!" Or maybe we are only three months away from National Barbecue Day. If so, Julie is busy pitching local nutritionists in different affiliate regions, loading them up with pitch docs of their own so they can offer their services to local TV stations for a segment on how we as a nation can have a healthier barbecue on National Barbecue Day.[30] A segment Julie conceived for the sole purpose that it may or may not allow the nutritionist to debate the merits of mayonnaise in coleslaw and thus perhaps offer an aside about Slawsa as a healthier alternative. It is always opportunity by giving someone else an opportunity, the natural medium of all PR, but Julie understands it on an intuitive level. She lives it. This most American mixture of sincerity and manipulation, opposites bound up by the energy of this tiny, cheerful dynamo. Helping people in the

---

30 Hanging out with Julie, I get a true understanding of exactly how many of these moronic commemoratory days exist out there, speckling our calendars with the legislative equivalent of pigeon shit, as if legislators had nothing better to do all day than to sit and roost above our calendars, caking them. To take a date entirely at random, the day I am writing this, November 1, is National Calzone Day, National Authors Day, National Family Literacy Day, National Cook for Your Pets Day, National Vinegar Day, National Deep Fried Clams Day, National Brush Day, and National Stress Awareness Day. This is not a joke—in some smug pagan lobbyist vision of the world, we would all donate five minutes from our lives each November 1, to reflect on brushes and calzones and the rest. Of course, hanging with Julie, I see their manic profusion as shockingly useful. "You have to know your days. That is basic," she tells me. "For instance, I know National Crab Cake Day is tomorrow. It has nothing to do with Slawsa but I made a pretty damn good crab cake recipe that has Slawsa in it. It's very moist."

hope that it might help Slawsa. I am alternately awed and troubled and always have to refrain from taking advantage.

At this point, Julie's sole conduit to actual food is her co-packer. She uses Golding Farms, which is housed in a cavernous cement building off the side of I-40 that is not the least bit farm but is run by a Mr. Tony Golding. Tony bought a small canning operation in 1972 and used it to begin churning out his own line of salad dressings and steak sauces. The Golding brand is a modest local success. I see the full lineup at a nearby Piggly Wiggly when I visit, looking a little dusty in metaphor if not fact, two shelves below all the national brands. But over the years Tony has expanded his facilities considerably. He has always been methodical about modernizing his operations, and with each upgrade, the ever-longer strides of technology meant that soon he was capable of producing far more output than he could ever need. And so slowly Tony's business evolved from manufacturing his own product to selling time on his line and manufacturing the products of others. The day I walk into his plant, the whole place is stinking of fermented soy, and I see an unending stream of tiny unlabeled bottles of black liquid chattering forth on the conveyors below us. They are destined to become a variety of Kikkoman soy sauce once the labeler hits them, that ubiquitous national brand found in sushi restaurants everywhere.

Most national manufacturers contract out work like this. They optimize their own in-house facility for a single item—that core brand-defining mayonnaise or classic marinara—needed in extreme volume. Then they contract with smaller facilities like Tony's to make the offshoots—the garlic mayo or the puttanesca—that would waste the talents of an industrial line so specialized and massive.

Golding Farms does a lot of private label. Grocers come to them with an idea, perhaps some new salad dressing they have seen and want to bring in-house. They then work with their team of food scientists and industrial chefs to create a parallel product: one that Golding Farms makes, but the grocer sells under their own proprietary label.[31]

In the best-case scenario, a facility like Golding Farms can then use these larger clients to update and expand their machinery, taking on debt for that expansion, knowing the big runs will keep them profitable. But in practice, especially with bigger brands that have the financing to contract with competing facilities simultaneously, it also leaves them vulnerable.

"There is always someone out there who is willing to do it cheaper," Kent Vickery, the Golding Farms plant manager, tells me. "They'll come to a supermarket and say, 'I know you are buying Golding Farms

---

31 This brings up a point that requires mentioning even if it is a little dry. The rise of private label in the post–Joe Coulombe world—where retailers attempt to make not just cheaper generics but own-label products that are rivals in quality to the national brands—has occurred simultaneously with this outsourcing of manufacturing duties by national brands. And these two trends have collided in the facilities of co-packers like Golding Farms, placing them at the center of a latent, never verbalized ethical quandary that is basically impossible to negotiate but which has completely tipped the balance of power in the grocery industry away from powerful brands—like Kraft, Campbell's, etc.—and toward powerful retailers—like Costco, Kroger, etc. The intellectual property involved in creating successful branded products is huge, time-consuming, and costly, but by definition must be shared in its most nude, vulnerable details—from pricing decisions to unique processes—with the third-party producer whose assembly lines will actually be making it. At the same time, retailers are no fools, can read between the proverbial chains of supply, and will approach the very co-packers who specialize in the national branded products they want to replicate on their own, beseeching Tony and his team of food scientists to help them design a product that is similar but even better than the national brand he may or may not also be making. All the NDAs and secrecy in the world start to fail here because the point of convergence is the same facility, perhaps even the same industrial chef, and thus the retail manufacturers get to draft off the speed of the national manufacturers and their R&D, making similar products at a cost structure that suits them. Naturally nobody at Golding Farms wants to talk about any of this stuff when I ask, and the conversation quickly falls back on old saws like respecting the integrity of relationships, trust, a family-run business, and of course pointing at legal NDAs. But even with the best intentions, there is an effect, and the last twenty years have seen a fantastic rise in the negotiating power of major supermarkets for precisely this reason.

steak sauce, I'll sell you a similar thing for twenty cents a bottle less.' Now, this facility may actually be losing money on that steak sauce, or coming close, but they are just trying to get their foot in the door . . . And that is a compelling argument for a buyer."

And so, to hedge against this squeeze, Golding Farms maintains an essential fourth strand of work: co-packing for the Julie Bushas of the world. Co-packing is essentially outsourcing all aspects of a fledgling business's food production. It allows Julie to focus exclusively on marketing and growing her brand, without the insanity of trying to run her own factory. In terms of line time, Julie might be a riskier proposition for Golding Farms, but she isn't going to nickel-and-dime them—she isn't capable—and if they bet properly, as her needs grow, she will take over more of their capacity at that great rate. At the same time, using a co-packer allows dreamers like Julie to move their baby at national scale without knowing a lick about what it takes to actually make her product at national scale. In return, she merely needs to dream in a very specific industry-mandated manner that allows manufacturing efficiencies to accumulate.

Golding Farms can fill just about any bottle with just about any substance—liquid, food, paste. In an industry where production is often optimized for volume, this flexibility is its own advantage, allowing them to match, say, a Slawsa run with their own Golding Farms–brand coleslaw run with a private label run that also requires bulk bell peppers. Even though Julie might only require a single eight-hour shift every six months—an eight hours that disgorges more than ninety thousand jars of Slawsa that she will then have to place in stores—the convergence of ingredients combined with the minimal adjustments to their production facility allow them to offer her a competitive price.

"It's a big chess game," Kent explains. "I can make a certain amount of money off each of these different pieces. Some match each other perfectly, some offer reliability. You only have so many hours in the day. So who do you spend your time on?

"People might come to us and say, 'We want Clorox in a bottle,'" he continues. "Now, could we do that? Of course. Would we? It would have to stand on its own merits. We'd have to price it all out, the cleaning and shutdown of the line, nothing we are currently producing is even close to that . . . Or right now coconut oil has been so popular, all the national retailers are saying hey, can you private label this for us? We can do it, but does it fit?"

These pressures are a structural reason for all those waves and fads you see in food. There is enormous manufacturing incentive to conform. "Listen, if we are trying to work out a co-packing deal and I have to get cocoa powder from Cairo for your product, that's not so easy. It's probably not something I'm using for any of my other products," Kent says. But once an ingredient breaks into the supply chain, placing it into other food becomes significantly easier. "That is definitely something we think about. Okay, I'm sourcing this, well now it's worth it to put in everything else." And suddenly avocado oil gets worked into everything from popcorn to crackers to mayonnaise.

When we walk the floor, decked in snowy white hair caps, snowy white beard protectors, and long white nylon gowns, a troop of ghosts inside a literal machine, the immensity of our desire as a species weighs down. Golding Farms is a small to midsized facility. But it is unlike anything I've ever seen before: 205,000 square feet of manufacturing space, whirling with machines, all working in powerful physical incantation. The speed and complexity of the line—bottles ratcheting up so they blur together beaded, robots swiveling to cap them in never-ending precision—expands the mind almost like meditation. It is enveloping and deafening, and as we walk through, every one of us sinks our necks a little lower into our shoulders in acknowledgment of the added pressure in the air.

Unlike so many other industrial spaces I've visited while researching this book, it smells like food. The line is impeccably clean, polished cement and shined-up stainless steel, not so much as a stray drop from the thrashing machines just inches away. Instead of smelling like machinery, the space is sweet and heavy and makes me oddly hungry. The muckraker in me wishes I could write about dirty conditions or workers throwing themselves from the scaffolding into bubbling vats to escape their drudgery, but alas, this was simply not the case. Instead, my overriding memory of Golding Farms is of order and precision and of almost-perfect cleanliness; a cleanliness that really did harken to godliness if only in its approach to an absolute state of being.

Eventually, after following the line upstream, we arrive at the beginning. This is a pantry area, but pantry for the gods. Shelving units thirty feet high are packed with giant drums labeled "spicy brown mustard,"[32] or "caramel color," or "honey," or "garlic." On the floor, we pass two thousand pounds of "granulated sugar" in a bag about the size of a twin mattress, next to a 12' x 12' pen of cabbage. I put the quotes around the "garlic" and other pantry items not to be snotty but because—excepting the cabbage—none of these ingredients are what we use at home. They are industrial analogues, produced and designed for machines at volume, not for pots and pans at a home stove. On the floor next to us, we pass two penguin-sized bottles of something called Aqua Clove and Aqua Allspice. "You might say, 'I used some vinegar to make this sauce at home.' But that just doesn't work here," Kent explains. "We need ingredients that are more precise, more consistent,

---

32 Given their versatility, the decision of a co-packer like Golding Farms to make or buy a given sub-ingredient once again hammers home the power of commodity products. For almost every ingredient, like that spicy brown mustard, there is a factory out there that specializes in just that and only that. Their buyers have cornered the world market on mustard seeds, have modified their machines exclusively for the particular viscosity of spicy mustard flow, and thus, although Golding Farms could make it in-house, even at their massive scale, it never makes financial sense.

and with better shelf life. A half a cup of your vinegar when you start doing it at six hundred gallons simply doesn't mirror. It wouldn't taste right."

This mirroring reveals a final industry truth. As a co-packer Golding Farms is a soup-to-nuts operation. If you are capable of handling their thresholds, i.e., ready to graduate from a commercial kitchen, they will work with your product at every stage, from recipe design to shipping. And once you sign off on their decisions, they will handle all those details for you, working to source every major input from ingredients to glassware.

"I could never in a million years get the prices they get," Julie tells me. "So I just piggyback off them."

In practice this places the power and responsibility for negotiating quality standards in the hands of these facilities. That is, whether the ingredients coming in are local, organic, ethically compliant, comes down to how co-packers source and how well they are held accountable by third-party inspections. Golding Farms seemed like exquisitely respectable people; I don't think they would have let me in the door if they weren't both proud of and confident in the products they were making. When I asked about audits, they kept accurately pointing out that this was not the type of cleanliness you could suddenly fake. But they also seemed concerned by the overall dynamics at play in the industry. They knew better than anyone that audits were largely paper with no teeth, and that despite all the extra work they were doing, a contract largely came down to trust. They saw and spoke freely about how competitors who were less honorable could exploit that trust. And, worse, how buyers who were under bottom-line pressure might blink and unconsciously collaborate with those suppliers to give themselves a deal.

"Retailers rely on us to maintain the quality of the food," Kent says. "For instance, the industry standard for local is 40 percent local ingredients. But nobody regulates that. Nobody . . . At Golding Farms, we do buy our ingredients for local runs in North Carolina. But does everybody? Who would know?"

For retail buyers already overwhelmed by logistics, there is a compounding effect of all these lean efficiencies: I'm stressed, you're stressed, and my stress actually pushes me to ignore any unease around what you are saying and instead enthusiastically accept this lower price you are only able to offer me because you are cutting corners due to your stress.

"At this point buying is an international market," Kent continues. "There are a lot of concerns that we didn't have to worry about before. Fraud is a very real thing, and the sourcing of product comes through an incredible number of channels. We sent people to China when we were considering buying ingredients there. And we decided we couldn't buy in China. Or at least not from the suppliers we visited. They were cheaper, but how often could we reasonably check on their quality? On the other hand, if you are one of those guys trying to knock out a price, get your foot in the door, that is exactly the type of ingredient you might source."

On the way back from Golding Farms, we pass a supermarket and Julie announces, "I'm going in to check on my jars. I'd like to take a picture for the website."

So we pull off the highway, hop out of the Ford, and head in. Julie walking across the parking lot at about 1.5 times normal speed, her pace increasing the closer we get to the store as if pulled by proximity, by the lure of her baby, and then the glass doors open, and I see it all with her eyes: an utterly drab supermarket transformed into pure anxiety. Products all yelling at the top of their lungs from the shelves for attention. Naked competition of the type you don't typically see except in wildlife documentaries or middle school recess.

As I'm processing this, Julie is moving up and down the aisles with long, quick strides, a look of perplexed concern on her face. You never know quite how big a supermarket is until you are searching inside one for a few bottles of Slawsa with their producer. The variety of similar but not exact items is staggering.

"I'm not real worried about competition," she tells me as we stalk the aisles. "It takes General Mills about four years to knock off a product like this . . . The midsized guys, they worry me a little. But the big guys, they would rather buy you out before they'd knock you off."

I'm nodding and panting, trailing Julie. Her speed has increased now that her first attempt to find Slawsa in the produce department failed. We head to the meat section, Julie's next-best hunch, and see plastic bags of coleslaw snuggled against coiled sausages, a promising adjacency. "Those big guys, they are companies of brands," she continues. "Dozens and dozens of brands. So adding one more isn't very risky for them." Julie is pawing past jars in a pickle display, double-checking to see if there is any Slawsa behind them as she says this.

We walk away from meat, Julie wrinkling her nose, maybe in annoyance, maybe to sniff out her Slawsa among the chaos of this store.

"A big guy can do BOGOF . . . But not me. I can't discount it a full 50 percent. I don't have the money. And it'll put in the wrong perception to consumers. I can't cheapen my brand." We stop abruptly. "Oh, up there with the kimchi! That would make sense . . ." Julie is frozen like a pointer, eyes scanning the shelves of one of those quintessentially American "ethnic" aisles where the Mexican green chilies are packed next to the black fish sauces of Southeast Asia. But there is no Slawsa. "Hmmm, let's go back to the produce . . . I know I've seen it there."

We spend the next ten minutes spinning around the produce aisle. I know this precise feeling well, losing something I just know I have, and don't particularly need to find, and feeling the anxiety of the search rising up my chest the longer I can't find it. Here in the produce department, Julie is lifting the figurative cushions on the couch, and on her literal knees to scope out the lowest shelf.

And then suddenly, there it is! In the local section, a sub-category within produce. Three rows of Slawsa, Original, Spicy, and Fire, on the lowest shelf of a fairly shabby display made out of used slatted boxes. Julie is clearly disappointed. I feel embarrassed to be there all of a sudden and want to give her a hug, though she would no doubt be horrified by even the idea. "I'm okay," she says. "I don't need to take a picture. It's here." And we head right out the entrance doors, back to the parking lot, triumphant at finding it, dejected from the search, our pace slowing back to normal the farther we move away.

At some undefined moment, Julie's buyer meetings began to produce results. "I thought, 'Should I reach out to Walmart? Just to make sure they know we exist?'" And after spending four months to research price, Julie approached them. Rather than just acknowledging her existence, Walmart placed an order. Then Kroger bought in. Then Safeway got excited. Julie stopped driving to stores and instead built out a network of brokers—agents who would rep Slawsa on commission, who had preexisting relationships with buyers, who could give her sales data about how her items performed on the shelf. But the better the news, the greater the pressure. Her spending increased with each production run, and she now had to manage the team of brokers on top of her marketing work. And so right around the time she signed with Kroger in 2015, Julie started taking sleeping pills. She hadn't been sleeping well for months, but suddenly it got to the point where even a single hour escaped her. "I just lay there thinking," she says. "My brain wouldn't stop. I'd get up and make a giant list of all the things I needed to do the next day to release the stress." Unfortunately, even the medication did nothing. And so for months, Julie would slip out of bed at four a.m., shaking her head as she walked around her house in the dark, trying hard not to wake her husband or the dogs. Then she'd stare at her to-do list in a pool of yellow light on her living room desk, and count up the hours she was getting back by not sleeping. That made her feel a little better. Then she'd sit down and get back to work.

Over the next two years, something very unexpected started happening. Things began to fall into place. Influential blogger Hungry Girl, author of six *New York Times* best-selling cookbooks, gets ahold of Slawsa and names it one of her Best Low-Calorie Condiments and then follows that up with Best Health Food Product. Walmart slowly expands her product into more and more stores. Then Lowe's Home Improvement decides to feature Slawsa next to their grills. Buyers return her calls quicker. She hires more brokers in more regions. And then, just a few months after we were frantically searching for her product in the aisles of her own local supermarket, Julie hits PR pay dirt. On some forgotten Tuesday, Dylan Dreyer, co-host and resident foodie on NBC's *TODAY* show, professes her love of relish on-air, and Julie reflexively, instinctually sends out one of her thousands upon thousands of routine, sincere handwritten notes affixed to a jar of Slawsa. And somehow this does not get lost, or discarded, or eaten with a spoon by some lonely overworked PA, but instead gets tasted and enjoyed by none other than Dylan Dreyer herself, backstage in her dressing room. And she promptly orders more. And so suddenly, on July 14, Bastille Day for some but National Hot Dog Day for those in the know, the *TODAY* anchors—in a perfect row of smiling faces behind their anchor desk—chow down on hot dogs positively smothered in Slawsa. It is the number one–rated morning show at the time. Co-host Natalie Morales gushes as she chews. Dylan Dreyer comes up for air and says, almost befuddled, "I said 'relish' on the air one time. And this company sends me this . . . It's like everything I love in one jar!" And she says this holding Julie's baby in her hands, label facing out at *TODAY*'s 4.5 million viewers, so blatant a plug it almost looks staged, except that the two other hosts are pigging out at this point, saying things like "I love this Slawsa," "How good is this?" and we see Al Roker shaking the whole goddamn jar out on his dog like he is trying to bury the thing, exclaiming, "This is fantastic! What a great idea!" between chewed mouthfuls, and it is obvious this is not a staged display of enthusiasm at all.

Julie basks. It feels like a dream. Around that time, though entirely unrelated, *Progressive Grocer*, the leading grocery trade magazine, names her winner of their Top Women in Grocery award for the executive category. This doesn't do a thing for her sales, but it does signify respect and that people in the industry have been watching her hustle. She is onstage with women from the major CPGs, executives of true multinational, multimillion-dollar companies. Kroger expands her line. Suddenly Slawsa, which was in all of zero stores when she got involved, can be found in over eight thousand; it is sold cross-country, including three different chains in Alaska, and Julie starts fielding offers to get into the Australian and German markets. She tells me in an email, offhand, as an aside, "I'm still not taking a salary, but I've started meeting up with friends again."

The last time I see Julie in action, we are back at the Fancy Food Show. This is two and half years after our first meeting, on the other side of the country, at the sister show in New York. Julie is in another small booth off the main hall. Even for booths, I am guessing there is a slotting fee she refused to pay. She stands, hair pinned back, smile affixed hard, but I notice something new in her enthusiasm. There is a calm to it. And she is dressed slightly fancier. Her smart suits upgraded to something almost un-Slawsa, something sleek.

Are those pearls in her ears?

As I approach, Julie is trying to hammer out new deals to move Slawsa beyond retail into her next frontier: food service. That is, selling directly to restaurants, cafeterias, hospitals, and stadiums so that Slawsa might sit on a table or get spat out of a pump anywhere you want a relish alternative. She also has two mentees who are helping her run the booth, both found from a Facebook entrepreneurship page she now administers. As they wait for passersby to approach, the two holding serving trays like caterers, Julie gives them their compensation in the form they most want: advice.

"You can't think of food service as a moneymaking channel," Julie tells them. "The margins are so low it is basically marketing. But that is exactly why it's important. People will eat Slawsa at the places they love, and then when they see it on the shelf, of course, they will pick it up.

"Plus, it's consistent business. As long as you are pricing it right, you might not be making much money, but you are keeping your volume up with your co-packer, which is a way of honoring that relationship."

The women nod, their trays bobbing slightly along with their heads.

"Can't you see Slawsa at the ballpark?" she asks.

And suddenly I can. With an exciting clarity. Even the amateurish lettering on the logo is starting to make retroactive sense. It looks like an old-timey ballpark script. It's like Julie has dreamt long enough and hard enough that she has changed my imagination and the very way I see her product.

Lost puppy dog no more.

As the day continues, I can see, however, that despite the sleeker suits, she is still very Julie. When a vegetarian comes by and accidentally eats a nugget of hot dog with her Slawsa, Julie scrambles for a napkin so the woman can spit it out into her waiting hands. That accomplished, Julie closes up the little mound of half-chewed food into a napkin canapé, tosses it no-look into a trash can in the corner, and in a smooth swivel worthy of a Golding Farms robot, presents a fresh meat-free cup for the woman.

"Beep beep beep. Come back here. You still have to taste. Slawsa is the perfect topping for all things vegetarian!"

A man walks right up between both of them and sticks his face real close. "What is this stuff? Some type of pizza topping?"

Before Julie can answer, he ambles off. "No, no, sir, not a pizza topping," she says to no one in particular. But then she arches her eyebrows. Stands with her hands clasped, looking off into the distance. I can see Julie's brain turning, trying to figure out if it makes sense. "Not a *traditional* pizza topping, at least!" She giggles at last. The vegetarian swallows her dose, smiles at Julie placidly, and continues on. Later, I hear Julie laughing with a long-haired dude about Slawsa on fish tacos, and after that, laughing with an older man about Slawsa on his wife's deviled eggs. When a vendor hawking some form of marinated pork loin stops by, Julie turns to me. "Every time I see meat, I get so excited. That is what Slawsa is made for!"

Eventually we have a moment alone. No mentees, no samples to be given out. I point out her clothes, tell her she is looking more relaxed than I've ever seen her.

At first she says nothing. Then slowly, with great relief: "I made my last payment to my former partner for the buyout," she says. "Just this month. That was the last of the big hurdles. Now we can start building up our savings again.

"If my husband had lost his job at any point over the last seven years . . ." She puts her hand on one of the jars of Slawsa, taps the top with her fingers instead of finishing the thought. "I wouldn't say I feel comfortable. But I'm no longer worried about being one of those 89 percent who get on the shelf and still fail. You know? We're here."

She picks up a jar and holds it in her hand. Then sets it back down.

"Did I tell you I'm playing tennis? Exercise! That's new." She gets a wicked gleam in her eye. "Turns out I'm pretty good. Beat the pants off my husband. Ran out of gals in the area to play . . ."

Just then, a group of chunky men with clipboards roll up. It's late in the show and everyone is a little tired. The man in the center of the group has his badge twisted over, the front facing his belly, ostentatiously hiding his identity, basically the only signifier of the true VIPs here.

"So what is this . . . this . . . Slawsa?" he says.

Julie whisks away from me. Sticks out a hand.

"What is Slawsa?" she says drawing out the question long and delicious. "Slawsa is the condiment that will change your life!"

PART IV

The Retail Experience

What does it mean to have and display a consumer attitude? It means first perceiving life as a series of problems, which can be specified, more or less defined, singled out, dealt with . . . It means secondly believing that dealing with such problems, solving them, is one's duty . . . It means, thirdly, that for every problem, already known, or as may still arise in the future, there is a solution—a special object or recipe, prepared by specialists, by people with superior know-how, and one's task is to find it . . .

—Zygmunt Bauman, 1990

Health Is Wealth

Orientation begins in a drab corner of the second floor "yoga room" at the Whole Foods on the Bowery. We sit at little rolling desks, our intro packets and pens smartly in front of us like we are about to take a standardized test. There are twelve of us new hires, a heartwarming range of ethnicities and ages, everyone channeling the first day of school, nervous and glancing and slightly overdressed. If I had to guess, I'd say we're all less curious about what we will be required to do on the job (earning our then industry-leading $11 per hour) and more about what in that work could possibly require two days of classroom-style instruction to instill.

This is the Whole Foods new employee orientation. It is the third and final stage in the hiring process, though completing it successfully—we are reminded frequently—does not guarantee us a "place on the team." There have already been two phone interviews, an in-person group interview replete with role-playing, a background check, and now this, a two-day twelve-hour orientation into the mission and philosophy of Whole Foods itself. But to actually become real live team members—I'd be working the fish counter—we still have to make it through a three-month probationary period, after which our coworkers vote on whether we should be brought on in a more permanent capacity. Passing the probation vote requires a two-thirds majority in which each team member fills out a skills sheet anonymously ranking our abilities. "This is a great thing," we are informed by a chipper green-haired human resources manager, "because it will help you understand where your weaknesses lie."

Joury, a young man I recognize from a previous group interview, because he didn't speak much English and relied on me to unreliably translate crucial moments, walks in. "Hello, Benjamin," he says. "Will you do the same thing?" I give a "*Sí*" between clenched teeth, not wanting to give off the impression to the surrounding Whole Foods managers that one of my weaknesses is an inability to sit still and listen.

Then Andy, our trainer, wide-eyed, ginger bearded, takes the floor.

"Welcome, welcome, welcome!" He begins with a cheer that verges on rage, "I so am excited to welcome you aboard!"

This feels a little off since we were just explicitly told we weren't officially aboard anything yet, and wouldn't be for quite a while, but the force of Andy's cheer, plus the knowledge that we can all be let go at any moment, causes everyone to lean forward and put on their best smile. Joury looks side to side and then follows suit.

"I started here just like you, as a part-time cashier," Andy explains.

"Now I'm leading trainings—all in two years! It's the type of position that at other companies might take five years to get to." Andy stops. "What I'm saying is that at Whole Foods you have a future if you want one. If you work for one."

At this, the green-haired human resources manager waves us a friendly goodbye and departs. We are alone with Andy, who shouts a few more greetings at us and then dives headfirst into an icebreaker. Andy tells us to partner up; one person is asked to talk continuously for three minutes while the other person doesn't speak at all. It is supposed to teach us "active listening" as well as serve as introductions, but almost immediately the human resources manager pops back in, Andy gets pulled out of the room on some errand, and the three minutes grow to ten. We are never told to switch partners, and so, with half the room ordered not to speak, the other half utterly exhausted from being ordered to speak continuously, everything gets awkward. There is mumbling. Then total silence. Finally, Andy pops back into the room and says, "Okay! Wrap things up!" to a room where most people are staring at their desks, necks hanging like narcoleptics, before adding without a drop of irony, "Unless you are in a heated discussion!"

He then fiddles with the PowerPoint for a moment and we begin.

The rest of the morning is a blur less for reasons of speed or overwhelming information than for the concussive effect of repetitive dull content. We are given a charmed version of the WFs story, learn that it was founded in 1978 in Austin as Safer Way (quoth Andy, "Now, that is really sarcastic. I love it!") by John Mackey, a "conscious capitalist" (Andy doesn't mention whether we should receive this epithet with sarcasm as well). That it survived a vicious flood in 1980, opened just nine stores between 1980 and 1992, and then went through a rapid period of growth that led to our present moment in winter 2015 with 427 total stores, and a new WFs opening every eight to ten days. It is a lecture that alternates between extolling the greatness of Whole Foods as an organization and extolling our greatness for being selected to interview at Whole Foods. At one point we take an actual moment of silence to marvel at this combination of our good fortune and Whole Foods' discernment. "You are here. Think! Think about that for a moment," Andy beseeches us. He stares off to the side, giving our thoughts the necessary space to expand, and I can almost feel him counting to five in his head before barreling forth.

At some point, we turn our attention to customer service. We learn about the 7 Different Types of Difficult Customers, a sort of late-capitalist version of Snow White and her dwarfs, featuring Angry, Whiny, Hysterical, Very Important, The Chatterbox, The Know-It-All, and Mr. Multitasker. We learn that we must treat these "challenging guests" with respect because it costs six times more money to attract a new customer than it does to keep an old one, and because, above all, Whole Foods is in the business of saving money—phrased here as "efficiency," and linked heavily with the mission of being green.[33] From there, we learn that Mr. Green is the Orwellian name for the Whole Foods internal security team, and that if we see something shady, we should head directly to the loudspeaker and page him. An undercover security detail will swoop on the scene and pounce on the troublemakers. This is followed by a crash course in the modern organic movement, which is shockingly—even movingly for a cynic like me—nuanced, calling out the idea that organic does not mean healthier, but rather is an option to pay extra to limit the externalities of production, and

---

33 The conjoining of efficiency and green becomes a leitmotif throughout these sessions, and serves as proxy for both the central tenet of Whole Foods the organization writ large, and the subliminal message being whispered to each Whole Foods customer writ small, namely, that by serving yourself, you are also serving humanity, that it is only a lack of ingenuity and concern that prevents us as a species from having it all. All meaning honoring mother earth while eating really high-quality squash in the specific sense, but which, in the general sense, is more about the life we deserve as intelligent, well-intentioned Americans living in 2020, where gratitude and giving back are two of the many things included in the concept of abundance we have come to demand from both our lifestyle and our grocery store.

which focuses on unsexy aspects of organic like soil conservation and groundwater runoff rather than borderline falsehoods like nutrient density and/or the overblown pesticide claims that we could use to up-sell customers. This moment of integrity is ruined the next minute by a bumbling lecture on GMOs, including a weird aside where Andy puts up the ingredients list for a non-organic, probably GMO box of cookies and says, "Your body is going to have to work a lot harder to break down all those ingredients with long names," as if there were a relationship between linguistic and gastric digestion. Everyone, including Joury, nods along in appreciation of this information.

Then a lecture on landfills and recycling or "the greatest thing we do," Andy says, where we are told that it takes one million years for a single glass bottle to biodegrade. When I get punchy from the boredom and point out that this is clearly not true, vis-à-vis beach glass that seemingly gets eroded on a days-to-weeks time scale, Andy handles me, The Know-It-All, with deft customer-service charm. "Huh. I'll have to look into that. Important point."

I want a wink from him, but Andy never gives in. He's incorporated customer service into his entire being, and charges on to tell us that recycling is good not just for the environment but for business—four cents per pound for compost and recycling, compared to ten cents for regular rubbish.[34] He goes on to list other efficiencies the store pri-oritizes, from freezer insulation to lighting fixtures. Efficiencies that above all save money. I wait for it. Wait for it. Then suddenly, "Health

---

34 Sad but totally predictable note you already know in your heart: recycling in practice at WFs and every other grocery store I worked at for this book was entirely and hope-lessly fucked. I don't care what corporate claims, or the rhetoric in the training, trash at the fish counter got placed liberally in every bin, less the result of apathy, more from the blitz of the job/day. This was true of employees and customers alike, and inevitably each night most of the bags from the blue recycling bins would be taken and placed in exactly the same landfill dumpster as the bags from the gray non-recycling bins.

is wealth!" he exclaims, to my relief. "Health for the planet, wealth for the store!"

We break for lunch and I excitedly use my employee discount card for the first time, accidentally ingesting 1.5 hours of salary at the hot bar. My coconut milk hoki was tasty, but I decide I'm better off brown bagging it from now on if I want to actually earn money on the job. Then it's back to the "yoga room" for a role-play around food safety.

I partner with Joury. We largely stare at each other, my Spanish not up to the task of translating "grease trap." In the middle of this, Joury's future supervisor walks to the door; he calls to Joury in Spanish, beckoning him. There, at the lip of the door, while the rest of us pantomime various food safety violations, the two have a long conversation of the type that looks actually instructive. Joury runs back in the room and gets a pen to write down information. I learn later that the supervisor specifically chose Joury to work the very same overnight grocery shifts that he, the supervisor, first worked ten years ago when he began at Whole Foods, when he also spoke almost no English. And despite the banality of our training, despite the hours of Whole Foods hype, I flush with the magic and possibility of these low-wage, low-skill grocery jobs—jobs laboring to create a myth of abundance for all the high-wage people with high opinions who populate WFs on the Bowery by day— and how there might actually be a path to this abundance, how Andy's cheer and rage might be the very mechanism of the American Dream in action after all. Soon thereafter, my brain buzzing on this notion, day 1 dead-ends into a thick packet of forms we are told to fill out while a video in the PowerPoint plays, featuring all sorts of eager faces who climbed the ranks to become management.

The next day we return and do it all again. I'll skip the blow-by-blow except to say, by hour 5.5 on day 2, I look up to see we are at slide 27 of

145 of the PowerPoint and I want to cry. Unlike day 1 with our ice-breaker, we have opened our mouths perhaps twice. The mood of the room is about what could be expected—bored twitching—except Joury, who, despite understanding not a word, stares with wide-eyed intent directly at Andy, his face a mask desperately conveying commitment. Then, somewhere in the mid-thirties slide-wise, it is over. We are given name tags, told they are all-important and that we must never come to work without them, and sent on our way.

Our department supervisors will call us within the next week and we'll come in again, this time to actually learn something about groceries.

Eight a.m., and I'm greeted by my supervisor, Ollie. He is a big dude, friendly and built like a wrestler. As a supervisor, Ollie will prove nearly flawless: kindly, flexible, reasonable, and completely absentee. I see Ollie on the floor only on the rarest occasions, when he gets tipped off that someone from Whole Foods central might be floating through the store or he wants to try some type of new promotion—like shucking oysters in store or filleting a whole fish as a demonstration. Beyond those moments, he largely stays up in his second-floor office ordering product, and fiddling with the schedule, tending to logistics we are neither privy to nor he is willing to describe, only fluttering down now and then to call us "boss," and make sure the display case is beautiful.

Accordingly, Ollie hands me off almost instantly to a deputy, a "supervising team member" in the nomenclature of WFs. Walter is a scrappy guy, slightly balding at twenty-seven, trim as a piece of copper wire, and all smiles and endless energy. He bounces around our section in knee-high rubber boots and a thick vinyl apron, straightening shelves, collecting garbage, and wiping up stains with unconscious action. Walter has been working seafood for six years. He hates it. He hates the smell. He hates leaving encrusted with fish guts. He thinks it is destroying his love life. But he has finally crested to a point in the pay scale where he is not going broke while working, and so wants to stick it out. It is also important to note that Walter is 100 percent upbeat about this hate; he was selected well by the WFs hiring squad, and hence has an irrepressible, smoothed-out version of Andy's caffeinated enthusiasm that makes everything that comes out of his mouth feel cheerful no matter how black the actual subject matter.

Walter guides me to the back of the fish counter. From here, standing on iron-grated platforms that boost us up an extra three inches to serve/loom over our customers, Walter runs me through the basics of cutting, weighing, and washing. The product slopes down and away from us. It sits on a plastic mesh designed to resemble ice, which itself sits on the crushed ice from this book's metaphorical beginning. The fish counter is a world of constantly melting and pooled water, every inch of the stainless steel dappled, every square foot of floor streaked. There is a definite funk, but the smell is for the most part the smell of clean. Of clean, not actual clean. That wet mix of industrial strength soap and chlorine you find in old folks' homes that lets you know on some chthonic level the place is absolutely crawling with buggies.

Smells aside, the work is simple. We have two primary missions: serve the customer, fill the case. Serving the customer is self-explanatory but primary. Anytime, anywhere, no matter what else we may be doing or thinking, if a potential Whole Foods customer needs help, we are to attend.[35] Filling the case is the background activity we return to when

---

35 At the fish counter, this service is equal parts ballet and crisis: You take the fish in gloved hand and hold it aloft for the customer to see. Then, whirling around to the back, you slice a chunk, amazing yourself every time that there is a hidden human skill for estimating weight from volume that you intuitively develop within hours of working with the fish. Then you pop it on the giant gray scale to verify your intuition was indeed within a few ounces of the request—which it almost always is—then rip off a big old piece of butcher paper. If you are me, this is where the crisis begins. I'm one of those dysfunctional

customers are not around. It is the sole command Ollie barks on the occasions we see him. The fish counter relies on volume to project fresh-ness, so any moment we are without customers, we race to the back freezer and grab new fish to fill any gaps on the ice. To do both these missions, we use box after box of vinyl gloves. They are consumed by our hands, almost like air that we breathe, constantly putting them on, ripping them off, the plastic skin becoming as familiar as our own. When the two primary imperatives are satisfied—the case is packed tight with fish, there are no customers in sight—we fill out the cracks in our time with tons of smaller jobs: blasting the plastic tubs with hot water so they don't stink; flooding and then squeegeeing the floor so it doesn't stink; picking out expired mussels from the stand so they don't stink; and if all else is finished, and there is really truly nothing left to do, perhaps using a handheld thermometer to check the cases and enter food safety data into a log. But truthfully, excepting my first day when I am taught this is a Very Important Thing We Do, I can't remember ever seeing it done again.

With Walter's guidance, it doesn't take long to realize that more than anything we are maintaining a mortuary here at the fish counter—keeping all our skinned dead friends looking glam for the customer. We retrieve their corpses from the back, and then begin coaxing some semblance of "fresh" or "life" out of them. Time, oxygen, and room temperature are our enemies. Techniques range from endlessly reposi-tioning them, slicing tired, flabby pieces into nugget-sized chunks, or,

---

left-handers who never properly learned how to use scissors in elementary school, and who feel almost genetically incapable of either budgeting the amount of wrapping paper for a given gift, or folding the subsequent swatch into anything neat and orthogonal, and has therefore spent an entire lifetime handing over presents that are both endearing—for the obvious amount of labor and Scotch tape involved—and puzzling for the sheer in-eptitude of the result. During my time at Whole Foods, I never get it. Often my results are so out of whack with the clean and expert Whole Foods image that I lose sales; per-fectly good fish that upon presentation in a clusterfuck of butcher paper isn't really needed after all.

when things get really bad, the fish mortician's makeup of cut lemons and squiggly halos of sliced red pepper.

It turns out each supermarket department has its own version of this cosmetic work. In produce, where I do a brief stint for a Whole Foods competitor, we pick at moldy blueberries in their cartons, smearing the white fuzzy fungus against our pants, before moving on to the next one. Here the command is "pack it in" (rather than "fill the case"), and there are intricate rules about how to stack the cucumbers (with the dark gray end out) versus bananas (letting the ends cradle each other). Instead of refurbishing the fish, we pluck melons just on the verge of rot and take them into the back room, where a woman who speaks no English stands all day carving them up into chunks and packing endless grab-n-go containers. In produce, we are constantly making secret stashes of over-aged items around the store to avoid sending them back downstairs to the walk-in fridge and facing reprimand. It is obvious work, but shockingly satisfying, handling all those vegetables. In the way of service animals and Japanese cat hotels, I think stressed-out and anxious New Yorkers should consider volunteer shifts in the produce aisle, letting all those leafy greens flood their parched cerebrums with calm. Likewise, center aisle grocery is all about "fronting," pulling those bags of beet chips forward to present a smooth face for the customer. There is no biophilia or satisfaction here for me, but the work feels like it would appeal to the neatniks among us, those who reflexively square stacks of papers to align with the corners of their desk and/or relax to a YouTube of Marie Kondo folding socks. A neurosis for every department, I suppose.

I finish the day in the back room, washing tub after tub in the hot stainless-steel sink. My glasses fog from the spray, fish oils and stray parts spatter everywhere. I end exhausted, the ankles of my jeans soaked through at the exact point the rubbery apron cuts off. A few more spritzes to clean the sink itself and I am done. I bundle up the trash, lug it back to the giant yawning dumpsters, and then run for the locker room. A process that continues every day for the two months that I work there.

One of the first things you realize working retail grocery is that people, in general, are hideous and insane, but their depravity almost miraculously balances out in the ledger of the day so that aside from bruised feelings and egos, which never really balance, the store itself makes out just fine. You'll have a tiny little man who can barely see above the counter berating you to cut a slab of the $32.99 per pound King Salmon into progressively smaller and smaller pieces as if to prove some volumetric version of Archimedes's paradox until you are left with reams of unsalable King Salmon that he promptly walks away from because you fucked it all up and that isn't what he asked for at all. And then minutes later an old woman with a blue beret and a lakeshore lockjaw accent will eye that very mincemeat and declare she'll take it. When you double-check to make sure she realizes she is about to buy a pound of wild King Salmon ribbons at $32.99 per pound, she'll note curtly that while she does have children there is nothing she adores more than her pet turtles and no food is too dear for them. This actually happened, by the way, but do not let its veracity get in the way of the lesson: a grocery store is a finely tuned instrument to serve human whim, and the diversity of human whim often allows it to do double duty, serving one through the act of serving another.

You also come to understand that unlike other professions, such as waiting tables or bartending, where you are confronted with the hideous and insane aspects of humanity, this will have no self-reflective benefit whereupon you go through the rest of your life generously overtipping the waitstaff of the world. This is partly because the particular demands you face in retail—or at least fishmongering at Whole Foods retail—are seemingly so idiosyncratic that you can't ever identify with them, much less imagine partaking in them. But more, because an inescapable part of the whole retail dynamic is an offer to step outside your normal self and get swept away imagining an enhanced version. Retail consultants never tire of discussing the three-act play of sales, but the truth isn't in the structure as much as the setting: retail is a performance, the very embodiment of some long-caricatured avant-garde "theater of the now," where, rather than passive audience, you as person are cast as the lead in a piece revolving around you as customer, targeted at you as financial instrument, and supported by a wide ensemble of living and nonliving players out to solve your problems and satisfy your dreams. This is obviously amplified to metaphoric heights when shopping for clothes and twirling around in actual costumery, but playing dress-up is part of retail no matter where it happens, certainly occurring in grocery, where we don various diets and identities, ethical approaches and fantasies, as hosts, guests, caretakers, and homemakers. Depending on the chain, employees are told to smile. To make eye contact. To WOW. To Smile Smile Smile. One manager repeatedly tells us, "We live in Yes town," which he always clarifies by saying, "That means we never say no," in a way that makes him sound like even more of an imbecile than it makes us feel. We are told to apologize for any and every mistake, especially if it isn't our fault, unless, of course, the customer is complaining about injury or food-borne illness. Then we apologize for nothing, the charade ends, and we run to get a manager.

"If a customer is angry," Andy explains, "you are calm. If they are saying something they think is smart, you are interested."

And like theater, customer service comes with a script. During research, I come across retail prompt sheets with phrases to memorize and protocols for responding to various situations. Listen; rephrase; empathize; apologize; etc.; with starter sentences and innumerable variations to address the full panoply of human neediness. In practice, however, it is very rarely, if ever, about memorizing lines. Instead it is method acting: forcing a look of concern, or suppressing a tic or involuntary reaction of annoyance. It is demonstrating empathy, and combining that with an utterly welcome condescension. "Think of customer service like how you would talk to a small child," one WFs trainer explains. "I pretend they are a little boy in elementary school I am caring for." Andy gives us a secret phrase to use whenever we are stumped: "Sounds important." It can be deployed almost universally to respond to questions we don't fully understand, hectoring we don't necessarily deserve, demands for advice we don't particularly have, and especially the long-winded rhapsodizing from lonely grandparents about children we don't at all know. At one point he leads us in a chant, "Sounds important. Sounds important. Sounds important." And the room fills with this customer service insight.

We are judged for this. It is part of our official job description, and depending on the chain, determines raises, preferential shifts, and general position in the pecking order. Employees, we are told, are there only secondarily to stock and work—those functions could have been outsourced or mechanized yesterday. Primarily we are there as forces of support, fellowship, community, and the all-important smile. That is our role. And while there is something animatronic and Stepford about the whole thing from a distance, I want to be clear, for the most part, this is nothing but a pleasure. The odd thing about being nice to people—even *being forced* to be nice to people—is that it is *nice*. This is not me, by the way, testifying from my completely dilettantish experiences, but the result of conversations with dozens of people over a wide spectrum of the retail food industry.

In the middle of writing this book, the *New York Times* published an exposé of sorts about Trader Joe's employees. It discussed how employees at the famously cheerful chain were forced in some Disney-Dickensian mash-up to smile and display enthusiasm, while underneath it all they were secretly anxious about punishment their superiors might lash down on them if they slipped up. I don't doubt the *Times* found a few people willing to testify to that. Every field has disgruntled employees, and every employee has days where they feel annoyed, angry, and frustrated. But for the overwhelming number of people I talked with, being asked to smile and be nice to people didn't come close to tops in terms of a grievance. (And there were grievances! Job security, nasty managers, choppy hours, low pay, gossip from fellow employees, you name it.) At the big chains, they were hired precisely because that behavior came naturally to them. In fact, I'd say our willingness to buy what the *Times* is selling—to believe that we as customers are oppressing our retail smilers—speaks to an uneasy parallel dynamic going on inside of each of us when we shop: namely, there is something about the whole retail grocery experience that feels too good to be true. Something that makes us feel we should be oppressing someone to make it all make sense.

And, of course, that something is real. Actually there are many somethings. But the fact that the person serving you gets through their own shift by alleviating their own stress with a smile that their manager has selected for during hiring, and occasionally reminds them to give, is absolutely not one of them.

Walter's day begins at four a.m., creeping down the hallway of his parents' apartment in Flushing, Queens, while the rest of the house snores. He tries to get to bed by nine p.m. on nights when he opens, but last night he couldn't fall asleep until just after midnight. This is typical. He only opens once or twice a week so he never completely adjusts to any schedule. By 4:05, he's splashing water on his face in the small hallway bathroom. Then he gets the coffee going and picks up his phone, twisting in a pair of earbuds to listen to a track he laid down last night.

Walter produces music. It's the side gig that he wants to make full-time once he gets out of grocery. He works with a variety of artists, most of whom he recruits from Whole Foods. The store is a village, and he hobnobs through the departments making connections, giving daps and pounds, popping headphones over ears to offer samples. The steady turnover of employees ensures there is always someone new to collaborate with. Right now he's working with Derrick, an aspiring rapper in cheese. It's pitch-black out of the kitchen window as Walter drinks his coffee, and he bobs his head along to the beat he made for Derrick. He'll share the track with him during one of their breaks, collect any critiques, then iron it all out after his shift back home. Now, here, Walter washes out his mug under the bright overheads of the kitchen, a kind of leave-no-trace ethic for his parents. He then returns to his room, picks up a tiny stubbed-out pinner joint, relights it, and takes a quick pull. The weed takes the edge off his fish counter work. What I've always thought of as irrepressible cheer is also slightly bloodshot and lifted. "Makes me ready to say hi to a couple of hundred customers," he tells me. "Hi, I'm Walter. I'm mellow. Let me help you." Then he trots out of his apartment into the early-morning darkness, the neighborhood gleaming, almost wet from the streetlamps against the early-morning emptiness, past the steamed-up window of the Curry Leaf, a late-night Malaysian spot where he occasionally gets breakfast, then up the covered staircase to the 7 train.

By six a.m., he's at Whole Foods in the employee lounge, a dank cement room, jammed with lockers and wire hangers. He sits on one of the rail benches, pulling on his rubber boots, strapping on a greasy apron, still streaky with unsalable omega-3s from the night before. The earbuds come out for the first time all day. Like all long-term employees, he has a locker he's claimed for himself, and his civilian clothes get crushed inside. Then he punches in his seven-digit personal ID number and heads to the floor.

At this hour, it's a shining vista: long, empty aisles, glossy flooring, a blaze of saturated colors popping from the shelves, their riot contrasting with the regimented order of the product itself. Walter walks past it all, flicks on the lights at the fish counter, and picks up one of the two big snow shovels to begin laying down fresh ice.

The ice in the case thaws out overnight, the edges thinning down like old teeth exposed by receding gums, and Walter's first job is to cover all that up with fresh flakes. Once the case is filled, he grabs the metal pans, arranging them like chalk outlines where the dead bodies of the fish will lie. The pans are secured into the ice with a big mallet and for the next half hour Walter is banging down on them, inserting each firmly into the ice. Then, once he gets the pans in, he starts laying down product.

This involves racing back and forth from the giant walk-in freezer. Whole Foods management is no fool—they've figured out how much time an efficient opening takes—and so moving at a leisurely pace between tasks is not really an option. Every morning, no matter how expert he gets, by the time Walter begins stocking the case, there is a slight time crunch. So he multitasks, filling a giant stainless-steel sink with warm water to thaw out the frozen fish until they resemble fresh, and ferrying out the tubs with the fresh fillets to prep. With each run, he makes a quick check for bad product—accomplished via the sniff test—and sorts them out to match their price tags. The work is a little like shingling a roof, slapping down the fish one by one in overlaying rows, each slightly on top of the other, so everything is tight and neat and the counter comes to look a little like a fish itself, each fillet a scale. His fillets assembled, Walter begins to lay out the whole fish, fins on, skin on, eyes bulging empty, curling them into the ice so the counter looks like a diorama they are swimming through. In the middle, like a grotesque centerpiece, he plops down a giant monkfish, a fish whose skin is starting to pull off from handling if you look at it too closely, but which is not designed to be looked at too closely. The monkfish is atmosphere, a freakish thing; its mouth has been popped open, vicious teeth and burgundy gums channeling all the mysteries of the deep blue sea. Its presence announces that Whole Foods seafood is for real.

By seven thirty a.m., the fish is largely out and a second team member has arrived in support. Walter is now working on the value-added product. Although this is a fresh fish counter, fresh fish aren't where the money or the margin is. In some big picture respects, the fresh fish are just slightly more salable versions of that monkfish, triggering an association the store wants to sell: the appearance of a market where "real" food is bought, sold, maybe even if we really squint, *bartered for* by gruff men with seafaring know-how at some offscreen pier. The profit, however, is in all that surrounds. At the fish counter that means precooked and ready-to-eat product. This is the tilapia, catfish, and steamed shrimp, aka the cheaper farm-raised stuff, that have been marinated in various attractive-looking oils and seasonings, or the fish sticks battered just sloppy enough to look "home-style." Most of the precooked is shipped in from a giant processing plant a few states away. That said, the seasoning is still done in-house, and so for the next thirty minutes, Walter is rooting around produce, making a bouquet of herbs, picking out a few shabby-looking peppers and a sunken onion, all of which he'll snip over the otherwise plain fillets to create a proper upsell.

Walter is good at his job and by 7:55 a.m. the case looks glorious, the garnishes arranged with the care of a florist, the food basically begging to be taken home and cooked, the result of pure technical skill by a man who can't afford to cook this seafood for himself. At eight a.m., the store opens, and an initial flush of customers stream in. These are shoppers who have actually physically lined up for the opening, regulars with hard-core routines, an equal mix of the geriatric and the corporate go-fer. They pulse through as soon as the doors slide open, instantly distributed like particles going into solution, so everything appears as it did moments before.

The next hour continues this latency period. Then there is a slow, almost imperceptible increase in customers, as if the store is gradually awakening. By ten thirty a.m., you become aware there has been a shift; the store actually feels open now, with customers milling around, asking you occasional questions. This continues pleasantly enough for all of twenty minutes, just long enough to register, until suddenly you realize the number of customers is still increasing quite steadily, as if the day has a current of sorts, and actually you are headed toward rapids. And then, it's bedlam. Lunch hour. Customers as locusts on the field. The aisles being ransacked, shelves pulled apart by young mothers with the righteous loathing of cops on a drug raid. At the fish counter, we're in continuous motion, the morning's organization flung around until the case is gappy, the fish themselves tattered, and the back counter a mess of stacked tubs and abandoned orders. The whole thing takes you from idle to under siege in a matter of minutes. And then somewhere way south, the rapids clear. It is over. We exhale and begin to put everything back in its place.

It turns out there is an entire science to tracking these changes in customer foot traffic, along with a whole pimply contingent of consultants promising to model things to allow for more perfect staffing. It's euphemistically called Human Capital Management, or "just-in-time scheduling," and it applies the same glorious principles of logistics that brought efficiency into Lynne Ryles's world to the staffing decisions in retail. Thus, weekly schedules that in Joe Coulombe's day were set in stone, ironed out as part of his business plan, are now adjusted on the fly, constantly, as the promise of high-speed computing and Big Data grind down on human resources.

The Grind

Human Capital Management, "just-in-time scheduling," and "lean supply chains" all have their roots in 1950s Japanese automobile manufacturing. In many ways, they are beautiful, turning logistics into dance, where every movement has a purpose, impact, and precision, so the results achieve an actual grace. At the same time, their expansion from auto manufacturing to human resources shows just how punch-drunk we've become by efficiency, just how loopy our collective moral compass has come to swing.

But to see this, it helps to first understand the sheer magnitude of logistics it takes to construct a car.

A typical automobile plant contains about six hundred individual workstations, each of which involves a worker installing one of the ten thousand individual parts it takes to make a four-wheeler move. Even by the early 1920s, assembly lines were cranking out one new car every twenty-four seconds, or just over 1,600 new cars in a single eleven-hour shift. The complexity here in terms of parts per minute per station should become mind-bogglingly clear to anyone who has ever depended on more than two back-to-back meetings running on time during a busy day. Suffice to say, getting the right one of those ten thousand pieces to the right workstation at the right time required a precision that needed to recur millions of times a day. Every day. Too few parts and the line simply stopped. Too many and the factory was overburdened, the financial balance sheet bloated.

In America, as we Americans do, auto manufacturers answered this complexity by erring on the side of *extra*. The inefficiency of too much was not just tolerated, it was seen as strength. We had space. We had cash. And most important, we had a bulldozer-style optimism that insisted customers would buy all additional cars produced simply because we made them. Henry Ford's River Rouge plant was an actual kingdom, with sixteen million feet of factory floor and over a hundred miles of interior railroad track. Ford brought in his own coal on his own barges, smelted his own steel in his own plants, and cast, cut, and machined those ten thousand parts to fit his own internally created gauge. Which is to say, he attacked the logistical nightmare of mass auto production by dislocating his jaw and swallowing it whole: a quest for perfect vertical integration.

Where we didn't go big, we made things simple: homogenizing what was once a customizable product made by a small number of highly skilled generalist engineers into a single unvarying form capable of being assembled by swarms of men each skilled at exactly one twenty-four-second motion. These two forces fed each other: parts that were interchangeable were less of a burden to stockpile; plants designed to make a single type of machine were capable of digesting raw materials far quicker. The result was nothing short of a revolution in production.[36]

None of this was possible in Japan. Geographically, there wasn't the same physical expanse or westward ho mentality. Geologically, Japan had limited natural resources, so vertical integration—tying together the coal, iron ore, barges, and smelting plants—was impossible. Financially, widespread post–World War II inflation prevented the type of liquidity needed to advance purchase and stockpile tens of thousands of discrete parts. And perhaps most trying, the Japanese consumer simply did not share the American preference for the monotonous, homogenized, and mass-produced, valuing the customizable and unique instead.

These difficulties came to a head at the young Toyota Motor Corporation. Today, Toyota is the largest automaker in the world. In 1950, it was a small family-run business that had made a name for itself modernizing wooden looms with combustion engines. The loom business was small and shrinking, and so Toyota decided to expand its work into the more powerful engines of cars.

And for all the reasons listed above, Toyota was floundering. The company was heavily in debt. Forced layoffs led to workers who were

---

36 It's easy to sneer at the homogeny and simplicity that Ford and the other early mass producers worshipped, but in many ways it was intended as a gift to democracy. Prior to mass production, cars were crafted by hand, one by one, the exterior metal beaten into place by wooden mallets, while more technical work was accomplished in dozens of shops scattered around the city. The cars that emerged were unique, beautiful, and only for the filthy rich. Think about the market for satellites and supercomputers today. By first simplifying the car itself—Ford's abecedarian march from Model A to T was all about streamlining his cars into something so simple anyone could fix them with regular household tools sans mechanic—and then simplifying its production, he made the single most complex piece of technology of his era affordable for the average consumer. It was the first stab at a blueprint that has subsequently been followed for almost every modern convenience—from air conditioner to iBauble—and that has essentially built the expectation that the lifestyle and toys of the elite will be available to us all within a ten-to-fifteen-year horizon.

perpetually striking. The quality of the few cars it was actually producing was low.

In one of those odd, looping historical moments, one of the head engineers at Toyota, Taiichi Ohno, went to the United States on an R&D junket to visit automobile factories. This was 1956 and somewhere between stops on his trip, he stumbled into an American supermarket. Like those shrieking Italian women, he was stunned by the abundance. Nothing similar existed in Japan. But rather than the food, his engineer eyes were drawn to a different delight. The workflow. Women walked from station to station taking exactly what they needed, and as the items came off the shelves they were replaced by stock boys exactly as space allowed. In a flash, he saw it all as supermarket pioneer Clarence Saunders had: an inverted assembly line, where the goods stay in place and the customer trollies forth building a basket. Yet in contrast to the assembly lines he was used to, piled with excess inventory, a woman on the supermarket floor was confronted with only the items she wanted. Standing there soaking it in, Ohno had a vision: an auto plant where the worker operated with the same efficiency a supermarket offered its shopper. Parts would be available "just in the time they were wanted."

It would take another generation and almost twenty more years for the vision to mature, but just-in-time would eventually become the first of Toyota's responses to the American way of mass production. Just-in-time demanded a simultaneously tighter yet more flexible coupling of the pieces of the supply chain, emphasizing communication over conformity. It relied on cooperative problem-solving with suppliers to ensure they shipped only what was needed when it was needed. And it applied a relentless, obsessive scrutiny to all forms of waste. It would evolve from physical adjustments to the manufacturing process—like red kanban cards handed backward at each stage of production—to the electronic flags and integrated robotics of today. In the process, it made Toyota the most profitable automaker in the world; its net margins grew to be over eight times higher than the industry average.

These practices made their way to retail slowly, even as their eventual application was impossible to resist. For instance, managing inventory is one of the oldest, most central problems for any grocer. If your buyers purchase too much, you are losing money for all the obvious reasons: those cluttered racks of 70-percent-off markdowns, crates of near-rotten vegetables being hauled off to a food bank. If you have too little, on the other hand, you are losing opportunity: the products that aren't sold because they weren't there to begin with. Given the tens of thousands of SKUs at even a modest grocery store, and the need to forecast completely fickle customer demand, the logistical problems faced are even more extreme than those faced by Toyota. When America, like a bunch of carbonated lemmings, decides to jump off the seltzer cliff, and you don't have enough LaCroix in your warehouse because your buyer wasn't quite sure how much to advance purchase, nothing immediate changes on the balance sheet. But instead of minting money on each sale of sparkling, every day contains a shadow loss, all the more painful because you likely don't even notice it.

There is no magic way to eliminate this tension, but just-in-time and its descendants gave retailers new, more powerful tools to negotiate it.

But somewhere in the last ten years, just-in-time *manufacturing* morphed into just-in-time *scheduling*. Whereupon the glorious terminology of efficiency squats square on the face of the retail worker. Again the allure is unavoidable. For years, scheduling was done with all the nuance of mass production. Staffing "orders" were placed and then rarely readjusted; "lead time" for an employee receiving their schedule might be as long as a month, humane if you have childcare to arrange and a life to enjoy, but almost geologically slow in a world accustomed to minute-to-minute supply adjustments. To correct this ineffectuality, a slew of consultants rushed into the space, crowing about "optimized schedule generation based on customer demand," "variable scheduling," and "advanced labor forecasting," phrases that seem to glaze the ear harmlessly, the same waxy consultant-speak that's been dulling us for decades, but which upon reflection are simply sinister: applying the principles that worked so well for auto parts to human beings: desperately needed when in demand, yet obnoxious waste when piled up behind the counter with no customers to serve.

In practice, this involves swapping the standard weekly work schedule for something entirely tentative, often just a printed list of days when an employee may or may not be needed. "The employee then learns via email, text, or call when or whether to physically report to work," *HR Daily Advisor*, a chirpy blog on the subject, explains. Similarly, an employee may arrive at work to discover that whatever off-site devices are forecasting customer demand have decided today will be slow, and get sent home with the explanation their shift has ended early. Sadly for management, humans tend to react differently than automobile parts when ripped from one place to another according to algorithmic whim; happily for management, norms are such that low-wage workers can be replaced almost as easily as automobile parts if they complain much more than the metal.

"You're supposed to get the schedule two weeks ahead," Walter tells me. "I can't remember a single time in my six years that ever happened. And if it did happen, it would change the following week . . . Usually we get the schedule two days ahead. A lot of team members have to call in to find out if they're working."

It's certainly a lean efficiency, whittling employees on both ends, limiting the number of hours they get—thus pushing more and more into part-time work—yet destroying the ability to take on a second job since they have no set schedule for a second employer to work around. The diminished hours often make it easier to promise valuable benefits during hiring, but then hold them just out of reach in practice, available only, say, for workers who clock the magical thirty hours a week required. And thankfully there's some machine crunching the numbers to optimize the precise logistics of keeping that in check. One study found that workers in these conditions had hours that varied month to month from "usual" by almost 50 percent. Which of course also means their wages varied by that much as well. Another found that 60 percent of retail workers said that they needed to be available to fulfill *every* work schedule that might be assigned in a given week, and that a full third of all retail employees get less than twenty-four hours' notice for schedule changes. There are professions where we expect people to be "on call"—doctors, first responders—but they are compensated for that both financially and in civic respect. Retail workers are simply not.[37]

The cultural effects of the shift cannot be underestimated. Retail and service sector jobs have always been marked by petty managers and their indiscriminate hiring and firing. And scheduling abuses come part and parcel with low skills and wages in every sector. But just-in-time automates all that; it gives the most callous decisions the imprimatur of technology, offering not just individual deniability but an actual halo of progress, where literal dehumanization (i.e., treating people like

---

37 Note on sunshine and lack thereof. These are all ways efficiency is brought to bear on consumer-facing employees. Suffice to say, the exact same dynamics bear down in an even more oppressive fashion on those low-wage employees who operate behind the scenes. It is not hyperbole to say there is a concerted effort to turn the low-wage employees of the world's warehouses into real (mostly) living cyborgs, leveraging the fine-tuned muscle control of human fingers with the immediate feedback and surveillance of computing systems. This merger, once minute to minute, now second to second, is entirely to service the goal of accelerating their ability to fetch, wrap, and box products. These employees already have computers strapped to their bodies, pushing them to carry out repetitive tasks as fast as possible, tracking their performance in a manner that can be tied directly to their pay scale. But the tracking being done now is with first-generation tech. Amazon, leader in all things warehouse and efficiency, recently patented a wristband that gives haptic feedback as it tracks workers' hand motions, vibrating to nudge them if they fall behind, alerting them if they stray from the optimal path to, say, scratch an itch. It is a technologic integration that might finally be tight enough to choke out everything extraneous and ennobling that could get in the way of box fetching. (And, yes, a third generation of tech where haptic feedback turns biochemical via nootropics and/or low-side-effect stimulants does not strike me as hysterical or implausible or anything except a natural progression, possibly even welcomed by a certain self-immolating work-as-life contingent in Silicon Valley.)

parts) can be justified as "valuable for the team." And in doing so, it slowly shifts expectations across the board. When I worked at Whole Foods, for instance, just-in-time scheduling did not officially exist in nomenclature. But the rapid scheduling changes, the short notice, the sudden demands on time, were still very real. They were often against official policy as preached to us by Andy on day 1 and day 2 of orientation, but then they were also often relayed to us in the exact same language of "efficiency," "team play," and "smart decision-making" that defined his lectures. Most important, we on the floor knew and discussed the realities at the competition—Target, Starbucks, Walmart, and all the other nearby retailers who explicitly used just-in-time. And those conversations flavored the coercion; a soft demand to be a "team player" was always in reference to how much worse it could be out there if we were ever unlucky enough to do something that would force someone to ask us to play for a different team.

Or, as Walter says, "Nobody wants to say anything, because they feel like their team leaders are going to get them in trouble . . . They might pull up your lateness from the last four months. Or if they don't have you on lateness, maybe they will go over your food safety logs . . . All these things that don't really matter until you complain, and then they matter."

Which Bleeds into a Larger Question

As an employee, Walter is sharp. Unlike almost everyone else I work with at seafood, he knows where the fish comes from, and can pay lip service to the different ethical regimes that are advertised endlessly as guarantors of wholesomeness. This is a natural accumulation of knowledge from working the front, earnestly answering questions, the slow development of expertise. In a different era of America, Walter, even without his college degree, would rise through the ranks based on his endless energy, enthusiasm, and willingness to do just about anything asked. Yet, in our current era, his fate at Whole Foods seems like an open question. He receives regular raises, but they bump him up by literal nickels and dimes, not into meaningful money for the New York he lives in. And thus, while the vocabulary around his title might change from "team member" to "supervisory team member," he basically stays in the same place. And the entire experience has embittered him.

The reality of Whole Foods is that its myth of abundance and efficiency is based on the idea that there are an abundance of Walters out there, willing to pour six years of their life into a $15-per-hour job, yet remain cheerful, eager, ready to serve all that virtuous food to those who can pay.

My experience is that there *is* an abundance of labor. I went to three different Whole Foods hiring sessions, and each one was packed with hopeful applicants. But that does not translate into an abundance of Walters. Unfortunately for WFs, they don't seem to care about the distinction. Payroll costs are an immediately identifiable flag to any consultant worth their MBA, while the faint aura of having a Walter behind the counter instead of a clueless replaceable me is something built and lost over time. It isn't intangible. It just often evades eyes whose financial pupils have shrunk from long hours staring at spreadsheets and can no longer see qualities that do not have clear metrics attached to them. They also likely assume Walter's capacity can be trained in others for less than it takes to retain him.[38] Walter knows

---

38 This particular point is wrong, perhaps most critically from an economic perspective: research again and again shows that spending on payroll results in increasing sales. For instance, one 2006 study of five hundred retail stores found that every $1 increase in payroll resulted in $3.81 of increased margin. However, its persistence in spite of the research is not accidental, and alludes to the LARGER QUESTION of the title heading: Is this quest for efficiency always a race to the bottom? Or are there equilibrium points whereby efficiency—and outcompeting your rival—can coincide with dignity? This is not a moral question even as our general way of life may hinge on the answer. It is a question about optimization and consumer habits and how exactly the shoppers who purchase from WFs make their purchasing decisions; it is also a question in which my generation of MBAs, both incentivized to find quick earning fixes and insulated from the

this and has grown sour on the chain. Our last conversations are filled with how much Whole Foods has changed, how his health insurance and the slightly-above-average pay that he has ground out prevent him from easily leaving even as he feels completely ground down by management.

When I ask him if he feels like he has any job security, he says, "No! It frustrates me. It wears on me. I've worked here six years. I got no security. I work hard. So I'd like to know I have a place as long as things are going right . . . I don't feel that way. Not at all. I feel like they might cut me at any moment."

On a different night, I close with him. We pull in the seafood, a dramatically quicker process than banging down all those pans to open—tossing fish into tubs, washing down the pans with a high-velocity spray nozzle—all wrapped in less than thirty minutes. Then it is back to the locker room and the 7 train. I leave him at the Flushing stop a little after one a.m. Because of a scheduling change—almost certainly against Whole Foods policy—he has the morning shift tomorrow. Rather than waking at four a.m., he can sleep in slightly, maybe until six thirty, he tells me. He'll be the employee who comes in at seven thirty to help prep the ready-to-cook section, back at the fish counter, strapping on the apron, ready to do it all over again.

Then one day I am working with Lawrence, a West African who commutes an hour and a half from the Bronx, and my favorite person to close with, since he is all business and willing to start pulling product a

---

actual work of retail in a way that transforms abstraction into condescension, may not even be interested in considering. Conventional wisdom on retail staffing runs hard. And thus, whether it is necessary or not, staffing is seen as a cost to be cut rather than a community to be built, and an actual human matrix of voices and values that could represent the heart of a brand are overlooked in favor of more easily quantifiable attributes like real estate, merchandising, and advertising.

good fifteen minutes before closing rather than the five we are officially supposed to, when Andy walks up to us. "Lawrence, I just wanted to find you. It has been a pleasure," Andy says with a face as smiling and upbeat as our first day of orientation. "Today is my last day as a member of the Whole Foods team." For a second, his smile drops, then from the customer side of the fish counter, Andy offers a clumsy handshake that has to negotiate the rise between us. Lawrence laughs long and hard at this. "I'll miss you, man. You are the best trainer ever. I don't think this place can survive."

Andy nods, and walks off, heading at a slightly dizzy pace toward the customer service desk while Lawrence looks over at me. "Andy is such a funny guy. Always such a joker." I am squeegeeing the floor. "Andy is never going to leave. He loves this place," he continues. But Lawrence is wrong and Andy is out. Whole Foods has let him go. They are working on a new, more efficient way of training employees, and his position has been "restructured." And so the single most enthusiastic person, the truest true believer I met in my time in retail, the guy whose answer to everything was just work harder and trust that things will work out, has found out exactly whom to trust, exactly how hard things can work out.

PART V

When I Look in My Window: Backstage in the Theater of Retail

The pleasure-seeker will naturally be pushed toward acquiring greater and greater control over all that surrounds him. Such control is not merely a question of ensuring that others submit to his will, but it is more a matter of possessing complete power over all sources of sensations so that the continuous adjustments can be made which ensure prolonged pleasure. There will, however, be an irreducible element of frustration for even the most powerful of individuals...

—Colin Campbell

The route that brought me to Kevin Kelley is a little tricky to explain, so bear with me. Suffice to say, at a certain point in my quest to understand the grocery industry, I became so turned around, so confused by the multiple layers of motivation and complicity, by the good people working hard and the hardness that came from it, that I needed to stop worrying about everyone else and just get someone to explain my role in it all as a consumer to me—and that someone was Kevin.

But First Our Introduction

This was back at the Fancy Food Show in 2015, the very same one where I met Julie, although I hadn't quite met her yet. I was trawling the show, popping samples, collecting totes, and generally marveling at everyone selling their newer, rawer chocolates of ever more singular origin. Somewhere, amid the chaos, I retreated into one of those educational seminars. It was there I happened upon Kevin.

When I first see him, he is onstage, backlit by a giant projection screen. Kevin is prowling along the apron, mic in hand, cord trailing behind him, almost like a TV minister before his flock. As he speaks, he is clicking through slides of supermarket floor plans. The room is dead silent, staring at these floor plans. But unlike the other educational seminars I attend, it is packed in here, standing room only, and the audience is locked in, glued to Kevin and his architectural diagrams.

And so I decide to stay awhile, lean against the back wall, unwrap some caramels I've swiped. As my eyes adjust to the room, I notice a series of giant foam boards lining the aisles with Kevin Kelley's face smiling out. Across the top: "Retail Bliss: Understanding the Mechanics of Shopping Behavior."

The first thing I hear him say:

"We are here to facilitate the consumer and create joy . . ."

Kevin says this and everything else in a low southern growl. It's a difficult register to convey, both conversational and commanding, with a warm, fuzzy sort of authority that involves a lot of imperatives in the first person plural. It is not too far from the voice in a good guided meditation, booming and soothing and located as much inside you as apart.

"We're not trying to manipulate anyone," Kevin explains from the stage. "To get someone to do something they don't want to do? That's hard. Maybe impossible. Maybe not. But if you did it, would you like yourself?"

The room ponders this question. I chew my caramels.

"What we want to do is make lives better," he continues. "We want to give energy. And if you do that, do you think your customer will come back? We want to understand the subconscious aspects of how space triggers behavior. And then we want to use those triggers to create joy."

The room doesn't need to ponder this. Kevin keeps going.

"We want to create physical bliss points. Sensory cues that switch you into a certain kind of joy. A sensory environment that activates you."

At this, I catch something moving through the room, perhaps the very energy Kevin is talking about. All those silent heads are nodding along in unison.

"How do you make your customers feel like a hero?" He pauses to let the question hang. And then it catches me. Like a human ripple in the auditorium's pool. Even though I still don't quite know what we are talking about, my neck is nodding too.

"How do you make your customer a hero?" Kevin intones again.

And suddenly I see it: A hero in every store! A quest! Shopping as Mario charging toward the right, scavenging gold coins from the landscape in a hero's journey, left alone to fight the big boss of the register at the end. "Activated," Kevin Kelley booms. "A sensory environment that activates you. Where you come in with an empty battery and leave with a full one."

I am rocking back and forth in my pew now too. Flipping through my press packet of brochures, I find Kevin. He is an architect by training, but one who specializes not in constructing buildings but in crafting the retail floor. His practice promises a sort of marriage between psychology and architecture, combining ethnographic research on human behavior with interior design to create spaces that fuel sales.

Kevin starts talking about a project he worked on for Harley-Davidson. "Let them imagine how their life will be better! Let the customer crank up the bike! Every piece on the sales floor is deliberate. We use plywood because we must! We need a warehouse, not a showroom!

Who would buy a Harley in a showroom? Not someone in this tribe. Not someone who would ever buy Harley at all. So we make a space fit for a Harley man. And to do that we must listen to the Harley man . . . Remember, we're not trying to manipulate anyone. We are listening to people.

"All across America, I see checked-out shoppers. I see men and women wasting their lives." And at this, he clicks through a mountain of slides of dour men sitting in drabby shopping malls, plonked down and depressed into chairs as their wives and daughters presumably frolic in offscreen dressing rooms.

"Why are these men sitting like that? What type of prison is this? Look at their eyes!" It's inhuman!

Walking out, when it's all over, I see Kevin Kelley's smooth face on one more foam board and think, Huh, that was intense and weird and somewhere between really moving and deeply cynical. I should probably get in touch with that guy.

But at That Point I Was Deluded and Thought All That Was Distraction

I had come to the Fancy Food Show in search of something far more serious. I say serious with a smirk now, but back then I believed it absolutely. I wanted to understand the ethical dimensions of our food. Where the claims on our packages came from, who validated them, and what it really meant when something was declared organic, fair trade, rain forest friendly, or gluten-free. This felt deeply important in a way Kevin Kelley did not.

Let me try to explain.

For years, whenever given the choice, I just tossed the organic fair-trade version into the cart. I had read my Michael Pollan and Eric Schlosser. Kept up on my *New York Times* exposés. I knew the cost of industrial food. Paying extra to make the world a slightly better place seemed like the actual literal least I could do as a white American male atop the food chain in a financial, social, and caloric sense. It was an opportunity. A sign of my larger sentience and connection to the world. And so without even thinking, I ponied up. Every time. Ethics was habit.

But the habit always nagged at me.

I had watched organics and fair trade explode into billion-dollar industries. But it was hard to say the world was becoming a better place for the marginal spending. In fact, it felt like it was becoming a more insulated one. I kept thinking of the medieval practice of simony, where the wealthy could pay money to be released from their sins. The grocery store felt like it was becoming a smug secular update. The seals and certifications acting like some sort of moral shield, allowing those of us with disposable income to pay extra for our salvation, and forcing everyone else to deal with the fact that on top of being poor, they were tacitly agreeing to harm the earth, pollute their children via their lunch boxes, and exploit their fellow man each time they made a purchase.

And so to better understand, I decided to drill down into the world of ethical labeling.

What I quickly learned was that ethics were big business. Those certifications had booths right next to the hot sauce purveyors at conferences like the Fancy Food Show. In the same way a buyer for Safeway might stroll up and down the aisles looking for the next snack sensation, those hot sauce purveyors could shop for an up-and-coming certification regime that would guarantee the integrity of their product. This struck me as *serious*—worthy of investigation—and so I filed Kevin Kelley away as a distraction, and instead poured myself into these vendors of integrity, trying to get to the bottom of who they were and what exactly they were selling.

Vendors of Integrity

In many ways the privatization of ethics makes perfect sense. Government regulation of our food is as spotty as a fourteen-year-old boy's first beard. It has grown out of federal agencies with conflicting and conflicted mandates, and is driven by the political qualities of food and the political contribution of lobbyists, rather than, say, a public-minded quest for fairness or consistency. There are areas where it is quite strong, even overly aggressive, and then whole wide patches where nary a regulatory hair has sprouted.

To give some small context as to the relative gaps at play here, in 2009, the Government Accountability Office estimated that only 0.001 percent of all imported food products were inspected for fraud or mislabeling. A stat that sounds pretty damning on its own, but especially when juxtaposed with the fact that 50 percent of all fresh fruits and 80 percent of all seafood are in fact imported, and that when a voluntary fee-for-service seafood inspection program run by the Department of Commerce actually looked, it found fraud in over 40 percent of the products submitted to it. Nor is domestically produced food much better off: a whopping 4.5 percent of domestic food production facilities are inspected by government regulators each year. Better than imports, yes, but when one-thousandth of 1 percent is your bar, maybe stepping over it isn't quite the level of accountability we have in mind.

In response to this general failure of government regulation, pretty much the most American thing imaginable happened: lawyers, armed with sickening pictures of toddler food safety deaths, rushed in to fill the void. Starting with the 1993 Jack in the Box *E. coli* outbreak, tort attorneys have reliably brought class action lawsuits down upon the head of any food manufacturer even remotely responsible for a food safety violation. And the verdicts they have achieved, routinely in the millions of dollars, often in the tens of millions, forced manufacturers to implement reforms that weak government inspection simply did not. Bill Marler, the biggest, strongest, and savviest of these tort crusaders, estimates that he alone has won more than $600 million in food safety judgments. That is a $600 million incentive to clean up your act spoken in a language the food industry actually understands. Timothy Lytton, a professor studying quality assurance, tells me, forget the Food and Drug Administration, "Right now many would say Bill Marler is the de facto czar of food safety in America, and trial lawyers like him perhaps the most powerful guarantors of our health."

But as is so often the case, the means dictate the ends. And grocery buyers quickly realized that if the regulatory threat was a lawsuit, what they needed most was a way to limit liability. And so, following the great food safety outbreaks of the 1990s—in particular 1993's Jack in the Box *E. coli*, 1994's Schwan's ice cream's salmonella, 1996's Odwalla's tainted juice—buyers began tucking two new demands into their contracts. First, they required that companies submit to "audits" of their manufacturing process. These were in-plant walk-throughs by an outside observer. Second, they demanded that food manufacturers pay for these audits out of their own pockets as a part of the cost of doing business.

These demands occurred at the very moment that we as a culture began plumbing the depths of our supply chains globally. Beyond Odwalla's *E. coli*–laden juice, 1996 was also the year the Gap would be attacked for its labor practices, *LIFE* magazine would publish a photo essay of a Pakistani boy stitching Nike soccer balls for six cents an hour, and Kathie Lee Gifford would bawl the mascara right out of her lashes on national TV, half in attack, half in apologia for her connection to Honduran sweatshops. Kathie Lee, in particular, with her chirpy evangelical bearings and sticky-sweet intentions, stood for a certain American naïvety. We could mock her for being slow, insulated, and out of touch from realities most of us had only discovered a few short years earlier.

At the height of her crisis, during a special pre-taped prime-time segment, Kathie Lee proudly declared she would be paying for third-party inspections at every factory stitching her name in their product. There was nothing particularly new here. Just a gradual mission creep of the food safety audit. But in the late 1990s, with the rise of corporate

PR needing solutions converging with the rise of empowered consumers needing absolution, the social audit was an idea whose time had come.

And so from the dust of an anxious sanctimony a mighty industry rose. In 1996, famed financial auditing firm Price Waterhouse conducted exactly zero supply chain audits. By 1998 they were conducting six thousand different types. By 2020, PricewaterhouseCoopers' food audits are but a multimillion-dollar drop in the $50 billion-per-year bucket that is the for-profit auditing industry. There are now thousands of firms conducting hundreds of thousands of audits across almost every sphere of production. Everyone from the Smithsonian Migratory Bird Center to Certified Paleo by the Paleo Foundation (certifying food just the way the cavemen did it!) has gotten into the act with a set of standards, a high-design label, and a team of auditors willing to testify that a product meets their approval. As of this writing, the private auditing industry is about ten times larger than every form of federal inspection combined, and it is growing each year.

And like any growing industry, there is intense price competition, with each new auditing firm trying to corner the market by offering the cheapest, most efficient, least painful, and yet most noble, comprehensive, effective, reliable audit service out there.

Mildly Untrained, Mildly Invasive

Let me say this up front: auditing is tough. First, you need to be an expert in your field to have any business doing it. Then you need to be the restless type of expert willing to travel constantly from facility to facility, living out of hotels, heading to the desolate exurban spits around the globe where our factories and farms have been relocated, arriving at five p.m. one day only to leave by nine a.m. forty hours later. The work itself is hard. Since there is never enough time for a really thorough inspection, everyone compensates by cramming everything into one, maaaaybe two really horrendously long days. The factories are often gargantuan. The five main export facilities for seafood processor Thai Union house a total of forty-five thousand workers. And regardless of hours or expanse, it is physically and emotionally taxing work, walking around the machines or fecal lagoons, poking your clipboard into everyone's business, your job and professional demeanor viewed not exactly as the bad guy but as the guy who is affable and tells jokes to put people at ease, but hahahaha might have to shut down a production line at the cost of several million dollars if there is an area of disagreement. Suffice to say, it is not easy finding a good auditor. And so, when the auditing industry exploded, it became necessary to focus more on the restless-willing-to-travel quality, and less on the highly-trained-and-expert one. Or it became easy to justify asking that a true expert in poultry food safety to maybe consider cashing the check and conducting an audit on dairy cattle sanitation or the washing stages of lettuce, since they were in fact true experts at something that must be somewhat transferrable. Right? And of course, expertise being a humbling thing to achieve, these auditors were likely to know exactly how much they didn't know about lettuce wash cycles and thus subtly defer to the undeniable experts who were running the plants or farms in question when they noticed something borderline or suspicious.[39] Similarly, it

---

39 It's almost insultingly obvious to say, but the skills needed to evaluate the pathogen wash cycle on a harvest are very different from those needed to verify the animal welfare of chickens in a shed, or whether the permeability of the material used in a co-packer's walls are acceptable for allergen containment. Expecting an auditor to toggle between the highly technical domains of modern agriculture, modern manufacturing, and modern labor practices is no more intelligible than asking a top soccer referee to judge a cricket match before sitting down to mediate a divorce settlement. You might think this expertise problem would be limited to the bottom rungs, but you'd be wrong. Top standards organizations are issuing certifications in food safety, food quality, and environmental

became useful to hire independent contractors rather than nurturing long-term employees, thus pushing the question of auditor quality to another day. All of which combined to ensure that whenever the boom subsides, the standard of the mildly inexperienced, mildly untrained, mildly invasive auditor will have become the norm in the industry rather than a temporary thing.

And yet: in terms of food safety, there is a lot to suggest this hybrid system of weak government regulation, strong tort hatchet work, and private auditing to fill the gaps has produced positive results. Our food is safer than it used to be. In 1999, there were sizable recalls for meat occurring on a monthly basis—500,000 pounds, a million pounds. "They don't happen anymore," Bill Marler tells me. "I just don't get *E. coli* cases linked to hamburger. Something has changed."

But ethical claims around labor or, say, fraud against the USDA organic label, don't fit into the framework in the same way. For one, they don't produce sickening pictures of toddler food safety deaths. Nor do they produce a crop of grieving middle-class parents with the money and media platform to see a long lawsuit through to the end. Ethical audits also involve non-observable qualities that don't allow for sampling very easily. You can take a thermometer reading at a critical control checkpoint. It's much harder to determine whether a manager selectively withholds wages until his employees agree to work overtime.

It's harder still six months after the fact during a onetime visit.

These audits rarely occur unannounced, instead unfolding with all the spontaneity of a doctor's appointment. A date is set. Inspection questions previewed. When the auditors arrive, they are not true investigators. They cannot open locked doors. They cannot demand employee interviews, nor conduct them in neutral spaces. They cannot prevent retribution on employees who choose to speak out. They are

---

responsibility, but according to food scientist Richard Stier, "the auditors who certified them were experts in car batteries and electric lightbulbs."

guests of the facility and never left unsupervised. Retail brands often give auditing firms strict instructions about how deep into the supply chain to look. For instance, a labor auditor might focus on the payments a chocolate manufacturer makes to the farmers who supply it with beans. But the same manufacturer might insist that the auditor stop short of inspecting the farms themselves. Whether the workers there—the ones who are actually "hand harvesting" the chocolate pods as detailed on the label—are getting paid is never even considered.

But even if they aren't hampered by the brands who require them or the suppliers who are paying for them, it is still unlikely auditors could produce much systematic change. That is simply not their purpose. Auditors cannot launch prosecutions against legal violations they uncover, nor impose direct penalties. In fact, if true call-the-police violations are happening at your business, an auditor is basically the friendliest set of eyes you can get. They might uncover some terrible things, but they are duty bound to tell only you, so only you can decide whether to correct them.

Finally, for the most desperate, the most clumsy, or the smallest, most vulnerable family run facilities, there is overt fraud. Factory managers in China can buy software that allows them to keep multiple sets of records, attend trainings on how to falsify their books, or buy guidebooks teaching the best way to conceal a show factory. Or simply issue a bribe. Li Qiang, founder of the China Labor Watch, explains to the *New York Times*, "If a factory has 500 workers, to improve standards you might need to pay each worker another $20 a month. But 500 workers at $20 is $120,000 a year. It's much cheaper to bribe auditors."

My guess is overt fraud will always be a secondary or tertiary option. Who needs it when you have the tacit fraud of just shopping for auditors who give you the results you want? It's baked into the private audit system. Or as one former auditor told me point-blank, "People don't hire you to blow up their deals."

Which Brings Us Back to Kevin

The more I learned, the less sense it made. I had millions of obvious questions: Given these problems, how exactly were social audits used? How did grocery stores, so sophisticated about managing risk with shipping logistics, evaluate the risks around food quality and fraud? How did they determine if these audits were accurate at all? Questions that for equally obvious reasons nobody in the grocery industry wanted to answer. When I asked professor Tim Lytton, who had been studying these issues from an academic context, how to get more nuance about social audits, he essentially told me good luck! He explained that my best shot at any practical insight was to "become best friends with a supermarket Quality Assurance officer" and maybe get drunk with them, so that in the process they might divulge all their secrets. This is not the advice you hope for when talking to an academic about their area of research.

So I revamped my approach slightly.

I decided I need to get as close to the inside as possible. Essentially, I thought that since audits are so sketchy and hazy, and yet ethical claims are so important, I, neutral me, should try to act as an independent set of eyes. I could audit the auditors! If that strikes you as dubious to the point of deep stupidity, good for you, you are way ahead of me.

First, I poked around the world of food safety, bouncing from expert to expert, visiting them at their laboratories, heading out with them to the field. I thought that because food safety was empirical in ways that ethical claims were not, and because food scientists are called in to handle crises and therefore see corporate food at its most vulnerable, these scientists might have interesting things to say. They did. But mostly to call audits totally hostile, not-helpful-to-print names on background. (First-clutch non-attributable quote: "I wouldn't wipe my ass with a food audit.") From them, I learn the standard critique of the audit industry is most definitely shared by those who investigate outbreaks, but that food safety as an industry is in a slightly awkward place to actually make that critique out loud.

Then, a second-clutch non-attributable remark—"You want to talk about fraud!? I've been to poultry sheds with 25,000 chickens with a little door at the back that no chicken ever sticks his head out of. Some of those chickens are sold for three times as much money because they are 'pasture raised,' and the rest are sold as 'conventional' . . . Tell me, how is that not fraud?!"—leads me to ask for suggestions about how I verify that claim.

This sends me to Fayetteville, Arkansas, where I attend a four-day avian influenza training for USDA veterinarians and scientists. The training is ostensibly to arm the agency with enough information and practical experience to respond on the ground should another epidemic strike[40] but that necessarily also includes a sweeping overview of the entire American poultry industry as context, featuring lecture after lecture from poultry industry insiders at a depth of nuance that doesn't patronize the veterinarians and scientists and thus is a gold mine of insider details for yours truly. (Third clutch aside: over the thirty-five days it takes to grow a chicken to maturity, the floor of the shed will rise six inches in height simply from the accumulated chicken shit the birds produce, and this chicken shit gives off ammonia gas so strong that the "live catch" handlers who go in to gather the chickens for slaughter have to apply cornstarch to their skin to prevent the ammonia from peeling the flesh off their bodies.) Even more helpful, I get to talk with the various chicken farmers who attend, and watch slide after slide in aforementioned sweeping overview of their industry with them, marveling at what can only be described as really impeccably clean poultry facilities completely contrasting with the image blasted into my brain by animal rights activists. When I ask the chicken farmers—who don't know that

---

40 As reference, the last major outbreak, in 2015, killed 42 million birds in less than sixty days and essentially resulted in the mass euthanasia of America's henhouses.

I'm writing a book, and don't have any discernible reason to lie since they've already gossiped about all sorts of other weird things to me during our midmorning coffee breaks—whether the slides look accurate or not, they tell me they *do*, except for the ammonia smell, which of course can't be captured in a slide anyway. When I bring up the animal rights videos we've all seen, they don't deny them but say, look, we make our money on percent livability, which usually needs to be right around 95 if we are going to make a decent profit; the last thing we want are birds dying or kept in unhygienic conditions so that they get sick. Also, they add, there are sickos all over the place, you used to be a public school teacher, how would you like it if we assumed you were a pedophile just because we've seen news reports about that?

So I emerge from that experience quite turned around. These are USDA videos and slides, which are basically coproduced by Tyson Foods, the very definition of propaganda. And yet, I really don't think those vets and chicken farmers have any reason to lie to me. And so, after making a few discreet phone calls, I leave almost directly from the USDA training course to visit with a radical vegan animal rights group in California that breaks into confined animal facilities, liberates wounded animals, and promises to take me inside.

Our first trip is to a swine farm.[41] We arrive at four a.m., the smell of pig shit and pig meal coming in hard from the mile away that we park. After creeping in closer, and scoping everything out, we slide into light blue Tyvek anti-contamination suits, wrapping our footwear in soft sterile booties lest we track in some disease and kill the whole shed in the name of saving it. It is procedurally exactly like my USDA training. The only difference is that it is pitch-black out and we are wearing headlamps.

----

41 Note on timeline and accuracy: I eventually go on two trips with the group, first to a swine farm, then to a caged egg facility. In addition, the group was generous and credible enough to allow me to view reams of unedited footage from their visits to other feedlots, chicken sheds, and egg facilities that do not inform my descriptions in the text but do inform my general feeling of being overwhelmed by the complexity of the topic.

From here, I'm not sure what to say.

Pigs have intelligent eyes. There is no other way to put it. And walking through this concrete barn, dust kicking up in the red beam of our headlamps, the light is caught by those tens of thousands of pig eyes. They glitter like holy orbs in the dark. And our slow walk through, listening to the pulsing lowing, the scared stomping at our intrusion, is deeply moving, dreamlike and disturbing at the very same time. A sad communion with all these creatures we as a culture are going to eat. And yet, it is also exactly what I would expect. Yes, there are a number of grotesque tumors growing on certain pigs; yes, there are a few open sores on others, exactly the hellscape features I've seen in videos. But the vast majority seem healthy. It is also 100,000 pigs we are wading through. I simply have no frame of reference. I wonder how many tumors and wounds we would see among the humans on the subway if we all were forced to ride naked? There are pigs crowded together, but to my eye, that looks like it happened because we woke them up from their slumber and they are cowering together in fear. I remember vividly, and perhaps always will, a very happy young pig, or he looked happy to me, his pig snout in a sort of grin, and his eyes delighted with us as we passed, the rest of his face covered in giant pustulating warts. What do you make of even this one individual pig, much less an industry with hundreds of millions of others?

Which is to say, visiting the facility gave me exactly zero answers.

The volume of cruelty in any factory farm is so majestic that it echoes the larger human place in the world. You can be deafened by the noise of it, or close your ears completely. My subsequent trip to the egg house was no different. I could lay into the description or just let it be said: I saw terrible, weird things,[42] but I left just as I entered—capable

---

42 Eggs with shells soft as Jell-O from a calcium deficiency, so that when you touch them they quiver; air choking with particulate matter; panicked birds, again most probably panicked at our presence, shrieking and clustering in terror; escaped birds marauding around the floor; birds with huge clumps of missing feathers.

at moments of seeing it like the USDA slides and capable of seeing it like the vegans. It was not filthy, nor a hellscape. It was instead an intensely alien, highly functional place for animals to live a sad, short life before they were set to die.

As a group, we left the swine yard that night in silence. Everyone in their own separate mental space, driving back in meditation toward Los Angeles. All the vegans end up falling asleep, including the one at the wheel. So, without any discussion or protest, I retrieve my cell phone, which had been confiscated by the group, and drive the sleepy radicals to our drop site, a fantastically lavish mansion in the hills. Then we all strip out of our clothes, clothes I think are probably permanently stained by the trauma of the smells they've been subjected to, and pass out in various states of dress and undress as the sun rises. As I am falling asleep, in a miracle of double-booking, I check my phone and see Kevin Kelley has responded to a last-minute inquiry. He's down for an interview, and so I'll see him tomorrow—that is, today—at Le Pain Quotidien on Melrose Avenue.

And So, Caked in the Odor of Pig Shit Made Physical on My Skin I Meet Kevin in West Hollywood for Lunch

Eyes buzzing with exhaustion, skin still impregnated by the previous night's odor, I stumble into Le Pain Quotidien. Kevin is there, waiting for me in a soft blazer. Unlike the minister onstage exhorting everyone to "activate," the Kevin before me today has a dolorous face like a weary pooch, friendly, soft, and slightly worn.

Truly, I haven't prepared for this interview. I wasn't entirely expecting it. I'm disoriented from sleep deprivation, and while I try to get my bearings, I ask him about business. I expect he has a pre-baked promotional spiel he can launch into. Instead, he just shakes his head sadly. "It's like an alcoholic calling," he says. "These stores have nowhere to turn and so they call me. This is a dying business and nobody knows what hit them."

I'm aware of the current retail apocalypse, but it isn't new, nor what I came for. I want Kevin to talk about retail architecture, about marrying interior design with psychology, about creating bliss points that "facilitate the consumer and create joy."

"They all want to play the quantification game," he continues. "Well, guess what? You aren't going to out-quantify Amazon. And if you think you can run a lumberyard of food that is going to beat Walmart, you're crazy."

Right, I say, trying to steer our conversation back on track. So you help them take that lumberyard and add in bliss points? Kinda rearrange the design so people will want to buy?

"Bliss points," he says. "Yeah, we can talk bliss points if you want." And he looks almost bored. "But these guys don't need that. When I get one of them on the phone, and they ask about bliss points, I say, 'What do you devote your life to?'"

I'm not sure where this is going.

"These are retailers who've sucked the soul out of their business. Now they're like an alcoholic calling me for one more drink." He pauses. "You're writing about an American tragedy. But it's not the tragedy you think. It's a tragedy of imagination. We have a generation of guys that can only imagine being Walmart."

And then he breaks off.

Maybe he thinks he's losing me. Maybe he is.

"Okay," Kevin says. "But you want to hear about bliss points . . ."

And at this, as if pulling a scrim from the world, he introduces me to the Pain Quotidien we are sitting in all over again.

To begin, it is a Belgian country store. Not French. Belgian. Kevin maintains this is a very specific difference, evoked in all sorts of details, from the softer color of the wood to the style of fixtures on the white cabinet behind us. It doesn't matter that I don't know the difference between a French or Belgian country store, what matters is that somebody did, that it was a real and deliberate decision, and that person imbued the space with a cohesion.

But that cohesion is only a starting point. Kevin describes the next phase as "realm building," and it requires taking those ideas and crafting an experience. "Every stage of your interaction is part of a narrative," he tells me. "Your experience started outside, from the view of the building. There was a picket fence, a porch, maybe you consciously registered these things, but likely not.

"Then as you move in," he continues, "there are some big symbols to slam you over the head. This giant table." He points to the huge communal table that I never realized defines every Pain Quotidien. "Maybe nobody even wants to sit at it. That doesn't really matter. It's a symbol. It says something about this scene."

A scene like a movie? I ask.

"Exactly. That's the standard we are trying to hit . . . I want retail that can reorient your emotions in the same way that a movie can."

Isn't that manipulative? I ask.

"Let me turn that around," he says. "Are movies manipulative? Is art? And the answer is of course! Retail should be no different. It should move us. Emotionally. But to expand us. The real problem is nobody thinks about retail in those terms. Because there are a lot of bozos who only care about money."

And here he stops. "See, you were thinking bliss points. But bliss points don't exist on their own. They exist because a customer taps into something meaningful . . . Think for a minute, what do you tap into when you buy? What matters to you? And why?"

Buying into Meaning

At the grocery store we not only buy food to taste but also to demonstrate taste. Which is to say, our discernment. And in this way, it is like all-American consumption, deeply attached to our sense of self. We buy things to stake claims, to demonstrate autonomy, and to assert our unique experience. Sociologist Colin Campbell traces this ethic back to the Romantic poets who glorified self-discovery, instructing the writer to "express what he thinks and feels" and to "reveal the depths of the human soul." And our tastes do just that. We express them; they reveal us.

Back in the grocery store this gets delightfully complicated because taste also exists in a third dimension: the socially determined one. That is to say, in addition to the buds in our mouth and our outwardly exhibited discernment, we can speak about what makes someone have good versus bad taste. Which has nothing to do with an individual "expressing their depths" but exists insofar as their expression matches a social judgment. Anthropologist Daniel Miller studied purchasing decisions of Britons and Trinidadians and came to the conclusion that most people didn't even know whether they liked something until after they shared it with others. "I started with the assumption it was going to be a study of people wanting something, buying it, and then discovering themselves in it," he says. "That was not it at all. People hesitantly ended up buying things, and it wasn't until they had a response from others that they decided whether they liked it." And if we personalize this dynamic, the holy grail of American taste seems to be the type of person whose individual taste is both an expression of them as an individual and one that is socially approved. Two ideas that are, by definition, in tension. And thus taste—and consumption itself—is bound up in a paradox of sorts: freedom to express the unique self, but requiring approval from the greater conforming community.

Which itself is tied up in an even greater paradox: we believe we are individuals with an essence that does not depend on material objects,[43]

---

43 By "essence," I mean whatever makes you you, in whatever form you personally call it—experience, memory, genetics, soul, or some nuanced nature/nurture combo—much

but if that essence or sense of individuality is ever going to mean anything—if it is ever going to be demonstrated to our social group—then possessions and material objects are one of the few effective means of showcasing it.

It all works together to make our relationship to material goods very tricky.

Cultural theorist Grant McCracken grappled with a lot of these tensions and found that when you really got down to it, consumer goods carry meaning in a very particular way. He believed that as people we take our highest ideals—our most precious selves and valuable understandings—and remove them from daily reality. This removal is primarily self-protective; on some level we understand they can't live up to the assault of real life—they are ideals, after all—but they mean so much to us that we want to preserve them. And to preserve them, we place them in a different space or time, perhaps in a golden age when things were better, or perhaps in heroes, like George Washington or Beethoven, whom we'll never know personally and thus are less likely to fail us. He called these "displaced ideals." And his central idea was that we use material possessions to provide a bridge back to them.

Once I start looking, I see this everywhere: my city slicker aunt's collection of cowboy boots; a wealthy friend's pride in his $1.99 tube socks; my winter jacket designed for a Himalayan ascent, yet destined for snowy walks in Brooklyn. But perhaps nowhere do I see it more than in the grocery store. In the supplement aisle, of course—all those herbal, Ayurvedic, or neurotropic signifiers we grab at and swallow—but also in the food itself. The entire Michael Pollan ethos is, after all, a way of making food a bridge to the past when the world was simple and purer.

And of course, there are those certifications and seals.

---

of which I realize might depend on material objects in the atoms and quarks sense, but not, I think, in the Bloomingdale's Big Brown Bag sense.

Somewhere between the time I was in elementary school scampering up and down the aisles of our local supermarket, begging my mother to buy Salisbury steak frozen dinners, and a college freshman packing ninety-nine-cent cans of black beans in my cart, something shifted. I remember the first sushi restaurant in my neighborhood. Then I remember the first time little cartons of sushi appeared next to the Gatorade at checkout. Then the Gatorade went organic. Where once Julia Child helmed a single low-budget live-to-videotape television show on French cooking, suddenly there was an entire media empire. Food got its own television channel (or actually two: Food Network and the Cooking Channel), not to mention sixty-plus national level magazines, supplying content to compete with around twenty-one thousand food-centric blogs. Growing up, food had just been food. To use it as a tool for self-definition would have been deranged.

But that was then. This is now.

For many of us, this shift represented something of a discovery: food became the perfect stage to resolve all our tensions around consumption. It is, after all, a material good in the good old-fashioned purchase, flaunt, and self-express sense; and yet as you chop, fry, and chew it, food becomes entirely experiential. Then it is gone. And we are forced to do it all over again for the next meal. Where historically food signified a few narrow ideals, primarily around wealth and social standing, now it went impossibly wide, offering a blitz of expressive possibilities from our relationship to our bodies to our relationship with the natural world to every aspirational desire in between: thin, muscular, compassionate, worldly, closer to our ancestors, unique from our kin, food allowed us to advertise who we wanted to be—who we desperately believed we were—all while simply meeting our vital needs, side-slipping those larger consumptive clichés.

It was, in short, the perfect blank space for displaced ideals.

"The dark side of this aspect of consumption," McCracken writes, "is it helps enlarge our consumer appetites so we can never reach a sufficiency of goods and declare, 'I have enough.'" And so it is with food. Once we discovered this genie, we were in its thrall, and the grocery store was only too happy to supply bottle after bottle for us to consider, compare, and decide whether it was the one that our true self might pop out of.

"Retail is a giant reflection of society, what people are thinking and wanting and looking for," Kevin tells me when we meet back up a few months later in Los Angeles. "Fundamentally, I think we are a meaning-seeking species and I think we place a lot of meaning in consumption."

When I watch Kevin work with his grocery clients—those entre-preneurial "alcoholics" who've come a-calling—I see this search for meaning directly. What I find most surprising is that it is not unidirec-tional, not simply about targeting shoppers or getting people to buy more but about building something meaningful on both sides: creating an exchange where everyone involved can feel proud. Up close, it's al-most wholesome to watch. These big, chunky grocery guys huddled around a corporate conference table, Kevin's soft eyes like a crowbar on their souls. One says, "We couldn't have run a drier, more impersonal store if we tried." Another: "I just want to build a store I don't have to apologize for." This interpersonal work—reconnecting to a sense of purpose—then unfolds into soul-searching in a more literal survey sense: Kevin takes inventory of their brand and looks for anything resembling a soul there.

Sometimes this is easy. At one meeting, the management team from a grocery chain in Alberta, Canada, comes down to his LA offices. The founder, in his nineties, attends at Kevin's request. As the team dis-cusses the stores, Kevin pulls the founder in at every decision point, squeezing his personality back into the chain. "At lunch, they started making fun of our sandwiches. They were too small and dainty," Kevin tells me. "And I turned to him and said, 'Okay, what do you like?' He says, 'I like sandwiches so juicy the bread is soggy and you have to wipe your chin because the gravy is dripping on your face.'" Kevin seizes on this. It is odd and real and just what he is looking for. At a different meeting, one of the younger Albertan owners describes his home routine and says, "I like to make sauerkraut in the root cellar," and *bam*, in unison, Kevin's entire team puts pen to paper, scribbling. "Root cellar. That's powerful," Kevin responds. Minutes later another manager describes his bread-making process and lets slip the phrase "mother dough," and the designer next to me, a woman in a full-length wool dress that looks like it cost slightly more than my monthly rent, lets out a gasp. *Mother dough.* Kevin collects all these insights and anomalies, the sopping sandwiches, the root cellars, the bread that relies on a phrase so incantatory and out of time it couldn't possibly be made in a factory, connecting them like crumbs or clues, and uses them to build a realm. His team keeps giant "evidence boxes" of items they find during this exploratory phase, and sifting through one you'll see everything from internal stationery to pages from the annual report to employee ID badges. "It all feeds the beginning of a story," he says. "Once we have that story, we take it and make it physical." It will be a realm honoring the Alberta that the owners have introduced him to, and that will lead to a store that is real to them, that isn't competing with Walmart.

Other times the process is hard. There are no founders. Or the founders have been bought out and ignored. Or the current employees have become fixated on price alone. "The maddest I have ever gotten was with a manager at a health food chain," Kevin tells me. "The guy asked me, 'Will doing this help me sell more shit to more people?,' which is just ignorant, just strip-mining their larger purpose." In these cases, Kevin has to work harder to find that meaningful exchange. Instead of beginning with store leadership, he listens to the people they aspire to serve. Then he summons his inner salesman and sells their vision back to the higher-ups.

I watch this process with another grocery chain, a popular brand in California, recently bought by a private equity group. Here, Kevin's team, a collection of cultural anthropologists, interior designers, and visual artists, hits the parking lot. "We just followed customers out the door," he explains. "Saw the cars they were driving then saw the houses they drove to. Then asked a lot of really open-ended questions." From there Kevin goes on the same fact-finding detective hunt he used with the Albertans. Take one interview. "We called him Mythological James because we wanted to study him like an archetype. The real James was thirty-three years old. He leased a Porsche, then downgraded to a Lexus. He comes from a wealthy LA family. And when we interviewed him about the store, he said, 'I shop there because it's an expensive Ralphs.'"

Which is the type of cryptic statement that makes Kevin's curiosity drool. What does it mean? What are the needs behind this desire to shop at "an expensive Ralphs"? Why wouldn't you just go to Ralphs itself, a competing supermarket literally down the block? And so the study of James unfolds until, like all myths, it begins to speak to something larger. James self-describes as tasteful and classy, but if you look at what he actually craves it is lasagna and red wine. "Quinoa is an adventure and he doesn't want adventurous food," Kevin explains. "But he also doesn't want simple. Simple is a trap. Thinking of him as a boob is a trap. He wants the classics upgraded and reinvented." And then there is a crosscurrent of modesty in James. He is actually quite health conscious, but he doesn't have the vanity for Lululemon, prefers jogging to yoga. "We kept arguing about all this. My team kept saying, 'He's California classic,' but what does that mean? James isn't eating Alice Waters. He is a Wolfgang Puck frozen pizza man." Eventually the clues coalesce and a realm begins to emerge, just as it did with Alberta or Le Pain Quotidien, here in unpretentious Mediterranean California. And whether you love or hate James and his realm, it is a place where unconsciously he will feel at home. Or, as Kevin says, "It might look tacky to you, but that's because it is not for you."

The more I hang around Kevin Kelley and scratch almost any consumeristic itch, the more it bleeds pathos. At one point, Kevin talks about his work for Harley-Davidson, which hired him to help understand a prolonged sales slump. It is not grocery, but just like the search to understand James, Kevin began to haunt Harley dealerships. Soon he was going to hog meetings. The whole scene was very strange at first. He'd meet big, angry, swaggering Harley customers who were also terrified of riding their bikes out of their cul-de-sacs in their suburban developments. "I remember one of my first insights," Kevin tells me. "I had a long conversation at a meeting. An angry man. Wealthy but hard scrubbed. He tells me what I came to call a Harley story, like a Vietnam vet story, but about his bike. And instead of a punch line or a joke at the end, he leans in and gives me a hug."

Kevin was astonished. Just as with James and his "expensive Ralphs," the hug made no sense. But as he turned the moment over with his team, Kevin watched the anomaly turn into insight. "It's obvious now, but these are men that aren't comfortable with their emotions," he explains. "And that means they can't read emotions. Which means they don't know when they are validated by other men." Back around a table on Melrose, his team realized one of the few things that did validate these men was danger. Or rather, the image of danger that was a Harley. And so Kevin and his team began to pour themselves into rituals of man making, looking everywhere from the martial arts to precontact Amazonia, trying to connect their findings to the rituals in the Harley community. "Once we knew what we were looking for, we found manmaking rituals everywhere. But new riders were terrified of them," Kevin says. "We discovered that if we could make those rituals a little easier, we could build the community these guys wanted so badly." From here, the team got tangible, and prototyped a series of "Harley bars," carefully constructed to take a slight edge off the unspoken initiation rituals while still allowing the men to confront symbols of danger. Places where a wannabe rider could come, drink a beer, and for a moment, experience what it might feel like to belong.

Which Is What Kevin Made Me See

It's easy for me to nod along as Kevin talks about those Harley riders. They are safe and distant, and as a nice young New Age man who can express his emotions like a sneeze, I can barely recognize them.

But what about my own anomalies? What "activates" me?

Then it hits me one day as I'm thinking about audits: I want to use purchases to create a better world. I take it as almost as a given, this belief that through shopping I can somehow contribute to the general uplift of mankind. But what type of sense does that make? Buying something for myself to serve others? The more I reflected, the more I saw a self-serving riddle: as contradictory as any Harley hug, as cryptic as any "expensive Ralphs."

And if I mythologize my weird belief like Kevin did to James, apply the same compassion and introspection he gave to those Harley riders, I begin to see a greater meaning behind it.

In America today, our dependencies are multitude. Every single product we buy, every piece of food we eat, it all comes from someplace else. A thousand different fingers contributing to a few afternoon snacks. In another universe, that dependency could be reframed as connection, a mutualistic web or ecosystem. But here, now, for me, there is a deep powerlessness: all these systems from the political to the economic that we were born into, that we have not chosen, that we would not re-create, yet that operate on our behalf.

What I craved was a reassurance that the glut of pleasure and variety—from the ninety-nine-cent bag of chips to the heaps of grass-fed ground lamb—weren't an unfair bounty but an opportunity. That my passivity could actually be flipped into a chance to take action, validate myself; that despite all my taking, I could give back.

Which is, of course, precisely what those ethical, organic, and fair labor seals are offering.

Talking to Kevin about bliss points, I begin to understand: third-party certification does not exist to solve a problem in the world, but to solve one inside of me. Their primary purpose is not to make the world a better place. It is to make the grocery store a safer place for me to shop. They lower my barriers to buy by promising me two things I crave: a sense of control and a sense of destiny.

In reality, audits are faulty, easily gamed, expensive, cumbersome, and antithetical to creating trusting, mutualistic relationships. They are terrible at enforcement. Rather than connect me to others, audits align incentives in a closed loop: between manufacturers who pay a small fee to get graded on a soft curve, grocers who don't have to worry about rising prices from true reform, and customers who get the same variety and convenience, plus a sense of virtue for only a few extra pennies. We all win. Except those outside the circle.

Which is why you are never meant to examine third-party audits at all. The preferred level of scrutiny is a half glance at a tiny label on the shelf.

Like all displaced ideals, kept at a distance in order to be preserved.

It's easy to talk about the tricks and traps of market capitalism, the way we are being manipulated, but I needed Kevin to show me how much any manipulation begins at home. And I've come to believe that to the extent the system consciously "triggers" these needs in me, it is to the extent it believes in them too. If anything, this is a conspiracy of good intentions, convincing ourselves in circles that we are doing just enough not to require any uncomfortable action, replacing the terror of a gargantuan world with a feeling of control.

Tim Lytton, the professor examining certification regimes, said something in our first conversation that took a while to sink in. "People talk a lot about trust in the grocery world," he said. "It is a tremendously good-natured industry. But on another level, people talk about trust because there is basically nothing else you can do . . . If you have fifteen thousand produce suppliers out there, there is no way to handle the volume of information coming in . . . You talk about trust, but what's really going on is flying without instruments."

There is an aphorism attributed to the Buddhist monk Thich Nhat Hanh: "Our own life has to be our message," which I interpret to mean, while we may use material objects to "reveal our depths"—curate our clothing, meals, and pantry shelves to show each other whom we imagine we are—there is a more primary method of self-expression: how we choose to live our lives; how we treat one another; how we demonstrate care. Retail is one of the oldest, most important forms of human connection, one circle outside of family, and just as important in current society to meeting our vital needs. Its uniquely material focus makes it a bridge between these two forms of self-expression: between the possessions we flaunt and how we treat the people who make them. Right now the methods of bringing integrity to this connection—the signs and seals of certification—make no corresponding effort to span this divide. They promise us that moments of individual action can create a type of change that in reality only institutional forces like labor laws, unions, and trade deals can begin to approach. They allow us to purchase our ideals from others without ever having to enact them on our own.

"Humans have a desire to connect," Kevin says during one of our last conversations. "The mistake in retail is forgetting we need to help the customer do that . . . How do we get them to participate? How do you get them to say, 'I can't just show up and buy. I need to act. I need to effect this story.'" He pauses. "These companies who think they are going to win on price . . . I mean, you can try. But you will probably lose. And just to get the chance to lose, you will have to lower yourself." He concludes the thought with a statement that he inflects more like a question. "I like to think most of us wouldn't want to win that contest even if we could."

PART VI

The Bottom of the Commodity Chain

Homo sum: humani nihil a me alienum puto.
I am human: nothing human is alien to me.

—Terence

On the Swallowing of Little Fish: or, the Type of Invisibility That Occurs When Something Is So Big You Can't See a Meaningful Piece of It

Up here, we chew and chew and chew. Two hundred meters below the Andaman Sea, the benthic trawl net glides in service. A great maw of oceanic destruction, it greets the seafloor with a wide nylon grin: calm ahead, roiling on all sides, black plumes of sediment bursting forth like the seabed itself is exploding. The trawl net is many things to many things, but to the bottom of the sea it is bulldozer and wrecking ball, the giant steel anchor weights plow through the ecosystem, crushing coral, rock, smashing bivalves and crustaceans, obliterating the nooks and crannies where juvenile fish hide and teenagers sneak off to mate.

The steel stretches out the lower corners of the net, ensuring the trawl scrapes up everything its bottom lip touches.

Fish are attracted by the noise. They stream toward the trawl on instinct, their smaller fish mouths hung open, gobbling in the tumult. The trawl swallows them. The fish don't notice. They swim with it, gamely keeping pace, blinded by the turbidity and feeding. Eventually, unlike the trawl, they are satisfied, their muscles tire, and their swimming slows as they hang back. But the trawl continues, sliding over them steadily. Inch by inch they slip back into its belly, until finally, they find themselves out of room, pushed up against the cod end, that final narrowest opening in the back: the net within the net. Here the reality of the trawl changes. The density of fatigued fish increases as they accumulate one by one; first a thick swarm, then fish pinned horizontal to the water flow by the steady addition of newer fish pulled on top of them. If you subscribe to the agony of fish, now is certainly the time, as fatigued fish crowd backward, sideward, and lack of volume turns to pressure, compacting the fish, so much that, by the end of the trawl, the first fish captured are nothing more than mash, measured in inches and torn pieces, not salable as species, their smeared bodies coating the net, flesh pulverized by the relentless pull of the trawl and the succession of maws above.

Upward and ahead, following the trawl line at forty-five degrees, Tun-Lin is on his knees, rocking on the choppy surface of the Andaman Sea. He is in his ripped shorts, a gray-green T-shirt, both his thighs and his arms scabbed raw with a rash from the salt water he is perpetually kneeling in. All around him endlessly in every direction the sun bounces hot off the water. Before this boat, Tun-Lin had never been on the ocean. He had never seen a living fish, only the dried ones they sold at the market in his village in Myanmar. Now he is head down and intent, staring at the deck, sorting through a mountainous pile of sludge. Of sludge fish. Some bending slowly inward, drowsy at death, some thrashing like a dog's tail, some plastic bottles, some blocks of coral, kelp, the membrane of plastic bags. Tun-Lin picks through it. Sorts. Different species of fish go on different trays. All are taken back by other men to the freezer.

This is Tun-Lin's second year on a boat out of what will eventually be fourteen years at sea. At this point he is a slave in the only meaningful sense of that word. He cannot leave. He is not paid. He was brought here a prisoner. He was sold in a cash exchange. He works under the threat of violence and he has seen those who fought back against that violence killed. His best friend on the boat and the only person he knew before boarding is slowly being driven mad. Eventually this friend, Tu-Lek, will get beaten to the point of unconsciousness and then kicked in the chest off the side of the boat to die as the boat chugs on. Tun-Lin will feel sad about his best friend's death, he will be terrified by it many years later when we discuss it while trying to reimagine his life on this boat, but he will also feel relief. Tu-Lek has been getting increasingly deranged, laughing and crying continuously without warning. His death by the captain has been all but certain for weeks. The death will also open up a spot in the bunk they are sleeping in. Tun-Lin shares a crawl space with Tu-Lek and the rest of the crew, some slaves, some closer to indentured servants, some free men who signed on of their own volition, some who enforce the captain's orders, many in more than one role, depending on the precise time you look, all sleeping together in a space less than a meter high. To get to the bed they crawl on their hands and knees for about twelve feet into the darkness through an opening that can fit at most one person at a time. This is where Tun-Lin sleeps when not working his twenty-hour days; when I visit a similar sleeping hole on the Thai docks, the opening comes up just above my knee and it is warm, exhaling the dark yeasty-manure smell of the unwashed human body. In 2015 when I connect with Tun-Lin for the first time,

NGOs estimate 17 to 60 percent of Thai shrimp includes slave labor like Tun-Lin in its supply chain. Seventeen to sixty percent might sound like a wildly high error range, but nobody knows anything in this world. It is divided between those who know nothing and are desperately trying to find out more, and those who know nothing and are financially incentivized to maintain that state. Once imprisoned on his boat, Tun-Lin estimates he sleeps less than five hours a night. While other Thai fishers I speak with will report being given amphetamines to keep up with the pace, Tun-Lin is not given any drugs. The captain provides his crew with instant coffee to eat by the scoop because there is always fish to catch, nets to mend, a deck to clean.

Tun-Lin operates the mechanical winch that pulls the swollen trawl net out of the sea, a gargantuan teardrop of dying fish. After guiding it in and dropping it on the deck, his job is to sort the mass. He tosses the large intact fish to other men who take them for freezing. The smallest fish, of which there are the most these days, the waters exhausted by the trawls, are unsalable for grocery buyers. Instead, on many boats, these get placed in a series of blue barrels, collected along with ripped fins, mashed tails, crushed mollusks, and other organic debris to be sold for fish meal.

Fishers like Tun-Lin never see these small, unsalable fish make it to port. They are passed to a sister boat at a rendezvous, traded along with food, cigarettes, Thai baht, and fuel. This is called transshipment at sea. It saves fuel for the larger refrigerated fishing vessels, and it allows some boats to stay out almost indefinitely. Resupplied by others, they turn into floating prisons for trafficked workers.

The sister boat, the first aggregator among many, will chug off with the catch. From there, the trash fish will get bought by a broker, combined further with others from similar ships, until all are unloaded at a small private dock, tossed barrel by barrel onto a long ramp with rollers that guide them from the water toward a fish meal factory. There, finally on land, they will be dumped into a giant pile in the hot sun.

Within a day, a man with a rake and wearing dark rubber boots will push this pile of fish and fish pieces toward a growling mouth in the cement dock. It looks like a hole in the ground with two grinders in it for teeth, and it takes the rotting fish and pulverizes them further. The scent near the hole is deafening. It blocks out other senses; you close your eyes near this smell; you say excuse me I cannot hear you or even think very well to your translator. It is the smell of thousands of tiny rotting fish piled ankle-high in the ninety-degree Thai sun on a space that has held ankle-high levels of tiny rotting fish for years. It is a hot smell, not just from the climate and the decomposition, but because there are furnaces just beyond. You can see them glowing behind the man with the rake. The pulverized fish will pass on a conveyor belt toward those furnaces, getting cooked into a paste, then baked into meal. This will then be sold to yet another broker, bought by a feed mill, and blended with inputs from dozens of other facilities, all to create the protein base in pet food, food for fish farms, and feed for hungry little shrimp.

Thus is the beginning of the Thai shrimp industry, a billion-dollar complex of activity that pumps 350,000 metric tons of shrimp into the world market each year, just under 10 percent of the total global supply. It is, depending on when I look during the writing of this book, the second- or fifth-largest producer after China, and always a top supplier to the United States, which buys more than 50 percent of its product each year. Shrimp are the single most popular, profitable, and widely consumed seafood in America, more ubiquitous than wedding salmon, tuna for carton sushi, or New England cod. And Thailand is our most sophisticated, developed, and integrated trading partner, largely the result of giant foreign investment developing its aquaculture sector.

Once there is fish meal, actual shrimp production can begin. In aquaculture, with the easy ability to transport millions of tiny developing larvae from place to place, this is an oddly disjointed process, completely unlike a farm where animals are raised in a single place before being taken elsewhere for slaughter. Shrimp are raised everywhere, shipped to new, more specialized facilities at each stage, combined with others, then separated back out. The concept of traceability barely makes sense.

The first step is the larval stage, and it occurs in a large, humid warehouse-like space. The one I visit is filled with what look like plain cement sarcophagi, about forty to a room. Approaching and leaning over the sarcophagi, you find thick troughs of nutrient broth, the color of cola, roiling away with oxygen bubbles. This is a brood stock facility. The air inside is held to a steady, sweaty eighty-eight degrees. If you pull a sample from these larva pools on day 1, it's Sea Monkeys: motes floating in water, about 500,000 per tank. By day 4, these motes will look just slightly alive, like gnats, flicking around in Brownian motion visualized. The cola color has faded slightly, and when extracted to a glass beaker for presentation, I think, *Ah, hairy champagne.*

My guide here, an American aquaculture entrepreneur, is leading a tour of businessmen looking to bring shrimp production to their home countries. When a Burmese worker walks in and begins flicking food into the troughs, the entrepreneur incorporates it into his tour seamlessly. "Workers don't get a salary," he explains. "They get a bonus based on the survivability of the tanks they manage." The owner of the facility, our guide's friend, chimes in explaining the details. "Rule number one when hiring people is you do not hire locals. They will want to go home. They will have families. You want someone who will live here twenty-four hours a day. If they come from a place at least twelve hours away, the chance of them going home is way down."

The businessmen scribble notes.

"These are farmers. They don't work eight-hour shifts. They don't leave the farm. You must think of them that way. If you hire three people to work three shifts on a twenty-four-hour day, all of sudden you are paying six hundred dollars, not two hundred dollars, and that is a cost you can't maintain."[44]

Then it's back to our lecture on shrimp. As they grow, the larvae are moved to successively larger tanks to accommodate their size. By day 25, they look like black seeds, maybe the size of rye grains, and at this point, if you squint very closely, you can tell each grain of rye is attached to a tiny translucent tail about the size of a fingernail clipping.

To harvest them, workers use fine-mesh nets, swooping in to collect the seeds, draining them like pasta, and then flicking the remainder into a sloshing plastic bag of broth. This bag is then inflated with enough oxygen for shipping, tied off, and packed in a crate. All of this happens by hand, totally efficient and low-tech, with workers squatting on an open-air dirt floor, whipping the bags around, pushing them in tight, flies buzzing. To get the count, the workers tally each net by hand. I watch two Burmese girls, cheeks stroked with thanaka, doing this at speed, ladling the larvae up, squatting, and counting those little black dots before tossing them into bags again and again until the harvest is complete. Behind them, a buyer leans against his pickup truck, chatting lazily with the owner. Behind them both, a young woman sits at a microscope on a foldout plastic table. Quality control, brought along at the request of the buyer's buyer's buyer three notches upstream. And while the Burmese squat and count, and the buyer schmoozes, this woman slices open random bags. At each, she uses a pair of tweezers to prepare a slide, dabbing down the alcohol, smearing the slide cover on top, and cranking the microscope in. There she jots down notes on color, gut-to-muscle ratio, and size distribution while a few dogs lie in the dirt beside her, everything and everyone baking in the heat.

---

44 That is two hundred and six hundred USD *per month*, as reference.

From here, the black dots head to a hatchery. They are officially no longer larvae, but post-larval shrimp, or PLs for short. As we drive across the Thai countryside following that pickup, we pass a wreckage of dark lagoons. Long stretches of highway lined on both sides by perfectly square ponds, all a murky stagnant green. We stare out the window at them, all knowing just a little bit about the shrimp industry.

One of the businessmen asks, "So is that the water for the hatcheries?"

The American guide laughs. "No, no, no. The water for the hatcheries must be clean. That is wastewater." Miles upon miles of it, gridded out across the landscape like Iowa corn.

"That's left over from someone who didn't know how to run their pond right," our guide adds. "It used to be so simple. You'd throw some food in and the shrimp would grow. Now you have to learn to do it right."

At the farm, the shrimp are dumped into a pond in a tumbling black rush. Food goes in next—delivered now by men in a canoe—and finally a foam aerator is placed on top, beating the water like miniature paddle wheels on a ferryboat. The shrimp continue to expand reliably, gobbling up the fish meal delivered five times daily, excreting lagoons of black shit below. They'll make their home here for the next three months. The limit in yield is purely space; ponds are packed dense with shrimp, up to ninety per square meter, and in the smaller ones, if you mistime or overstock, there are stories of the ripened shrimp rising right out of the water as they grow, like dark popcorn kernels bursting over the pot edge. When they are finally whisked out in large nets at harvest, dipped in a succession of freshwater tanks for cleaning, the long and translucently blue-brown shrimp we know from the *Nature* show emerge: part whiskered alien, part beady-eyed friend, wriggling one thousand to a bushel, each armored in its own hazel shell, curling inward like a beckoning finger.

These are killed instantly. The same style of plastic barrels used to transport trash fish at sea are filled now with an ice slurry and packed full of the harvest. The temperature shock provokes an immediate and final spasm to each shrimp heart, a cap comes down, sealing them in darkness, and barrel by barrel they get jammed in the back of a truck for processing.

From here, a clock starts ticking. There are ten hours to get the shrimp from the farm into a bag and then get that bag frozen to −30°F for export. If it's all done in smooth succession, the shrimp can sit in a deep-freeze locker for just over six months, finally assuming the status of commodity, ready to be traded around the globe at the whims of the market. If there are hiccups, it all crumbles. Each hour of delay translates into weeks, even months, of lost shelf life. A bounty crop responsible for an entire farming community's income can be rendered worthless from a slight glitch.

To hedge against this, the harvest is conducted by yet another broker, a woman who temporarily buys each farmer's product, aggregates them with others in the region, and then transports the whole load cross-country to the industrial regions where shrimp is processed for sale. The broker evens out kinks in supply, perhaps selling the bulk of her product to a single plant, and then spreading the remainder across several competitors who are looking to "top off." Her first stop is a "preprocessing" plant. Preprocessors are smaller operations, responsible for peeling and beheading. They are often located in temporary sites, hence the local term "peeling sheds," and range from the truly underground and illicit—dank, fishy spaces where whole families of migrants live on-site and are paid per kilo of shrimp they peel—to meticulous industrial spaces proudly shown off in Western annual reports. Peeling shrimp is delicate labor, and despite all advances in technology, nothing can yet do the work better than small, nimble fingers.[45]

The product from these facilities will be bought by even larger processors above them, those with the giant factories that sell directly to exporters. These facilities operate aboveground and aboveboard, registering with industry associations and inspected frequently by teams of auditors. The space I visit is operated by one of the largest seafood producers in the world, a company that buys directly and exclusively from brokers, processors, and ponds that operate under its specifications. It is a model of vertical integration borrowed from the American poultry industry, and allows for far greater oversight and control. However, even here, where explicit exceptions are never made, I'm told implicit ones do. If an upstream buyer, e.g., your grocery store, is in need—say, the holidays have come and the people need their shrimp—there is no hesitation to apply pressure on brokers to increase their supply. That broker must go out and execute, augment, find product somewhere to appease the mouths beyond.

The final "high-risk" room of the factory is the cleanest place I've ever been. Shrimp from all the previous phases of production pass through it, as if collecting a blessing before getting bagged for export. To get there, we walk down a series of highly chlorinated cement steps

---

45 This multichannel system exists to meet foreign demand. A supply chain expert explains, "The smaller sheds smooth out risk for the entire system. Suppliers who can't commit to regular volume do not get deals with major grocery buyers. And so they turn to the smaller sheds to supplement." When I speak to a Burmese man who worked in one of these sheds, he described hygiene standards as nonexistent, the smell terrible, and the work variable, depending on demand: one day six hours of peeling, the next day ten. And yet the supply chain expert is right. The spaces are empirically critical supports: in one of the few investigated cases, the product from a single illegal peeling shed was found to have made its way to four other, more regulated preprocessing plants and forty U.S. brands.

to a basement and then push through glowing yellow plastic curtains into a dressing area. Here we disinfect, leaving our earthly bodies behind. We strip down, removing exterior layers. We wash our hands and forearms up to the elbows. We dab antibacterial gel on our faces. We slide on blue gummy rubber boots, then apply a face mask, a hairnet, a beard protector, then on top of all those a beekeeper-like headpiece with veil. Finally, I am helped into a gauzy smock and gown. Every inch of my body feels contained. We leave, not via door, but by wading through a crystal-clear, ankle-deep pool to disinfect our boots. The solution remains as perfectly transparent and wavy after we move through it as before we entered.

On the other side, we head through a sealed door to the line. Walking out, I can see the formerly "low-risk" shrimp pour into this room through another mechanized hole in the wall. The main line itself is maybe a hundred yards long. Today, the workers are preparing shrimp for sushi. Some slicing them further, others removing them from steel frames designed to straighten out their natural curl into something more aesthetic. I focus on one woman among the hundreds. She spins and slices a shrimp every two to three seconds, fingers twirling, head down, a living cog in my diet. Behind her, in a separate process, pink precooked frozen shrimp are being produced by the ton. They spill out of a kettle hot and steaming, before being channeled into a long freezer. I am told the freezing takes thirteen minutes, but of course the continuous input and output make the whole thing look instantaneous. Thousands of shrimp pouring in one side hot and pink, thousands of shrimp bouncing out the other, now frozen white, plinking down the chute into a succession of plastic bags that shudder past with the automatic rhythm of the factory. They are bags familiar to the frozen aisles of grocery stores across America, complete in every way except one: brand name and logo—afterthoughts to be applied later, just before they are bought, torn open, and dumped into a cook pot for dinner.

Huddling and Bundling

To fully understand the bottom of the commodity chain, it is helpful to take a step back and look at the concept of commodity as a whole.

Whether wheat, iron, almond, or swine, commodities are rooted in fungibility, in an inherent similarity that allows them to be swapped interchangeably without thought or trade-off. The word comes to us etymologically from the French *commodité*, meaning convenience, and like many conveniences it stems from simplifying the world. For each good, a series of details are selected, and once chosen come to define the whole. An apple for juicing is no longer simply an apple but a discrete series of apple-y details from the pH of its flesh to the amount of wax on its skin. A bucket of trash fish becomes protein content alone. The details that are excluded—perhaps the place of origin of that apple or precise species of fish in the bucket—quite intentionally vanish. In this way, commodity is an agreement around nuance, a willingness to fix the depth of our scrutiny, and without it in some form trade would grind to a halt, fixated on endless, diminishingly small differences.

With it, we receive the blessings of uniformity: purchasing at scale, stability through advanced buying, industrial engineering predicated on regularity, the comfort of consistency.

The trade-off is one we accept almost unconsciously. After all, as the cliché goes, out of sight, out of mind. But this process has effects. At each step in the chain—through the maze of brokers, agents, and other aggregators who swap goods on our behalf—our visibility grows thinner. The branches of supply transition from manicured arrows on a corporate flowchart into a gnarled thicket on the ground. And rather than fight to see in those spaces, we hire professionals to gloss them over with their professional imaginations, replacing the abstraction of commodity with the colorful inventions of marketing. Suddenly a hundred scattered groundwater reservoirs become a single magical Poland "spring." And since we largely accept this trade-off reflexively, or allow others to make the trade-off in our name, it is worth considering how the simplifications of commodity—its selective abstraction and filtering of our reality—change not only how goods are bought and sold but also how they are created to begin with.

The Simplification of the Eyestalk

"The story behind seafood in this country is almost entirely hidden," Katrina Nakamura, an expert on Thai seafood and ethical supply chains, tells me. "If you pick a regular everyday seafood product you grew up with—like a can of tuna or a bag of frozen shrimp—it looks the same as when you were a kid. Or when your parents were kids. But the way it is produced as a commodity is completely different."

Shrimp were, until very recently, a luxury good. As far from commodity as you can get. This is easy to forget in our current era where runty gray knuckles of the stuff get tossed in everything from five-dollar lo mein to plastic-domed airport salads. But just thirty years ago, fresh shrimp epitomized class. They cost more than steak, were served at country clubs on silver, and existed as the defining hors d'oeuvre of the Upper East Side: elite, elegant, expensive.

These shrimp were not grown but caught, trawled for with nets that swept the middle of the water column—less bulldozer, more butterfly net—kinder to the ecosystem than the benthic trawl, but still indiscriminate, inefficient gobblers, ensnaring five pounds of unwanted bycatch for every one pound of salable shrimp and widely hated for killing sea turtles. The boats were also expensive to operate, relying on domestic labor from the Gulf of Mexico, and only out seasonally. Two qualities that limited the shrimp supply further, boosting its status as luxury.

Aquaculture represented the promise of technology to liberate this luxury and make it available to the common man. And in many ways the promise has paid off: since 1980 prices have fallen while production has increased some 3,000 percent.

Shrimp farmers like to point out that some form of aquaculture has been practiced in Southeast Asia for millennia. And certainly this is true. Historically, coastal communities seized on and enhanced tide pools and inlets to create protected ponds for shrimp to grow. The best of these would be washed out naturally, existing as little more than sculpted features of the landscape. And, in its early days, industry merely attempted to scale these practices, i.e., maxing out densities, applying consistent management techniques, sharpening the quality of food, and when in doubt lining everything in plastic.

But there was a problem. When shrimp lived in these more confined habitats, their sexual development was stunted by stress. The females simply refused to develop ovaries. Which meant humans still had to head to the wild to scoop up natural brood stock. This is a little like farming, if farmers first had to scour the forests for crops and then take them back home to replant. It was neither more efficient than trawling for mature shrimp, nor able to guarantee the large quantities needed by the global market to lower price.

The single great breakthrough came in a fittingly bizarre and brutal manner. Then, as now, those trying to make aquaculture work raised their shrimp in overcrowded tubs. And as their shrimp swam round and round in circles in these tubs, their outside eye would rub against the side of the tank. And slowly, after god knows how many circles, in god knows what type of crowded environment, the outermost eyeball of the outermost shrimp in these tubs would eventually get rubbed right off. Erased by friction.

And from this misery, an industry was born.

It turns out for as of yet biologically unexplained reasons, a female shrimp who loses a single eyeball gets fast-tracked through puberty, her ocular loss unleashing a cascade of hormones that begets ovaries in as little as three days. This was not predictable, nor does it fit with some grand anatomical theory of shrimp endocrinology, but it is very real. And some supremely attentive farmer noticed it and began snipping eyeballs off by hand in an attempt to replicate it. Soon, the process was studied and verified in the lab, and although nobody could quite explain "eyestalk ablation," the quirky stride of science skipped merrily forward, pushing shrimp aquaculture into a new age.

Now, instead of relying on natural habitats for brood stock, farmers could breed them indoors. Trawling through estuaries was out. Genetic selection was in. After a decade of highly controlled domestication, shrimp with abnormally large and fleshy tails, fast growth rates, and tolerance for odd diets and turbid water were genetically selected and emerging.

The result was nothing short of an economic fairy tale. A once humble farmer could eschew his family's rice paddy, wall off a pond, lower a plastic laundry basket in, and come up with a basket of gold. Or at least a basket of "pink gold," which is what the tumbling heaps of flesh came to be known as. A boom ensued. Ponds were dug. Mangroves razed. Seawalls torn down to allow the salt water to flood in. It was all too easy and too lucrative for the market to ignore. This new shrimp was four times more profitable than rice farming. And like any other rush, from gold to diamonds to land, the years that followed were a sordid thing.

For this was one of those fairy tales with an ugly moral waiting at the end.

First there was the fuzzy math of ecology. "You would think, gee, if we can produce them in farms then we no longer have to fish as much," Steven Webster, of the Monterey Bay Aquarium, tells a PBS camera crew in *Empty Oceans, Empty Nets*. In fact the opposite is true. Regardless of where shrimp are raised, they are still carnivorous, and thus, rather than silencing the trawls, the bloom of aquaculture encouraged them to take an even larger catch. It takes two pounds of wild-caught fish to create one pound of shrimp. And with aquaculture increasing the total supply of shrimp five times from the late 1970s, it forced the fish trawls to operate at ten times capacity.

Daniel Murphy, an expert on Thai seafood supply chains, explains the ripple effects: "There were never—and there still are no—exclusively trash-fish boats. They are a by-product of boats willing to do market with a lower level trade, and they exist because there is money there." To wrangle the trash fish arriving in uneven amounts from tens of thousands of unaligned boats, the industry relied on brokers who in turn relied on sub-brokers traveling port to port. These brokers and sub-brokers blended product from different boats, each finding their edge by upgrading a substandard catch, or merging bad actors and honest fishermen alike.[46]

Then there is disease. As with any group of animals raised in a concentrated, confined space, and especially one soaking in a broth of its own feces, shrimp in captivity became far more susceptible to disease. And when a pond spoils, it spoils all at once. One day you have several hundred thousand healthy, wriggling post-larvals, the next day you pull up a net to find your shrimp listless and deformed. After that, all is rot. The entire pond is not just worthless but toxic, a stew of dead and dying animals that need to be drained and shoveled wet into disposal. And then the disease spreads to your neighbor.

A cycle of spectacular growth, overnight riches, and then sudden collapse came to define the Asian shrimp industry. It is a cycle that rolls across the globe, seeking out new, untouched territory—from Thailand on to Vietnam on to Indonesia, then India—a moveable gold rush of pink gold, where the promises remain the same, and the failures come in new, innovative forms as the diseases continue to mutate. Jonathan Shepherd, former head of the International Fishmeal and Fish Oil

---

46 I'm sure the more observant can already see the horrid ecological sidebar here: as the boats began receiving regular payments for their trash fish, they trawled for them more intentionally, exhausting the local waters of smaller fish, degrading the fishery. Over the decades, a cycle developed: the more the fishery degraded, the harder it became to land the more expensive species everyone originally came for, the more the trawls relied on netting smaller fish for aquaculture. Eventually there was a crash. Catch per unit plummeted. And with waters barren, the boats chugged on to do it all again somewhere new.

Organisation, has estimated the collective toll as ranging up to $20 bil-lion and calls shrimp aquaculture "virtually uninsurable." It is an indus-try for gamblers, betting they can ride a region hard before some new ecological crash.

But as any gambler knows, the house always wins. And for shrimp, the crash and boom are regional events, while the global story is one of growth, continuous output, and considerable wealth. And so amid the individual ruin, an industry arose: those preprocessors, brokers, ex-porters, fish meal factories, and trash-fish boats all forming a beating economic heart that didn't care where the aquaculture farmers were located or what ecological havoc had been wrung, but did have new, much-needed jobs to offer and did need the blood of able-bodied men and women to run.

An Able-Bodied Man

I first meet Tun-Lin sitting on the side of a barbecue in a cement alley-way in exurban Thailand. It is well over ninety degrees in the evening and the mosquitoes hang big and fat in the air, lethargic from hours of blood sucking. I have come as a guest of a local NGO called the Labour Protection Network, or LPN, which promises to show me around the area's shrimp production plants. We are all drinking warm beer with crushed ice out of highball glasses. A long picnic table is laid with all the fixings for a Thai feast: white tendon meat stacked in swatches, pats of lard, bowls of gray-yellow sprouts, and three giant stainless-steel pots simmering away with red oils and coconut milk. Everyone mills and chatters in the way of NGO gatherings around the world. There is a man with a guitar and a group of interns gathered around him. Tun-Lin is sitting by himself on the side, hunched and apart, not so much lost in thought as eyes darting and nervous. He looks lonely and non-threatening enough that I, who know nobody here, feel like I can drag my translator over and approach him. He is holding a baseball cap in one hand, and my first thought meeting him is that he's balled his fist so tight holding that cap it looks like there is no hand at all. I think, This is a man so tightly wound he's erasing himself. It's only at the end of the night when I go to say goodbye that I realize the cap was resting gently on his knee and rather than being balled up tight—he was missing his hand completely. It was torn off at sea.

We meet again the next day, and then on and off again for the next two months. I learn Tun-Lin isn't nervous so much as he's a blank man. He exudes a negative charisma. There are several other fishermen I hang around with that I might even say I am friends with. We get along. Drink. Laugh. Not Tun-Lin. He agrees to meet and tell his story. But despite the succession of lurid details, he is desensitized to the point of almost being boring at it. He is, however, patient, and I think that's why I am drawn to him. I get the sense he neither wants to exaggerate nor escape his past. He corrects me too often. Mostly I spend my time with Tun-Lin thinking how the questions I am asking him are just illusions of understanding. Figuring out the precise way a trawl net is hauled in, or how he felt the moment something unimaginable occurred, just magnifies our differences. It invites me for a moment to feel like I might connect and then reminds me how false that is. And I appreciate that failure. It feels like the most honest exchange we can have.

He tells me he is from Mwabi, a tiny village in the Mon State in Myanmar, just north of the capital, Mawlamyine. His father is a soldier; his mother is a *morphi*, which is alternately translated as "shaman," "fortune-teller," or "necromancer." He remembers his parents as reasonably happy. Life was not easy, but there was a minimum sort of stability his father's post provided. Then in the late 1990s, the army calls his father to serve. There is no simple frame of reference for rural Myanmar at this time. It is feudal and corrupt, trapped in time without electricity, running water, or paved roads, yet bedecked with assault rifles. Tun-Lin doesn't grow up with a floor, but does remember his father's M16 leaning against the walls of their hut. Transportation to the front is largely on ox-drawn carts. The country at this time is in perpetual civil war: between the government and the Communists, between small mercenary armies funded by industrialists and rival tribes, between ethnicities and religions in the different subregions, all of whom ally with each other and disband and realign to create chaos. When his father leaves, his mother runs off, leaving him with his older sister. They lose their house. And suddenly at fourteen years old, Tun-Lin has almost nothing. After a week of homelessness, his older sister finds a small house outside the village, and she takes him in. The house is made entirely of bamboo, dried and woven, and when it rains, the water comes through the roof in fat, slow drops.

Or as he says, it is fit for people to sleep in, not to live.

In the village, he becomes an outcast. When he stops going to school, people say he is stupid and illiterate. When things go missing, people call him a thief, an accusation he denies years later with an anger that is heartbreaking. A friend's mother tells him his mother was a prostitute and that he is a bastard.

Then his father returns with an aunt who was also displaced by the war. And all of sudden, there are four people in his sister's tiny house.

It is at this point, wet and cramped each night, that he begins to dream of working in a Thai factory. The way he describes these dreams, they feel so universal—almost charmingly adolescent dreams of becoming the family savior—and yet so agonizingly specific to Myanmar during its civil wars. In Mwabi at this time, there are simply no jobs outside the army. Most of the people Tun-Lin knows collect wood from the forest, which they take to the state capital to sell as firewood. If they are lucky they earn a few pennies. It is a community undone, starving to death. Tun-Lin tells me he doesn't really know what a factory is, only that people work hard there and make good money. But he dreams of a factory every night. He thinks he can make money and bring it back to his family and buy them a real house. And so after weeks of four people living under a roof that had barely fit two, Tun-Lin decides he needs to make his dream real.

He leaves without telling anyone, bringing three T-shirts, three pairs of pants, one blanket, and the shoes he is wearing. He doesn't have a proper bag, so he uses a plastic one. He crosses the border at the town of Myawaddy. It is easy. He does that by himself without a broker or "snakehead," just a matter of hitching a ride and dashing across a river a few meters down from the official checkpoint. When I visit Myawaddy eighteen years later, I see several people doing the same thing.

From there he walks up the steep bank, and emerges on the Thai side of the border into a town called Mae Sot. He is alone. The reality of being in Thailand, of the language being different, of knowing absolutely no one, hits home. And as that reality hits, a broker waves to him. Tun-Lin says it seemed like he was waiting for him. Tun-Lin says it was such a relief. The broker is about forty years old, his eyes smart and handsome, dressed in a blue long-sleeve shirt that is clean.

So Tun-Lin approaches. And the broker asks him in Burmese, Where would you like to go? And Tun-Lin says simply, Thailand, not totally realizing he is already in Thailand. Then he realizes and becomes ashamed and tells the broker he wants a job but doesn't have any money.

The broker says that doesn't matter and puts his arm around him.

The two of them walk back to a two-story brick house in Mae Sot. They walk side by side like they are on a date. The whole time, they talk in Burmese about Thailand. Tun-Lin is very excited. The broker is laying out a future, telling him about the different cities in Thailand, the resorts in the south, the skyscrapers in Bangkok, the factories in Samut Sakhon. And, of course, he is telling him all about the jobs and money there. When they arrive at the brick house with the red roof, the broker lets him inside. There are over a hundred other migrants there. Waiting. Spread out over the floors. Some with bedrolls and suitcases, most like Tun-Lin with little more than plastic bags stuffed with clothes. The broker explains to Tun-Lin that he doesn't live at the house but that he will be back. And so Tun-Lin takes up a place on the floor.

The first thing he is told while sitting on that floor: he is very lucky. One of the migrants near him explains that Tun-Lin has come at a very good time. It has been hard at the house. Some people have been waiting on the floor for over a week, but Tun-Lin learns he should be very excited because the next day they are set to leave.

True to the word, the next morning the broker arrives. He tells them they are going to Chiang Mai, a city in the north. But he tells the group that the police are looking for migrants. They are making his job very difficult and dangerous. He explains that the military is pulling vehicles to the side and checking papers, so to get to Chiang Mai without being arrested, they will have to go by foot. It is a 210-mile trek through a jungle, over several mountains during the heart of the rainy season. Tun-Lin does not know this because the broker does not say this. The broker does not take any questions or explain anything beyond how they are to leave town without attracting attention. Tun-Lin is just excited to start.

It rains continuously the first day of the walk. And quickly the group begins to break down. Many were sick and starving before leaving. Every night, they sleep outside, huddled in groups under trees, or in small caves and overhangs in the mountain areas. The only food comes at two checkpoints per day where the guide has arranged for meals to be stashed. Each of these meals is identical: tinned mackerel in tomato sauce. It is not one man per can. Tun-Lin says they split cans three, four, or five people per can. Tun-Lin estimates that a group of one hundred people left the house. By the end of this trip, he knows for a fact that he saw six people die of hunger or disease.

On the last day, they have to cross a pass near the tallest mountain in Thailand. They are in the Op Luang National Park and told to move very fast because there are police looking for them. Tun-Lin's legs ache. What were blisters on day 2 are now wet blood. The skin on his heels is sloughing off, and at the top of the mountain, he remembers a final person dying of fatigue when all they have to do is walk downhill.

That night, they arrive in Chiang Mai and are told they can sleep and do not have to walk anymore. The next morning several trucks arrive at the campsite. From here, the group is divided and everyone is told to get into one. Tun-Lin describes his truck as small, more of a pickup with a shell. Inside there are benches, and the shell has no windows so it is impossible to see out. His group is about twenty people, and Tun-Lin is certain it is impossible for them all to fit. But they file in anyway. They sit in rows so tightly packed it is hard to breathe. Then the door is closed. It is dark. No one speaks. Tun-Lin is not on one of the benches but sitting on the floor with his knees tucked to his chest. He closes his eyes and tries not to think. Estimating from a map, driving with no traffic, their trip lasts twelve hours. He tells me there are no rest stops, and that people cannot control themselves, and they urinate and defecate in the truck. When they arrive, the back of the truck is opened and they are told to get out. One by one they unfold. People are crying. A woman near Tun-Lin has died. She was suffocated or crushed, Tun-Lin does not know which. Only that he sat so close to her the entire trip and that he had not thought about her.

They emerge from the darkness of the truck into the darkness of a gated parking lot. It is night and a new broker, a man to whom they have been bequeathed, begins dividing them into smaller groups. Tun-Lin and several other men are separated out, placed in a car. They drive a few short minutes, then are brought to another house. This is Samut Sakhon, shrimp processing capital of Thailand.

Tun-Lin is led to a room with twenty-five others. The door is opened and he is locked in. It is only now, looking around at the twenty-five other men in the room, that Tun-Lin realizes something is wrong. The room has no bed and no mattresses, but does have a partition for a toilet. There are no blankets. Just a room with a wooden floor and twenty-five grown men starving in it. By this point, Tun-Lin has lost his plastic bag and has been separated from all his possessions except his traditional Burmese pants, which he has been wearing continuously since crossing the border into Mae Sot.

In the room, he makes his first and only friend, Tu-Lek. A small man, Tu-Lek is also Burmese and from the Mon State. Later, when they work on the boat, they will sleep next to each other, share food. When I ask if he has any good memories of Tu-Lek, whom he calls his best friend, Tun-Lin says no. He says from this point forward, there are no good memories. Then he stops and thinks and tells me sometimes at night when they are lying quiet but awake, Tu-Lek turns to him and asks for his sister's number and jokes that he would like to call to ask her out.

Their door opens twice a day when food is delivered. Two large pots are pushed on the floor to them. One has rice. The other is filled with a Burmese stew of pork and curry. It is the same stew each day. Tun-Lin calls it delicious. Despite twenty-five men sharing two pots of food, there is no fighting. Tun-Lin says everyone understands that getting in a fight among themselves will provoke the broker and they will be beaten.

After a week in this house, he is called out of the room. A man tells him he should be very happy because he will make a lot of money. The man gives him more food. Tun-Lin tells me that years later this man will be murdered by another fisher seeking revenge. The man tells Tun-Lin that he will work on a fishing boat for three months to pay off the debt of being smuggled, and then after those three months he will be paid. Tun-Lin doesn't believe him. But the next day, the man takes him and several others from the room to get their pictures taken for a seaman's log.

From there, he is placed on the boat. It is midsized, about sixty feet long, with a dark blue hull, a white band around a two-story pilothouse. And before Tun-Lin fully understands, the boat has left. He has received no training. Very quickly he learns he doesn't want to work on the boat. But it is too late. They are out at sea. During his first night in the boat, he is convinced he will die there. He is terrified of the water. He cannot eat because he is seasick and throws everything up. And he is not allowed to sleep. This continues for three days. It is at this point the captain puts out the big canisters of instant coffee for the crew to eat. On the fourth day, doing work he does not understand, among men who speak languages like Khmer and Lao he can only partially communicate with, nauseated, starving, exhausted, Tun-Lin says he becomes physically unable to continue working. And so he stops and goes to the crawl space to take a nap.

This is his first beating. The captain finds him asleep. He then wakes Tun-Lin up with a weapon my translator insists on calling a yo-yo. It is a steel ball on an elastic cord and he swings it at Tun-Lin, catching him across the face, then repeatedly on the shoulders. Tun-Lin shows me his scars. He says he is beaten many times over the years, but he will always remember this first one.

Tun-Lin says he is not beaten again after this—the captain merely has to point at this yo-yo for Tun-Lin to increase the speed of his work—until, after waiting six months, he makes the mistake of asking for the salary he was promised. For this, he is beaten even harder than before. He learns now the captain owns him, that he bought him when he acquired his debt.

His friend Tu-Lek simply can't handle it. He is only a teenager, and is weak, which means he is beaten more frequently. As the captain whips him, Tu-Lek slowly loses his mind. After a particularly bad beating, Tu-Lek gets very sick. He can't walk. And he is allowed to rest for two days straight to recover. The ship captain provides Tu-Lek with medicine and lets him sleep in his own bed. For the next week, the captain lets him do light labor like helping him supervise and release the net. But Tun-Lin knows things are wrong. Whenever he asks Tu-Lek questions, the boy will only laugh or cry. Soon after, Tu-Lek refuses to work. It is now that he is beaten until he is unconscious and kicked into the sea.

Months at sea pass into years. Tun-Lin adjusts. He never enjoys life on the boat. But he learns it. He becomes good at it. He comes to do every job, sorting the fish, carrying them to the freezer on trays, patching, folding, caressing the net looking for rips, and supervising the entire six-hour process it takes to haul it in. He learns the rhythms. His boat goes to port every four months, and Tun-Lin watches new men come on. He knows when these new men will be beaten, and he knows the work they must do to avoid it.

It is tempting to wonder why, when the boat comes to port, Tun-Lin does not jump off, flee, escape from this nightmare. But he, and many other fishers I speak with, correct this misunderstanding. "You can escape, but you cannot escape," one fisher tells me. They are at ports in countries thousands of miles away from Thailand, which is itself a country that is not their own. They do not speak the language, they have no money—and no possessions they can barter for money—and they are illegal in body and mind at this point, without papers or passports, living in constant fear of arrest. There is also great collusion not only among boat owners—who enforce a code, looking out for one another's men—but also among boat owners and police. I speak to one fisher who was on a boat stopped by Thai authorities for environmental violations and who took a desperate risk to tell those authorities he was being held against his will. Instead of rescue boats, NGOs, and the media helicoptering in, the captain pays a bribe—to preserve his catch and make the environmental violations go away—and, as an aside, one of the authorities tells him about his snitch. When the fisher tells me this story, he says that he feels lucky to be alive. Others tell me stories, perhaps fictional, perhaps real, about fishers who escape only to starve, forced to live in the jungle on the edges of ports thousands of miles from home, eating stray dogs and attempting to dig for cassava on beaches. These stories of failed escapes are literally beaten into fishers by their captains. Rescue workers who help repatriate them will talk about this fear even when long off the boat. I hear rumors of hidden tracking devices placed on them by the captain and private jails run by the owners where they will be detained. The message is: We will find you. We own you. There is no hope out there for you.

So Tun-Lin never escapes.

But then after five years on this boat, an odd thing happens. It catches me off guard in the interview and so I'll just write it the way Tun-Lin explains it. He is let off the boat. Tun-Lin says he waited until the boat came to shore. He believes that if he asked at sea, his captain might kill him, but at port with laws, he feels he will be safer. Other fishers tell me that after five years on a boat, you had worked off your debt. But Tun-Lin insists this isn't the case for him, and that he just asked. Either way, after five years on this boat, without pay or sleep, when in a port in Indonesia, Tun-Lin asks this captain if he can leave, and the captain says yes.

He is given no wages. But since he is let off, not an escapee, he is also allowed to board a sister boat in the fleet going back to Thailand. In Thailand, he finds work in a fish processing plant where he stays for two months. He works with one other man, pulling meat from the bone and shoving it in one-kilogram plastic sacks. Because Tun-Lin is illegal, the owner insists that he live on the premises and he locks the door at night from the outside. His own room is a cell. But this does not seem to bother Tun-Lin. What does bother him is that the owner charges him for this room and for electricity and because of that he makes no money at this job.

And so he asks around. Finds another captain. And returns to sea.

And if your head is spinning, let it spin.

Tun-Lin has no documents and no way of getting a legal job. He tells me after five years at sea, he feels like he knows which captains will be abusive and which will be fair. He says he knows the job of a fisher-man and is experienced. He says he has learned bits of Thai, and he can ask to work on a different part of the boat, doing easier work. And he also tells me that on the new boat he can become a boss.

And so he enlists. On the new boat he trains the new fishers. He says this is very hard. That they learn slowly. And when I ask if the peo-ple he was training were legal migrants or men enslaved just like he had been, he says he doesn't know. Then, after a moment of silence, he says he asked the ones who spoke Burmese, "How did you end up here?"

And they told him they were tricked.

At this point, he is twenty-two years old.

He continues working on this and then other boats for the next twelve years. He is now a supervisor. He tells me he is nice and does not beat his men. At one point, he loses his hand. It is ripped off when he is adjusting a rope called the "yaw-yap." He is wearing gloves so he doesn't even know he has lost two fingers until he takes the glove off. At a re-supply, he is placed with his heavily bandaged hand on the transport boat and taken to an Indonesian hospital, where the doctors amputate the rest of his fingers to save his arm. Then, after a month in the hospi-tal, he checks out and gets on a new boat. Fishing is what he knows.

Tun-Lin finally gets off all boats in November 2014 when a high-level diplomatic dispute over environmental damage causes Indonesia to aggressively cancel Thai fishing concessions in its territorial waters. Tun-Lin's boat happens to be there. When it is detained, he realizes the ship's captain will be unable to pay the crew their wages and unable to pay a bribe to wriggle free. And so Tun-Lin becomes a whistleblower too.

From this he meets the LPN—the NGO hosting the barbecue where I meet him—who are working with international aid organiza-tions and the Burmese embassy to help trafficked fishermen aboard these boats. No doubt due to his lost hand, he gets outsized attention from authorities looking into illegal fishing. Then he is sent back to Thailand, and sent to live in a camp for trafficked migrants. He is officially labeled a victim, which becomes a new form of paralysis: he is still illegal in the eyes of the Thai government, still unable to get work, and while he could sneak back to the boats, that would prevent him from getting any compensation for the five years he was enslaved. Instead he waits. Lately he has been volunteering with the LPN, helping educate other migrants.

Once, after talking for hours on a patio, I ask Tun-Lin whether he thinks his story is typical or exceptional for fishermen. It is a question I almost immediately regret because there is no way for him to answer. Tun-Lin just nods.

All the fishermen have different stories, he says. But mine is not typical. I feel very lucky.

Replacement Theory of Migrants

If we pull back from Tun-Lin we can see the outlines of something much larger than just his story. Up through the 1980s much of the fishing in Thailand occurred right off the coast. At this time, the Gulf of Thailand was still quite resource rich and trash fish were still trash—pushed right back off the deck to the water because they were not worth their weight in the hold. The workers on these fleets were entirely Thai. Some worked year-round, but most were from the northeast, participating in a great seasonal migration that stretched back centuries. The work these fishers describe was hard—northeasterners are famously the poorest Thais—and there were certainly abuses like underpayment and withheld wages. But even in the worst cases, their boats went out for two to three weeks at a time. And since everyone spoke the same language, word of an unpleasant employer spread quickly.

But then things changed.

First there was the storm. In 1989, a monsoon over the Gulf of Thailand hits an exceptionally warm air pocket and rapidly intensifies into Typhoon Gay. One-hundred-sixty-two-mile-per-hour winds rise from nowhere to catch the Thai fishing fleet unaware at sea. Hundreds of boats sink. The tragedy is not something that really comes down to numbers; it is a national shock, an unthinkable disaster, almost in the way of September 11. Every Thai fishing family loses someone. There is talk of ghosts at sea, of carnivorous fish living off the bodies of the dead. Fishing becomes stigmatized. Many in the northeast stop eating seafood altogether.

At the same time, the first aquaculture boom finally hit. Thai shrimp production leaps, and foreign investment rushes in to catch it: refrigerated docks are erected, export facilities built, and hundreds of processing plants spring to life to cater to the heaps of product coming in from the rapidly developing farm sector. These all need workers. Now, instead of going down south to fish, the northeasterners have the choice to stay on land. And in the shadow of Typhoon Gay it is an easy one.

Which means all of a sudden, the fishing industry is hit with a massive labor shortage. And it comes at the very moment the job itself has become much less attractive. After decades of overfishing, catch volume in the Gulf of Thailand flatlines. Nets that used to come up wriggling now come up flaccid. As we enter the 1990s, the fishing fleets are forced to move farther out into deeper water. And so, purely out of economic necessity, the industry moves to a new model: one boat acts as a mother ship, another carries fish to and fro. The era of transshipment at sea has begun, and boats that were once rarely out for a single month now routinely stay out for a year.

And so now, in addition to the physical storm of Typhoon Gay, we have a perfect causal storm of events. A huge labor shortage hits at the exact moment international industry arrives, job quality plummets, and a massive vulnerable population of migrants waits desperate at the border.

The final factor isn't part of the storm at all. It is a universal constant: racism. Despite being geographic neighbors, the Burmese are slightly darker-skinned, wear a different style of clothes, use different forms of makeup, and speak in a hundred different dialects and languages, all incomprehensible if you are Thai. Nationalist politicians in Thailand seize on this and call migrants "a danger to the public order," responsible for "high birth rates, disease, and crime against Thais." It is overheated rhetoric that successfully leads to brutal enforcement. There is the migrant code I hear: never look a police officer in the eye; you will be hit for it. Legal migrants are stopped for papers when they go out, detained on completely illegal pretexts. Illegal migrants face an even deeper web of threats from arrest, physical abuse, extortion, and extended detention. "Police patrol like sharks," Phil Robertson, deputy director of Human Rights Watch's Asia division, tells me. "They make a lot of money this way." When a migrant is stopped, the squeeze begins. The migrant either loses money from their job for lost wages, or they lose money to the police directly as a bribe. Or if they cannot pay the bribe, they may become money, sold from prison to a labor broker who will sell them on at a profit.

From here, everything proceeds reasonably to completely unreasonable ends. As the boats become progressively worse places to work, their owners are forced to offer more money up front. These are lucrative sums, six months to one year of salary in advance. Enough to ruin the fleet if the men don't appear. Since many migrants are illegal, don't speak the language, and are often smuggled directly from their home countries, they cannot negotiate with boat owners directly. Instead a broker is used. A single profession responsible for balancing the giant vortex of need that is the Thai labor shortage with the giant vortex of need that is the poor Burmese looking for jobs. And this broker is often doing that balancing illegally, as a service to both parties, while hated by the state. Suddenly, it becomes a system where everyone is owed something, and thus everyone can feel aggrieved: the owner who might go bankrupt if the men he paid for in advance do not appear (or if they appear and flee because they decide they hate the work), the broker who is risking his liberty dodging the police and smuggling men who asked for his help, and the migrant, to whom so much has been promised but who slowly comes to understand that none of those promises came free.

Of course, it is this last piece—the migrant's obligation—that is the most profound. Even in the softest sense it acts as a restraint, a stay that keeps him working a job he might otherwise leave. And since employee turnover is one of the highest costs of production, this very fact makes him a more desirable class of employee. It is a testament to the retina-scarring brilliance of market capitalism that this tiny source of value cannot go unnoticed even if one wants to look away. It needs not ever be explicitly stated or accepted. It can in fact be hated. But eventually even an ethically upstanding factory owner might give in and let sub-contractors handle hiring, opting to be grateful for the efficiencies they bring. After all, the first-world grocery buyers above never come to offer owners like him *more* money. In fact, every few years it seems the buyer visits to offer him less, as that buyer is competing for customers back home. And so paying a living wage makes it impossible to compete. Then one day minimum wage becomes too much. And to supply the workers they have slowly become addicted to, a new class of brokers emerge. Brokers like Tun-Lin's, who sell men to other men and wipe their hands clean.

And here grocery has one last trick: it allows us to hate our shrimp and eat it too. The image of the bad polluting aquaculture farmer or vulnerable exploited migrant gets imprinted in our first-world brain, while the fungibility of commodity goods—that maze of brokers and agents—gives the entire system the plausible deniability it craves. We might demand action about horrid conditions, but the idea of asking us to forgo shrimp, even momentarily, and fill our nonstick woks with some other protein is precisely the type of inconvenience the entire system is built to protect against.

And the store is left alone to figure out a solution.

"Big supermarket buyers feel tremendous pressure from their customers to improve these situations," Corey Peet, an expert on Thai aquaculture, tells me. "And they turn to third-party certification, the only tool they have . . . It may be a bit ridiculous to show up at a Thai shrimp farm with standards that are a hundred pages long in English talking about proper format of a pay stub, but that is what happens."

In the buyer's hands, those certifications become a magic wand. They empower and absolve at the same time, shifting an enormous burden onto a single participant in the exchange. "I've seen buyers for major American retailers say, 'You get this certification or we won't buy from you,'" Corey tells me. "That's not corporate responsibility, that's extortion."

And as each new first-world demand comes down, each new certification gets put in place, the farmers, brokers, and boat operators have to figure out how to be profitable yet again. But when you peer into their cost structures, there is very little these producers actually control. Pathogen-free brood stocks, environmentally friendly medications, enhanced refrigeration systems, and payments for the audits of each, are all new top-down demands that do not lead to higher selling prices. They are costs paid to gain entry; paying them simply makes a product acceptable enough to play the commodity game along with everyone else.

One of the only places a producer feels in control is labor.

And so labor is where cuts occur.

"These producers are caught in a nightmare," a shrimp supply expert tells me. "Facing increasing demands from buyers, trying to lower the cost of labor to pay for them, all while trying to retain people who don't want to do the job to begin with."

The Most Unusual Aspect of Thai Slavery Is That You Are Hearing About It at All

The LPN started as a children's educational camp, a kind of after-school program targeted directly at migrant children. In 2004, Patima Tungpuchayakul, known to everyone as P'Aon[47] and her partner, Sompong Srakaew, moved to Samut Sakhon, a vast industrial city outside of Bangkok. They were recent university graduates, idealists, and had decided to try to raise awareness for the growing plight of migrant labor in Thailand. Neither had a personal connection to migrants, nor to the seafood industry that defined the region. It was just a place with a need. They did know about childhood education and community development; this was their area of training. And so, with the help of a tiny grant, they began running a series of camps and activities for migrant children. In many ways, they offered little more than a warm place to go. But that was more than anyone had ever offered the migrants in the area before. P'Aon and Sompong led the children in games and songs, taught basic language skills, and worked to enroll whoever was willing in school. It was the most basic curriculum, teaching love, respect, and above all offering children who had never belonged anywhere a place where they were valued.

Almost immediately they discovered something. Working with children was a back door to building trust with their parents. These parents were migrants whose fear of exposure made them even more marginalized than their children. P'Aon and Sompong watched as they skirted the edges, wary of surfacing enough to even pick up their own kids. But as trust was created with the children, the parents started coming forward. They often relied on their own children as translators, and they often came asking for help from these two teachers who their children promised would listen.

47 Pronounced "pea," like the sprout, and "on," like the switch.

The help they asked for was beyond anything P'Aon or Sompong had ever heard. These were stories I've just related: of being held captive, of breaking free, of beatings and threats, of pay stubs with only deductions, of being unable to speak the language well enough to ask why.

And dutifully, P'Aon and Sompong would take those stories and go to the local police and make a report on behalf of the migrants.

And watch as nothing changed.

There are two very understandable paths here. One is to continue listening to these stories, continue reporting them, and realize that in this world there are forces bigger than you, forces beyond your control, and that fighting against them directly will only wear you down. That is, to resign yourself to making the small, meaningful contributions that make up day-to-day life, continuing to fight through the kindness of one-on-one interactions.

Or you can hear these stories and become radicalized.

P'Aon is not what you think. She is small. There is just a hint of snaggletooth on a perfectly round face. She has a black patch of a birthmark under her left eye like a shiner that has spread across her cheek in a smudge. She is in her late thirties, but there is a crinkle around her eyes, hair that is just going gray, and with her small size and friendliness, her careful motions and baggy clothes, there is something grandmotherly there. She persistently avoids TV interviews, always pushing others in front of her when asked, always saying her story is unimportant and will only get in the way. It all fits together so when she smiles at you with those crinkly eyes and snaggletooth, you will think P'Aon is very kindly. But it is a kindness that feels a little shy and awkward. Like maybe you would have to look out for P'Aon at a busy event, check in on her to make sure she is okay, because maybe P'Aon is someone who could become overwhelmed and needs protection.

Nothing could be further from the truth. If she didn't repeatedly explain how terrified she was, I would take P'Aon to be fearless. This is a woman who has led midnight raids on illegal processing plants, who has faced down men six inches taller than she, twice her weight, and who has pushed past them without a glance. Who has had men who kill, and men who hire killers, scream at her to mind her own business, to do something else with her life, to stay away from their workers. Who carries a screwdriver and hammer on every raid because she personally is adept at using them to pop open the locks that are keeping the migrants inside. Who, if necessary, will do these raids unaccompanied by the police and press because, although she always alerts the authorities, she has found they do not always follow through. A Pulitzer Prize–winning journalist tells me, "P'Aon goes in. She does the really dirty stuff. It is dangerous." Fishery owners, the multimillionaires who run Samut Sakhon, have shown up at her house with cash, cars, and gold. When she refused one, he calmly explained he would chop her body into small pieces. And for each threat like this, and there have been many, she has reflected on the experience and decided to go back out and do it again. It is the type of swallowed fear, or perhaps tolerated fear, that teaches a lesson about the difference between bravery and bravado, between persistence and confidence, about how completing difficult tasks has less to do with complicating a situation with reams of affirmations, and more about starting with whatever is in front of you and accepting there is always more. Over the last ten years, P'Aon has personally rescued more than two thousand migrants, and has been indirectly responsible for the rescue of thousands more, facts that seem to sadden her more than give her peace if you bring them up, because she sees her ability to have an outsized impact as precisely the point, the most obvious representation of the scale of the problem, a question that she will never directly pose, because that is not P'Aon's style, but that goes a little something like *If she personally has had this impact, just by listening and following through, what would the world look like if others acted on their instincts too?*

When P'Aon and Sompong radicalized in 2006, they decided they were going to build a network of migrants. They wanted to build something strong on the local level that could take care of its own. And the first step they took down this path was to help migrants to document their own experiences. Rather than make a series of isolated reports, they started bringing in workers to give testimonials, compiling their experiences with others to build cases. It was participatory action research, and the very process created the network they envisioned: using action to build trust, and trust to give those marginalized and voiceless a reason to speak.

One of the first cases they began documenting was on beriberi. Beriberi is a disease where the hands swell and delirium sets in. It comes on with sudden immobilizing pain in the arms and legs and can be devastating. And in 2006, the LPN learned there were thirty-nine returned fishermen in Samut Sakhon who had it.

This did not make much sense. As conditions go, beriberi is rare, but certainly not unheard-of. It is a nutrient deficiency; it isn't contagious. It comes from a severe lack of vitamin B/thiamine. As the LPN investigated, they learned there were occasional clusters of beriberi in refugee camps, which did make a little sense—a common group starving together—but why fishermen? And why in Thailand, where there were plenty of cheap foods that supplied the needed thiamine?

And so the LPN got out and investigated. They talked to migrants. And because they were trusted, people opened up in ways they hadn't to the medical task force that had previously investigated. The more the LPN listened, the more they connected the dots. It turns out eating raw fish and seabirds also strips the body of thiamine. And soon, the LPN was documenting something much bigger than beriberi. Simply by talking to people nobody in official government positions was asking about, they uncovered some of the first cases of human trafficking in seafood.

From 2006 to 2012, the LPN rang the alarm bell to everyone they could think of. They told the United Nations, the International Labour

Organization, countless NGOs. They alerted the press. Reporters Shannon Service and Becky Palmstrom visited with them three times to create a brilliant piece for National Public Radio. Slow gears started moving. But, in general, despite uncovering an industry in the twenty-first century where human slavery was not just common but flourishing, things continued pretty much as normal.

Shrimp, Chocolate, Coffee, Cattle, Cotton, Timber, Sugar, Palm Oil, and Gold

In a parallel universe, the nonprofit Humanity United was attempting to tackle the same issue from the top down. Founded in 2008 by eBay billionaires Pierre and Pam Omidyar, the firm had spent its early years searching for a cause to anchor its endowment. At the time, modern slavery was getting considerable media attention from the war in Sudan. Women in Darfur were reportedly being captured by local militias and sold to troops in the capital. After a 2010 feature in *National Geographic* got the attention of co-founder Pam, the nonprofit set out to explore the issue in depth.

The more they looked, the more they were stunned. Slavery, debt bondage, and forced labor were not extinct in our world, nor were they limited vestiges enabled by the chaos of war; they were vital forces underpinning the global economy. Over 35 million people per year work under coercion, more than in the entire history of the Atlantic slave trade,[48] and their labor is responsible for some $150 billion in profits

---

48 Important, if morally tricky, point here: There is no legitimate way to compare modern slavery with the Atlantic slave trade, the latter of which is perhaps the single most destructive institution in the history of humanity, and so what I did up there was wrong and misleading and mostly designed to get your eyes down here. I have elected to use the word "slave" liberally in this text because I think no other word hits with the appropriate impact when describing a person who has been simultaneously bought, sold, imprisoned, and forced to work under the threat of violence. But the Atlantic slave trade with its basis

per year. Sex slaves, like the women in Darfur, represent less than a quarter. In many ways, the horror is so vast that it risks overwhelming anyone who learns about it.

And so Humanity United did something unusual. Rather than plow in and fund direct action, it began to strategize. How do you create change around a problem that is so pervasive, invisible, and damning that most people just want to turn away and ignore?

The first decision was to focus on forced labor in items we use, rather than the more sensational forms in the sex trade or domestic help market. At that time there was no sourcing information on most global commodities, and so the firm hired outside consultants to begin what they called a "strategic vetting process," producing quick snapshots of different industries. The result was mind-boggling. Twenty-five commodities emerged from this analysis as candidates with extremely problematic supply chains. To narrow down their efforts, they focused on industries that were likely to achieve a media hit: Was the product imported into the United States in significant quantities? Would the severity of abuse shock consumers?

Ten different commodities met these new criteria: chocolate, coffee, shrimp, cattle, conflict minerals such as tungsten, cotton, timber, sugar, palm oil, and gold.

In 2011, the group decided to elevate shrimp above all, publishing a

---

in skin color, with its dynastic heritability—whereby humans born from slaves are born enslaved—and most critically by the fact that it was legal and upheld by the state, is unique and distinct and should not be used as some gauge point for the awfulness described. I'm of the opinion that these descriptions speak for themselves and need no gauge. I think I'm particularly sensitive to the moral trickiness here because many modern advocacy groups lump all forms off trafficked labor together to get aggressively high numbers for marketing purposes—lumping together people smuggled across borders for a fee, those working off a debt, and those like Tun-Lin, imprisoned for years against their will—creating numbers that are at the very least manipulative and, at most, at odds with meaning: misrepresenting people who are actually active agents in their own survival as victims.

massive, engrossing report aimed at policy makers. Brian Edge, the lead author, visited with the LPN while writing; he tells me no other group influenced his thinking or gave him the access on the ground the way the LPN did. At the same time as it was publishing this report, Humanity United was also cultivating journalists, putting the Omidyars' considerable resources into media partnerships and developing stories behind the scenes. In all, it was an extremely patient, calculated effort to move the global conversation.

Which leads to the most unusual aspect of forced labor in the Thai shrimp industry: the fact that you are hearing about it at all. It took an unusually deliberate billionaires' campaign combined with the raw engagement of a small group of community organizers to pull one small portion of the bottom of the commodity chain to a place where it was visible.

Thus, by 2013, just as P'Aon and the LPN are hearing new, terrible reports of a prison camp for enslaved workers, a brilliant team of reporters at the *Guardian* leverage the Humanity United report to publish their own massive exposé. This gets the hit the Omidyars had strategized around five years before. The media crashes down. Suddenly seafood slavery is on the scene. The Associated Press comes next, digging even deeper to win a Pulitzer. The *New York Times* does a story. Then the *Economist*. Then everyone. Bangkok becomes a sea of white journalists and aid workers running around in metered cabs looking for seafood slaves to interview. I speak to one fisher who estimates he's given three hundred interviews. For a brief moment, shrimp are added to the list of things a certain type of good middle-class person understood they aren't supposed to eat.

This attention has made the people who study this sort of thing very uneasy.

It isn't quite the worry of overexposure. It is the fear that we will allow the horror of the specific to shield us from the horror of the overwhelming. A fear that shocking abuses like Tun-Lin's on a boat will

obscure the more mundane abuses of Tun-Lin in the seafood processing plant. Think back on that moment. Tun-Lin gets off the boat and
finds alternate work. But then, because of conditions that don't outrage,
conditions that fail the critical media test of murder, kidnapping, assault, just a paycheck being bled by overcharges for rent and electricity,
an exploitation endemic to every one of those twenty-five problematic
commodity chains, Tun-Lin voluntarily returns to the boats where he
was enslaved.

Tun-Lin isn't stupid in the slightest; he just needs to survive.

And he sized up those very normal, non-sensational, non-media-
friendly conditions and decided they were worth risking going back on
a fishing boat.

Or consider what one shrimp supply chain expert told me: "The
focus on Thailand has brought so many resources, so many journalists,
then policy makers here. But I believe if you put the same amount of
resources and energy into other countries you would find something
similar."

Another: "This labor is 100 percent necessary across the globe. The
whole system depends on it. It gives us the prices people have come to
expect. And the profits."

A third: "There is nothing special about Thailand."

A fourth: "I do think the boats are extreme. But only in the violence. On the farm you have the same exploitation, but you have people
living in family units, so there are more social connections. The abuse
can be quite terrible, the exploitation just as bad, but you don't have the
extreme violence."

A fifth: "What I can say is that production has shifted to India now,
and if you look at India and the volumes of shrimp they are producing,
their history with the caste system, and the prices they are able to sell
at, I don't see how they could not be having these problems. It just
doesn't make sense otherwise."

And as this media storm descends, and Thailand gets elevated in world attention, grocery sellers are among the least well equipped to respond.

The moral fantasy is to raise prices. Perhaps a sign posted at the seafood counter saying, "Due to labor abuse in Thailand, the price of our shrimp is increasing as we work to ensure every person in our supply chain receives a fair wage." And then the store raises prices, sells the same amount of fish in defiance of the laws of supply and demand, and dutifully passes the increased revenue back up the chain in reverse, to its importer, who passes it on to a manufacturer, who passes it on to a compromised supplier—one who has decided to turn a new leaf. Then the money is actually used by that supplier: reforming their recruitment process, expanding their human resources department, educating their workers on their rights, providing pathways to grieve abuse, and finally—if there is any money left over—increasing wages. But even if all goes right, the money arrives intact, nobody in between gives themselves a raise, that last bit of work done by the supplier is incredibly hard. It will generate exactly zero press since it is also searingly boring. And it is completely and utterly beyond the expertise of a grocery chain. There are NGOs devoted to this kind of work who openly admit they barely understand the complexities of how to reform a supply chain.

And then, even if you muster the moral courage to pursue this ideal, there is the entirely appropriate fear that a competitor down the street will simply hang a different sign, one that says, explicitly or implicitly, "Hi, valued customer! We have heard about the labor abuse in Thailand and would like to assure you that all our shrimp are sourced ethically," and continue to price right below you.

Consider Margie Mason of the Associated Press, who won a Pulitzer for her reporting on child labor in the seafood industry. "When our story came out," she tells me, "Whole Foods was calling us and pleading, saying none of the shrimp from that plant got into their supply chain. And we were just baffled. 'How can you be sure? We are the people who informed your supplier! Are you saying you have closer oversight of your supplier's supply chain than they do? If so, how? Your exporter had no idea. Your importer had no idea. So how can you be so sure?' But they just kept pleading and pleading. It was crazy making."

And so, to avoid the absolute hubris required above, most grocery sellers are much more likely to cut and run. Drop the stigmatized supplier or region and find a new area where they can make new promises. Industry observer Jim Prevor calls this "catering to the aesthetic sense of consumers who don't like to be associated with ugly things." It has the vanity of simplicity, the attraction of any moral absolute. But it rarely makes the world a better place. When the industry picks up and leaves, withdraws their money and purchasing power, the problems simply get shifted elsewhere. "As industry moves, so do the problems," Daniel Murphy, Thai seafood supply expert, tells me. "The global narrative is displacement."

"Too often during these media storms, I've heard people say, let's boycott this product," Simon Baker, a migrant researcher, explains. "Look at what happens when abused children get pushed out of labor markets. They typically don't suddenly find better jobs. They get pushed further underground. In my research, I've found this often means going into sex work . . . What you in the West have to realize is the entire narrative is backwards. In trafficking, the media focuses on why and where poor people get into difficult situations. But maybe we should be looking at why they are poor to begin with?"

And where was P'Aon during the *Guardian* media storm? Before the police, international aid workers, or media had heard of it, P'Aon left Thailand to follow up on reports about a prison camp run by boat owners. She went with one other friend to a lonely island at the tip of the Indonesian archipelago. For years, the LPN had heard rumors of men being held there, kept in cages, beaten for disobedience, in a place that had been chosen for its isolation, where there was no police presence, and where owners could punish fishers without killing them because killing a slave in a labor shortage is expensive, but the fear a prison instills across the entire industry is quite lucrative. Together these two women found the rumors were far worse than simply true. They found a private prison system with men held as long as seventeen years, uncovered mass graves, and found fishers starving in the jungle, surviving on leaves and rodents, who had escaped from the prisons but had nowhere to go. The two women brought back whom they could with them and returned to alert authorities. Then they went back on their own to help more.

At one point, P'Aon tells me, "We used to have fear. I used to be so afraid. Now we fear the fishermen will be dead. It has made us quite fearless."

And This Is How She Does It

Camp wakes around five thirty a.m. There is a slow gathering for breakfast, everyone crouching and scooping rice into bowls, going over the plans for the day as the sun creeps up. We are on the far edge of Sangkhlaburi, very rural, very western Thailand, just a few miles from the Myanmar border, so everyone is practicing basic Mon words over breakfast, greeting stragglers in unison with what I think means "Hello." This section of the border is famously loose, barely demarcated in many places, and while there are no roads across, families travel back and forth by foot every day. This makes it a major migrant route for seafood. Which is of course why the LPN is here. And so, a little after six a.m., still groggy, the whole group piles into a big church van, sixteen-deep, the aisle filled with interns, all scrunched into sleepy balls, heads resting on the thighs of the rest of us above in our seats. We hit the unpaved roads, jostling over ruts, the driver blasting crap Thai pop music that all the interns seem to know by heart and thus mouth silently and sleepily as we roll. By seven a.m., the van thuds up on an empty soccer pitch surrounded by abandoned buildings. Everyone piles out, shaking legs free.

After a brief inspection of the grounds, P'Aon selects a large building that is in the worst shape of all. This was once the cafeteria for a Mon elementary school, one that specialized in reaching out to that ethnic minority, but was abandoned from lack of funding, and corruption. Bottles litter the floor, the main room is covered in dirt, the bathroom with its one squat toilet is essentially a waste pit filled with rusted metal desks upturned on each other. Its identity as a school cafeteria is gone, and if you walked in and thought it was an actual junkyard, no one could argue.

And then, after agreeing this was the site, without so much as another word, everyone begins cleaning.

Spreading out with the power of enthusiastic numbers, brooms are located, pulled from the van in two sections and twisted together, then dustpans, then rags, then trash bags flushed open. Soon a team is sweeping while another strings up posters, decorating, wiping, and physically hauling away the junk. I think of the maxim of the Young Lords that the people may want liberation, but first they want their streets cleaned. And somehow, after only forty-five minutes of this—sixteen people bearing down with coordinated effort—there is something approximating a school shining back at us where previously there had only been muck.

Only once this space is reclaimed do the megaphones come out.

Everything begins moving pretty fast at this point. It being almost eight a.m. on a Sunday and nobody wanting to let the day get away, one team splits off to unload the large bags of donated gifts they have brought with them, another begins arranging informational flyers, T-shirts, and a game with pictures illustrating legal and illegal trafficking scenarios. Others continue cleaning, now wiping down dust from windows. Four of the tallest interns take the megaphones and split into the four cardinal directions from the soccer pitch, calling out to the neighborhood in every language, announcing their presence, announcing the event, announcing the LPN will protect both the Thai and Burmese workers. And sure enough, like the Pied Piper or the ice cream truck, a steady stream of Mon children come pouring forth in response.

These are little kids, no taller than my waist, and big kids in their teenage years, all coming into the now pristine cafeteria, many visibly taken aback by the cleanliness of the space, their space, recovered by this mysterious group with megaphones. As they come, the LPN puts the smallest ones into tight rows ten-deep, sitting cross-legged on the floor, and lets the big ones head to the back, where they can slouch cool against the wall. By eight-thirty a.m., the room is almost three-quarters full, and to corral the growing crowd, an educator stands in the front of the room leading clap-based call-and-response activities that have the pacifying and unifying effect they are designed to have, but which I had never quite seen effected in the real world.

While the children are the ostensible focus of the day, they are also reliable lures for the older and harder-to-reach mommas and poppas and curious neighbors who have been attracted to this schoolhouse awakened. This older audience is crucial, they know migrants about to cross, workers in dangerous situations, and all of this energy is directed at getting them to believe too. Finally, just before the presentation is set to begin—the room filled with maybe 150 people now, packed to standing-room capacity—three interns in salmon-colored T-shirts scale the walls by the windows, crawling toward the center rafter to unfold a giant banner: BORDER OF LOVE, BORDER TO SEA.

Just about then, the call-and-response activities turn into a solid clap, a single rhythm, and I'll confess to a lump in the throat as this small organization managed to transform a corrupt, neglected school into a venue for 150 five-to-twenty-year-olds sitting in neat rows, chanting "Brotherhood and Sisterhood" in Thai and then Mon. For a brief moment, this is a community where people show other people they are linked, and through those links will be protected and informed. Its maintenance of course depends on the extent to which the rest of the chain joins in, forming new bonds of exchange, connected less by what we'll get and more by what we'll give.

The Long Road from P'Aon to Amazon–Whole Foods

That corpse you planted last year in your garden
Has it begun to sprout? Will it bloom this year?
. . . You! Hypocrite reader! My fellow! My brother!

— Baudelaire, translated within Eliot's *The Waste Land*

Almost exactly one year after my last visit with the LPN in Thailand, I learn that activist investor JANA Partners has acquired 8 percent of Whole Foods stock. It will be the first step in a series of events that lead the Internet giant Amazon to swallow the grocer whole.

It is a deal that is portrayed with an almost eschatological force in the trades, and perhaps appropriately so. With it, retail grocery feels like it is closing in on some type of end point, almost a bathroom-drain-style singularity through which all supply chain consultants must pass before being evaporated to the cloud.

In many ways, and however earth-shattering, it is one of the least surprising developments of this book.

"Focusing on Amazon–Whole Foods is completely missing the narrative," Errol Schweizer tells me. "These changes have been going on behind the scenes for quite a while."

Errol is one of the very few in the position to know. For a moment he was Whole Foods grocery in a literal embodied sense, the head of the national grocery program for the entire chain, a man at the helm of some eighty categories and ultimately responsible for the buying, pricing, and shelf allocation of tens of thousands of products in the store's most profitable sector.

Then, after fourteen years, he jumped ship.

Errol is a little tough to get right. He is sharp. In the elbows sense as much as the analytic one. There's a receding hairline buzzed down to skull, a crinkly smile, and he talks quick. He's not actually small, but there is a little man inside of him, ready to jump up and lunge at you anytime he's challenged. I think there is something essential about the insecurity. Errol came up in grocery the old-fashioned way. "My parents didn't have money, but I had a young family right out of college. It was work or starve so I decided to work my ass off," he tells me. Which means he began on the retail floor, moved on to ring registers, stock shelves, and manage the night shift. It was a slow climb, but one where he worked in almost every aspect of the industry before hitting the corporate suites. Now, in his life after Whole Foods, he sits on the board of national retailers and advises dozens of multimillion-dollar suppliers. He's the stock boy who made good, and he can speak to both sides of the retail divide. As in it actually comes out of his mouth in the language he uses, toggling between an earnest grocer from the Bronx and a guy who has spent a little too much time on corporate retreats. Once, he tells me, "Look, I'm a bigmouthed Jew from New York. That makes me an asset in innovation culture and an asshole in maintenance culture," and really I couldn't capture the divide in Errol any better. But the beautiful thing about that path and divide, about Errol, really, is that as he grew, he never detached. He knows how hard those jobs are, and is one of the few people who can compare the eighty-hour work-week in the boardroom to the eighty-hour workweek on the retail floor and call bullshit on all those who are convinced the latter are replaceable and the former requires a sainted level of intelligence and expertise.

He's also just cynical enough about how business actually gets done that I get the impression he actually gives a shit. I'm wary about this at first. He feeds me line after line about Tikkun Olam, the Jewish duty to repair the world, and it sounds a little like another one of those in-novation buzzwords, but when he rattles off the planks of the Whole Foods mission he is quick to say which have been abandoned and which are still limping by in a way that seems nuanced and fair. And his out-rage at the intrusions of private equity, their insistence on applying a value-equals-price equation to *his* Whole Foods, where value meant a compendium of qualities that included treating people well, is unfake-able in the way it subsides from stream-of-consciousness rant to fidgety bitterness. Which is to say, on a kind of profound level I come to believe Errol really cares about using grocery to make the world a better place. And I believe that is why he got out. At one point, going on and on about his attempts to source chocolate without slave labor, a process just as agonizingly difficult as with Thai shrimp, he says: "Look, anyone can do this with their life. It amounts to seeing the world and being creative about how you engage with it. I just happened to have a platform in grocery and so that's how I made my impact."

I meet him at the Whole Foods Bowery—the same store where I worked the seafood counter and one of many that Errol helped build from scratch. When we walk the aisles together, there is something faintly touching going on: Errol reaching out to products like they are old friends, pausing to tell a story about their launch, turning the box over in his hands, checking how sourcing decisions and prices have changed, before moving on to greet the next one. A man wandering through some vast family reunion slightly estranged and overwhelmed.

As we talk through his history with the chain, this dynamic continues. Errol swings between "we," "they," and "me" so frequently in a single sentence it moves from being disorienting to speaking clearly about the emotion of being outside something that was once your own. And his negative comments about structure are always immediately followed by praise of personnel, a veritable grocery list of people he wants to make sure I understand he loves and learned from.

Nevertheless, all the love and learning could not prevent Errol from leaving in early 2016, directly after Andy, my ginger-bearded trainer, along with five thousand other employees who got the ax. Almost exactly a year ahead of the merger with Amazon.

The timing wasn't an accident. It was the first stage in a trend.

For most of its history, Whole Foods was a highly decentralized company. They put their authority in their twelve regions, each of which acted with a unique level of autonomy when it came to deciding what to sell and how to price. There are historical reasons for this: much of Whole Foods' growth came through acquisition rather than new store development. And there are deeper philosophical ones: the chain is far more Texas libertarian than it ever was East Coast liberal. The early organic movement, itself an outgrowth of late '60s counterculture, was a band of outsiders—the loners, seekers, and impassioned weirdos of the food world—who saw government as not just failing to regulate agriculture, but corrupt as an instrument.[49] And at Whole Foods the decentralized structure was critical. It brought buyers closer to the

---

49 This libertarianism got tempered at Whole Foods by its early expansion to California. As the chain grew, and early hires came up through the ranks to senior management, they brought their state's famously care-taking, progressive, slightly paternalistic values with them. This created the hybrid "conscious capitalist" machine that would barnstorm through the upper-middle-class kitchen, able to gratify the self, save Mother Nature, and delight Wall Street at the very same time. But it shocked nobody who knew the chain when CEO and founder John Mackey came out against universal health care and retail unions.

ground, allowing them to keep a better eye on quality, earning the chain a deserved reputation among entrepreneurs as the best place to premiere young brands; its genuinely local procurers wielded their authority to waive promotional fees, give advice on logistics, and otherwise nurture the products they personally loved and believed would help the earth.

But then the rest of the industry caught up. Whole Foods' very success allowed the products they premiered to scale up, and, once at scale, flee over to Target and its ilk: those massive chains that operated with a buying power and efficiency the Whole Foods decentralized structure couldn't match. And rather than double down on their strengths and continue to innovate—and since we are far from a sustainable world, it seems there is plenty of room left to innovate—Whole Foods decided to stand pat. And when you are suddenly playing the same game against everyone else, you play it on their terms. Which means you have to compete on price and convenience.

To do that, you have to get big.

And you don't get much bigger than Amazon.

"It's a middle finger to what Whole Foods stands for," a supplier who still sells to the chain tells me. "Big centralized buying is the opposite of Whole Foods. A giant fuck you to quality standards."

Ian Kelleher, co-founder of Peeled Snacks, noticed the same thing from the outside. "One by one, I started seeing all the good, smart people leaving . . . Whole Foods was *the* leader in progressive activism in the food industry. Then somewhere by mid-2016, everyone I knew doing that type of work got sacked."

Or, as Errol puts it, "I'd say they are no longer really interested in the 'conscious' part of 'conscious capitalism' because it didn't get them to where they want to be in terms of price."

And so at the same time Ian was noticing the best and most idealistic people leaving from the outside, Errol watched from the inside as they were replaced by a new type of hire. These were people from Home

Depot, Walmart, and Target. "They have talents," Errol tells me. "They do certain things really well. But they aren't always the type of things that line up with Whole Foods' core values.

"We always said if you are trying to be the cheapest, there are two stakeholder groups who are going to pay for it. Your employees and your suppliers," he continues. "With the Prime deals, they are just sending the bill to the suppliers. It is actually kind of gross. We are going to do a 10 percent deal and you pay for it. It is the opposite of the way we used to do business . . . Whole Foods has retreated so rapidly from their value of win-win partnerships, it is stunning."

It all reminds me of something that aquaculture researcher Corey Peet told me when we talked about Thai shrimp farmers. Corey sketched to me what he called a "pillar of sustainability." "All these NGOs talk about people, profits, and the planet," Corey said. "But for it to actually work, all three of those need to be equal. Our current model does a good job at maximizing profits. But to the extent that it works to protect the planet, which it often tries to do very faithfully, it almost always comes out of people."

When I relay this to Errol, he pauses. "That's not quite how I see it . . . For me the question is, do you want to win a race to the bottom? Or do you want to deliver the highest quality and be the best? Everybody has pressure from the competition. Always will. But it's how you respond. It can't just be about cutting things back. Humanity can't just play defense. We need a good offense too."

We get quiet for a moment and I wonder what that offense would look like. What it demands of its customers and whether it is incompatible with the abundance grocery promises. Then Errol continues, "The biggest problem in food is the financial community. They don't get any retail dynamics outside of price comparisons. It's not how they are trained to look at the world and so they totally miss it. But this stuff is obvious to people who actually work on the ground . . . Once you start chasing price downhill it rewards the worst practices."

When Errol says this, we are sitting on the second-floor balcony of the Whole Foods on the Bowery, munching on two ancient grains salads, looking down at all the men and women sifting through the deals below. And as we munch, we watch them shop—the price comparisons, the picky ingredients scans, the carts filling with unprecedented variety— and I wonder how many of those completely mundane choices map to the worst practices we decry in suppliers, and when exactly they pile up enough to slide downhill and become P'Aon's problem.

Two Paths

Back in 1970, Trader Joe Coulombe looked at the grocery industry and saw two paths: the first required becoming an "active retailer," which for him meant rejecting a passive role as supermarket landlord, and applying intensive effort to seek out or create "discontinuous" products that could not be imitated by competitors. The second was to grow big, "sell goods that are available in infinite supply," and compete ruthlessly on price.

This latter path was essentially what every single one of his competitors was attempting. They would spend the next decades scaling up to carry bigger and bigger inventories, gobbling up larger and larger warehouse spaces, forever looking over their shoulders at competitors and trying to shave down costs. He saw his own ruin there; the biggest chain would always win, and however many competed, there could be only one or two that survived to the end.

And so in 1977, he plunged down the riskier track. He slashed inventory. Shed warehouse space. And reoriented his entire approach from selling at cheap prices to buying what he believed consumers would find outstanding at the price he could sell.

I don't want to elevate Trader Joe's too much. For one, the chain has changed significantly since Joe's days, existing now in dilute design, where many continuous goods bask in a halo cast from that earlier image. The very week I wrote this, I went to a Trader Joe's and under "new items" found cans of plain seltzer. You simply can't get more mass-produced and continuous than that! For another, even in Joe's heyday, I am sure things weren't as rosy as his people remember. One of his buyers memorably told me a story about visiting a factory selling extremely profitable "handmade pies" that he watched get unloaded from a truck, unboxed, and reboxed into different, more "handmade" packaging. When he rushed back to tell Joe, the only response was one of those chuckles and, "Oh, maybe don't go visiting any more suppliers without calling ahead first." But Joe got certain big ideas about humanity and curiosity and individuality right. He looked at the retail landscape and saw that investing in those would allow him to survive while his competitors' strategy would only allow them to grow more similar. He created a store that bought *for* people rather than sold *to* them, creating new products when necessary rather than giving people what they already knew. He pushed his customers to stretch themselves, and then led them toward a life they wanted to be leading even if they did not know it quite yet. He then shrunk his offerings down to a human scale so his buyers could get the expertise needed to actually do all that.

Amazon, liberated by the virtual space of the Internet, has taken the path Joe surrendered to its logical, almost unrecognizable end point. It has no limits on inventory. It insists on the most efficient practices in warehousing. It uses size and scale and efficiency to get the lowest price. It is a pure selling machine. It does not buy for anyone, it buys for everyone at once, and the "displaced ideal" Amazon caters to is singular: liberty. In the form we most typically worship it these days: convenience. It is an ideal that says with a little help from Amazon stripping away the hurdles, barriers, inertia, and shipping time from your life, you can finally be free to make the best of your precious time on planet earth.

I saw it first in my prior book. That book looked at the world of yoga, and a particularly obsessive practice therein. Men and women who would enter a studio and bend for eight hours a day, busy doctors, lawyers, bankers who would sneak off to fit in an hour and a half on their lunch break. In yoga it was self-betterment, self-improvement, or becoming a stronger, more radiant version of yourself. And in it, I found a whole community based on this ethos; people reveling in the very real ways they had transformed from couch potatoes and addicts, remarking after every class about just how much more capable they felt now. But what was the end? What did you do once you became a better version of yourself? Where did all this self-improvement lead? The answer was always back to more yoga. Never volunteer at a clinic or a food kitchen, never for a studio owner to open more classes to the poor or injured. Never to take our radiant yoga bodies and put them to use in the service for others. And so those lawyers or doctors would go on to use that extra energy to bend for longer hours, and when they had a vacation they went off *in search of themselves*, spiraling deeper and deeper into the practice, becoming ever more capable humans, who could push their bodies into ever more drastic positions. In grocery, it all feels eerily similar. Instead of self-improvement, we have the god of convenience and efficiency, which everyone across the system is bending on both knees to serve—from customer to manufacturer and all the increasingly cog-like humans shuffling goods in between. Convenience is the great gift the grocery store gives to the consumer. Efficiency its great technique for delivering it. But when you make convenience itself an end point, what then?

In this sense, grocery is a story still being written. In the beginning, there was nature, powerful and cruel—that original destroyer of worlds—drought and predation, wind and disease. And so we built tools to subdue her: from jamming sticks into anthills to charting out agronomist tables and plows. And we built these tools so well and for so long that now nature, real nature, is mostly a dream, an uneasy longing, repressed and turned kindly by submission, the way terrible fathers crumble into grandfathers. Then somewhere, after centuries, we woke to the fact that our tools had become too powerful—our monocultures, pesticides, and mine scalings—the tools just as fearsome as the nature they set out to rein in, and we found ourselves cowering once again. This is the typical end point, with our Frankensteins and atomic Godzillas. A daily alienation updated almost as a background app into our iPhone addictions and queasy feelings about social media we just can't quit. But what we've begun to see, what I certainly learned writing this book, is that we've undertaken a new project. We decided that, caught between two awesome external forces—nature everlasting, and these new tools of our own creation—the one piece in the whole operation that was most malleable was us. Our selves. That we would happily trade away aspects of our lives—be it community or duty or eccentricity or care—for an ability to survive between them.

I came to see this as the very juncture where grocery sits, the store constantly recalibrating as we decide what of ourselves to trade away.

To think of it another way, ever since Eric Schlosser and *Fast Food Nation* came into my life, and of course there was Upton Sinclair and many other muckrakers before him, there has been a very American idea that the closer we look at our food, the more disgusting it will turn out to be. And this always seems to be the case! Every time the best food minds and investigative journalists dig into a particular part of the supply chain they find some new horror. From slave-grown tomatoes to subsidized corn. It always seems to be there, at the bottom, this disgust. But in this book I've come to see something else in that digging. It is no less horrible, but maybe the slightly sadder form anger takes when balanced by introspection: more of a clawing feeling of being trapped, a revulsion at our own immobility. It is this notion that at the bottom, after all that digging, the particular investigative horror we've uncovered is just a proxy. Something closer to a shadow cast off from all of us above peering down and doing the digging. The real object of our scorn might not be in our food safety standards, in the revolving-door regulators, in the rise of industry, or even in the abuse and commodification of men, but in ourselves as agents in this world: for knowing what we want and what we are willing to give up to get it, for understanding that this is a moral outrage we've been digging for all along because it verifies what we know but also don't quite want to acknowledge about ourselves.

This is to say, the great lesson of my time with groceries is that we have got the food system we deserve. The adage is all wrong: it's not that we are what we eat, it's that we eat the way we are. Retail grocery is a reflection. What people call the supply chain is a long, interconnected network of human beings working on other humans' behalf. It responds to our actions, not our pieties; and in its current form it demands convenience and efficiency starting from the checkout counter on down. The result is both incredible beyond words—abundance, wish fulfillment, and low price—and as cruel and demeaning as Tun-Lin voluntarily choosing to return to those boats. To me this is as hopeful as it is depressing. We are in a dialogue with this world, not at its mercy. We have a natural inclination toward what is right that is as powerful as any selfishness. But for those out there who bristle at this reflection, who want to scream the patently obvious fact that meat is murder, that labor without choice is exploitation, or whatever their own personal horror is, who want to shake the world awake to the fact that we are literally sustaining ourselves on misery, who want to reform, I very much don't want to dissuade you so much as I want you to consider that any solution will come from outside our food system, so far outside it that thinking about food is only a distraction from the real work to be done. At best, food is an opening, like any maw, that might lead us inside. Somewhere darker, more unknowable, a place where the real work of change may finally begin.

Climbing out to Fresh Air

When I talk to Lynne Ryles the trucker for a final time our conversation is filled with a new cough that rolls in like a sob. I ask her about

Waymo, Google's plan for driverless trucks and the automating of the industry, and she doesn't even pause to acknowledge the question. "They can take my steering wheel out of my cold dead hands," she says, channeling every cliché I could ever put into her. Then, just a moment later, in response to a question about Bella, her dog, there is a silence so long I wonder if her hands haven't gone cold and dead. "I'm going broke," she says, "and I don't have a clue what to do."

Labor Day comes and I get a hankering for some Slawsa, so I head to the website to place an order. Not five minutes after clicking send, Julie Busha writes me personally, "Ben, what are you thinking? I canceled your payment and am sending a sampler." I realize I should have known better. Her vigilance and generosity in the name of Slawsa knows no bounds. She signs her email with "Have a Slawsome day!" and I resolve to do just that.

In November, when I visit Whole Foods on the Bowery with Errol, we find it has a new seafood case. The old, inconsistent one was ripped out, and a brand-new beautiful counter installed. Who knows what it means for opening metaphors, but Walter is happy about it! He's still working there, no raise, but the rot doesn't accumulate like it used to. Soon after our visit, the newly merged Whole Foods–Amazon takes the next logical step in optimization and cuts medical benefits for its part-time workers. Corporate announces this proudly as an effort to "create a more equitable and efficient scheduling model."

Just after I leave Thailand, major reforms sweep in. Threatened by the media crisis, and the prospect of international sanctions, Thailand's military junta begins cracking down. Boats are docked. A new port-in, port-out set of paperwork is brought to the piers. And yet when I ask those who work in the space whether the reforms will stop the abuse, the answer is a categorical no. Analyst Josh Stride speaks for many when he says, "This is a fifteen-year project. Any retailer who tells you they have snapped their fingers and can give you a clean supply is lying." Others speak to something more depressing than prevarication: Thai producers who have poured themselves into costly reforms only to watch buyers balk at their new prices and seek cheaper product elsewhere. "I think you'll see the Thai shrimp industry pay for doing the right thing," one analyst tells me. Errol remains an optimist. When I call to fact-check, he tells me, "One of the country's biggest positive secrets is how amazing and fascinating the food industry is. People are working their butts off for other people. Amazon and Whole Foods might be chasing price for now. But that just creates an opportunity for someone new to move into the space they abandoned."

Finally, Tun-Lin. The last time we speak, something sort of like justice is grinding forth. We are standing in a backyard in Samut Sakhon, maybe a mile from the docks where he was abducted. It's home now. He is volunteering for the LPN. On his wrist there is a yellow rubber wrist bracelet, of the type I associate with Lance Armstrong, only this yellow bracelet was given to him to denote his place as a survivor of seafood slavery. He touches it frequently, flipping it around his wrist back and forth like the dial of combination lock he's trying to crack. In the time since I last saw him, he has become one of the few and rare fishermen to see some form of compensation for his time on the boat. He ended up successfully navigating the reparations system, not just because of the five years he was trafficked on a boat but because when he went back of his own volition he lost his hand. For the first time since meeting him, Tun-Lin is smiling. He used the money to return to Myanmar for the first time since he left at age fifteen. He is three days back now, having just seen his father and mother after twenty years. They wept. His father was shaking. Then Tun-Lin used the money from his lump sum earnings to buy them a proper house with concrete floors. He has decided to move back to Mwabi village to be closer to them. He tells me people there no longer make fun of him now that he has money of his own. What are you going to do now? I ask him. Tell me about your dreams now that you are free. He gets excited and spreads his arms wide. My translator nods seriously and then speaks in his monotone:

He says he will open a store. A big store with lots of food the people in his village haven't seen. Then there is another moment of translation. A conferring across time and language. And my translator says, he wants to start with one small store. But then he says he will collect the money to expand it to many. And so after twenty years of being hurtled around Southeast Asia, after hiking literal mountains, parting literal seas, losing his friends and limbs and all his hope many times over, after being enslaved and overseeing slaves himself, Tun-Lin is heading back to his home state to build a grocery chain.

ACKNOWLEDGMENTS

This book would have been impossible without the contributions of what, by the end, felt like a true community of entrepreneurs, analysts, activists, academics, and hardworking grocery professionals—all devoted in some way or another to understanding the chaotic ways we Americans feed. Accordingly, a few thanks to those who made this project possible:

Thank you to Joe and Alice Coulombe for letting me into their Trader Joe's adventure and to Lynne Ryles for allowing me into her truck and life. To Julie Busha for explaining every important thing in this industry twice while simultaneously being one of the kindest, smartest, and hardest-working people I have ever met. Thank you to Walter for being such a delight of a human being. Your openness, humor, and work ethic inspire. Thank you to Kevin Kelley for insight, access, and understanding; Kevin, we only scratched the surface. Thank you to P'Aon and Sompong of the LPN for your hospitality, grace, and inspiration; and to Tun-Lin and Sompong Linsey for your honesty, bravery, and witness. I tried to do you justice. Most of all, thank you to Ma Htay for safely taking me places I could not otherwise go.

Thank you to all those who shared the ideas that define this book but requested not to be named. This project would be impossible without your willingness to speak candidly to a nosy stranger.

Thank you to LeRoy Watson and Robin Guentert. To Ian Kelleher. To Daniel Murphy, Andy Hall, Katrina Nakamura, and Lisa Rende-Taylor. Thank you to Elizabeth Aud and Desiree Ann Wood for endless patience. Stay safe out there. To translators extraordinaire: Boong Chairattana, Sasivara Tulyayoon, Hannah Snow, and Anny Tar. To Phil Robertson of Human Rights Watch for patiently stitching the connection between Typhoon Gay, Thai police, and racism. To Brian Edge, Corey Peet, Lori Bishop, Simon Baker, Darian McBride, David Kawahigashi, and Josh Stride. Thank you to Mansour Samadapour—there is a whole book on you alone. To Errol Schweizer. To Kevin Coupe. To Tim Lytton and Wayne Hsieng. To the Whole Foods fish counter winter of 2015. To Carrie Gleason and Carolyn Wheeler. Thank you especially to Doug Rauch and his work at the Daily Table for inspiring this project into being.

Thank you to my beloved secret editors Liz Greenwood, Sukari Jones, Stephen Fishbach, Rachel McKeen, Missy Mazzoli, and Matt Stewart. Thank you to Alena Graedon for dealing with overflow crazy via tacos&text, and to Cecelia Watson for handling emergency grammar questions with aplomb. Thank you especially to Rachel Corbett, a champion of sanity, voice of compassion, my edit-hero of 2019.

Thank you to my indispensable real editors: Pam Krauss for acquiring this thing and encouraging it. Lauren Appleton for shepherding, crafting, nudging, and hassling it into completion. Lauren, I'm both sorry for my stubbornness and tremendously grateful for your persistence plowing through it. The book is so much better for it. Thank you to Marian Lizzi for your wisdom, scrutiny, and strong puns along the way. I am indebted to all of your eyes and insights, saving me from blunders and elevating my arguments.

Thank you to Mike Harriot, agent, stalwart, and kind, calm, unflinching voice of reason on the phone.

Thank you to the MacDowell Colony and to the Corporation of Yaddo, where critical parts of this book were completed. To Marian, Cheryl, David, Blake, and whoever thought to put a bathtub next to a screened porch in Calderwood. To Katrina Trask and her giant white room. Thank you to the Allen Room residency at the New York Public Library, because sometimes free office space is worth more than inspiration.

Thanks to Athas&Kat, Sol&Ash, Raj&Jo, Scott&Liz, Nad&Mike, Stephen&Julia, Josh&Julie, Matt&Whit, Mike&Lauren, Jon&Renana, Josh&Katie, David&Carla. You are anchors and guiding lights. To Joe R, and the rest of the Creaky Joint Rollers marathon crew. Thanks to mycologists Scott and Kenan: life examined with you two is life worth living. Thanks to Victoria for starting this with me way back when. Thanks to Vadis for all good things along the way.

Finally, thanks to my sister, Sarah Lorr, for being the best. And Adam Blumenkrantz for becoming family. Thanks to Franny the dog for keeping us all sane. And most of all to Kathy and Richard Lorr, the best two parents a guy could ever ask for. I love you more than you know: you are my sun, moon, earth, and stars.

Introduction: Between the Ice and You

1   **"In short, her shopping is primarily an act of love":** Daniel Miller,
      A Theory of Shopping (Ithaca: Cornell University Press, 1998).

1   **This happens every other month after closing:** The following
      description is based on the author's personal experience as well as
      conversations with fellow employees during his time working at
      Whole Foods on the Bowery from roughly September 28, 2015,
      to November 30, 2015.

5   **In 2018, Americans spent $701 billion . . . there are 38,000:** Jim
      Dudlicek, Bridget Goldschmidt, Randy Hofbauer, and Kat
      Martin, "86th Annual Report of the Grocery Industry,"
      Progressive Grocer, April 2019.

5   **the average adult will spend 2 percent of their life inside one:**
      Andrew Seth and Geoffrey Randall, *The Grocers: The Rise and
      Rise of Supermarket Chains* (London: Kogan Page, 2011).

5   **the way that most of us are introduced to the system:** Viz, farmers
      markets, oft touted as an alternative, account for less than one-
      fifth of 1 percent of grocery spending, and—at least when I visit
      them—seem largely patronized by people in a correspondingly
      marginal income bracket.

5   **We spend only 10 percent of our budget on food:** USDA Food
      Expenditures, "Table 7—Food expenditures by family and

individuals as a share of disposable personal income," *USDA Economic Research Service*, January 26, 2016.

5   **compared to 40 percent by our great-grandparents:** Derek Thompson, "How America Spends Money: 100 Years in the Life of the Family Budget," *Atlantic*, April 5, 2012.

6   **nearly 90 percent of the population worked:** Beth Waterhouse, "A Sustainable Future?" www.pbs.org/ktca/farmhouses/sustainable_future, accessed August 30, 2018.

9   **The average store has 32,000 individuated products ... The biggest have more than 120,000 SKUs:** Food Marketing Institute Information Service, "Supermarket Facts," *Food Marketing Institute*, 2018.

9   **Once, talking to a slaughter plant supervisor:** Conversation with author at USDA APHIS Veterinary Services, High Path Avian Influenza Team Training, January 21, 2016.

10   **140 birds a minute:** Kimberly Kindy, "USDA plan to speed up poultry-processing lines could increase risk of bird abuse," *Washington Post*, October 29, 2013.

Part I. Salad Days at Trader Joe's

13   **"These days, it's not enough to simply produce fruit":** Gustave Rivière, as quoted in Susanne Freidberg's exquisite *Fresh: A Perishable History* (New York: Belknap Press, 2010).

13   **This is late Friday afternoon, October 1965:** This scene was re-created based on interviews with Joe Coulombe in winter 2015 and 2018, and enhanced by his descriptions in his unpublished autobiography *The Wages of Success: How Trader Joe Coulombe Made It Happen*. Background and physical description on the Tail O' the Cock were additionally fleshed out through Southern California nostalgia websites such as Oldlarestaurants.com.

14   **frequented by Bogart and Gable, Bette Davis and Bela Lugosi:** Marc Wanamaker, *San Fernando Valley: Images of America* (Charleston: Arcadia Publishing, 2011).

14   **About 250 men running five hundred daily routes, six days a week:**
      Allen Liles, *Oh Thank Heaven!: The Story of the Southland
      Corporation* (Dallas: Southland Corporation, 1977).

14   **massive industrialized compounds with 100,000 cows:** The largest
      of which would be the Mudanjiang city dairy in China, spanning
      22,500,000 acres.

15   **they eject an especially rich and creamy milk . . . marked the
      Guernsey as premium:** Josh Harkinson, "You're Drinking the
      Wrong Kind of Milk," *Mother Jones*, March 12, 2014.

15n   **Merritt Jr. sits on the last crumbling vestiges of an empire:** Judy
      Pasternak and Jill Stewart, "A Lasting Legacy: Merritt Adamson
      Jr's Land Dealings Changed Malibu Forever," *Los Angeles Times*,
      March 16, 1986; David K. Randall, *The King and Queen of
      Malibu: The True Story of the Battle for Paradise* (New York:
      W. W. Norton and Company, 2016).

17   **Ice might feel like a modern luxury, but it's not:** Gavin
      Weightman, *The Frozen Water Trade: A True Story* (New York:
      Hachette Books, 2004).

17   **In 1890, it opened the first ice manufacturing plant in Texas:** Allen
      Liles, *Oh Thank Heaven!: The Story of the Southland Corporation*
      (Dallas: Southland Corporation, 1977).

17   **sold at its own proprietary chain of "ice docks":** Although the ice
      made for the Southland docks was artificial, its use by consumers
      was identical to the way they used the ice harvested from lakes,
      i.e., they would store it at home in an insulated wooden cabinet
      called the icebox. Home refrigeration wouldn't come into the
      mainstream for almost another fifty years, when nontoxic, albeit
      ozone-slaughtering Freon, was developed in the 1940s.

17   **By 1951, it was Texas's largest retailer of beverages:** Ibid.

17   **Southland will open 398 new stores in 1965 alone:** Ibid.

21   **That he can read 1,200 words per minute:** LeRoy Watson, former
      vice president of operations at Trader Joe's, to author. Listening to
      these claims, I heard them less as fact and more as a desire to

convey a sense of awe. Can Joe really read at 1,200 words a minute? It doesn't matter. LeRoy wasn't the only person to note Joe's abilities as a speed reader, and what I believe these men were trying to convey is Joe is exceptional in a way they can't really describe. He is a man who simply outmatches most men.

21   **That he adds, multiplies, or divides lists of figures in his brain quicker:** Robin Guentert, former president of Trader Joe's, to author.

22   **he called them Theory Papers:** Access to a surviving (but incomplete) set of Joe Coulombe's Theory Papers was generously made possible through Alice Coulombe and several early employees who collected and saved them.

23   **Joe disembarked in St. Barts . . . the opposite of panic:** Per Alice Coulombe, interview with author.

23   **From Ape to Man:** This section would have been impossible to write without reference to the engrossing works of Rachel Bowlby's *Carried Away: The Invention of Modern Shopping* (New York: Columbia University Press, 2002); Tracey Deutsch's *Building a Housewife's Paradise: Gender, Politics, and American Grocery Stores in the Twentieth Century* (Chapel Hill: University of North Carolina Press, 2010); James M. Mayo's *The American Grocery Store: The Business Evolution of an Architectural Space* (Santa Barbara: Praeger, 1993); Shelly L. Koch's *A Theory of Grocery Shopping* (London: Bloomsbury, 2012); Randolph McAusland's *Supermarkets: 50 Years of Progress: The History of a Remarkable American Institution* (Toronto: Maclean Hunter, 1980); Max M. Zimmerman's *The Super Market: A Revolution in Distribution* (New York: McGraw Hill, 1955); Susanne Freidberg's *Fresh: A Perishable History* (New York: Belknap Press, 2010); and Jeffrey M. Pilcher's *Food History: Critical and Primary Sources* (London: Bloomsbury Press, 2014). All praise to these more serious scholars, all errors mine.

23   **About two-thirds the size of a convenience store:** William Greer, *America the Bountiful: How the Supermarket Came to Main Street: An Oral History* (New York: Beatrice Companies, 1986).

23   **staffed by two to four male clerks, working for a dollar a day:** Ibid.

24   **the walls jammed with boxes of clothing:** Descriptions here cobbled together from a series of priceless photographs of general stores and primary source descriptions in: William Greer, *America the Bountiful: How the Supermarket Came to Main Street: An Oral History* (New York: Beatrice Companies, 1986); Julian H. Handler, *The Food Industry Executive's Pleasure Reader* (New York: Media Books, 1969); and Richard Longstreth, *The Drive-In, Supermarket, and the Transformation of Commercial Space in Los Angeles 1914–1941* (Cambridge: The MIT Press, 2000).

24n   **Rural areas might also have what was called a tree butcher:** Ibid.

25   **Prices were typically unmarked . . . The indigent and poor allowed to buy the rot everyone else had passed over for pennies:** James M. Mayo, *The American Grocery Store: The Business Evolution of an Architectural Space* (Santa Barbara: Praeger, 1993); William Greer, *America the Bountiful: How the Supermarket Came to Main Street: An Oral History* (New York: Beatrice Companies, 1986).

25   **transactions . . . were handled almost exclusively on credit . . . settle up only once or twice a year:** Shelly L. Koch, *A Theory of Grocery Shopping* (London: Bloomsbury, 2012).

25   **One early supermarket owner remembers his father's general store:** William Greer, *America the Bountiful: How the Supermarket Came to Main Street: An Oral History* (New York: Beatrice Companies, 1986).

26   **Paperboard . . . only began to be used for commerce in 1817:** Stanley Sacharow and Roger Griffen, *Food Packaging: A Guide for the Supplier, Processor, and Distributor* (New York: AVI Publishing, 1970).

26   Then, in the 1850s, corrugated cardboard . . . gentlemen's hats is: Matt Blitz, "How the Cardboard Box Was Invented," www .gizmodo.com, February 9, 2015.

26   **until, in 1890, Robert Gair of Brooklyn begins to manufacture:** Allen Smith, *Robert Gair: A Study* (New York: Dial Press, 1939).

26n   **packaged food is responsible for one-fifth of all manufacturing:** Thomas Hine, *The Total Package: The Evolution and Secret Meaning of Boxes, Bottles, Cans, and Tubes* (New York: Back Bay Books, 1997).

27n   **The brand itself is ancient:** Ibid.

27   **Robert Gair's own son tells the befuddled company "You need a name":** Diana Twede, Susan Selke, Donatien-Pascal Kamdem, and David Shires, *Cartons, Crates, and Corrugated* (Lancaster, PA: DEStech Publications, 2015); James Beniger, *The Control Revolution: Technological and Economic Origins of the Information Society* (New York: Harvard University Press, 1989).

28   **lauding the package as proxy for security, as barrier:** Early processed-bread magnate Edward Atkinson speaks for them all when he defends his less flavorful bagged product by nonchalantly saying, "I do not fancy paws or perspiration in my bread."

28   **Clarence Saunders, a classic American eccentric:** Charles Patrick and Joseph Mooney, *The Mid-South and Its Builders: Being the Story of the Development and a Forecast of the Richest Agricultural Region in the World* (Memphis: Thomas Briggs Company, 1920); George Morris, *Men of the South* (New Orleans: The James of Jones Company, 1922); John Brooks, "A Corner in Piggly Wiggly," *New Yorker,* June 6, 1959.

29   **a new type of novelty restaurant called the "cafeteria":** Charles Perry, "The Cafeteria: An L.A. Original," *Los Angeles Times,* November 3, 2003.

29   **In 1898, Childs Restaurant in New York City riffs:** Ibid.

29 **One day, watching beady-eyed piglets charge a trough, Saunders decides:** Michael Freeman, *Clarence Saunders and the Founding of Piggly Wiggly: The Rise and Fall of a Memphis Maverick* (Charleston: The History Press, 2011).

30 **Passing through the turnstile, the customer enters an unconscious bargain:** I'm indebted to Rachel Bowlby's wonderful *Carried Away* for this fantastic insight.

30 **saving money becomes an act of loyalty for family, picky acquisition:** And here I am grateful to Daniel Miller, whose writing in *A Theory of Shopping* on the meaning Britain's families gained from their shopping helped clarify my thinking on the subject.

30 **By 1930 . . . the grocery store leaves him to take one final leap:** Saunders, however, has an absolutely fascinating denouement, foreshadowing in form if not detail modern grocery's thrall and capture by private equity and cost-obsessed bankers. He would never finish building his Pink Palace. Instead, with the ballroom half constructed, the swimming pool half filled, he gets pulled into a Wall Street power play. East Coast "short" sellers target the Piggly Wiggly, spreading entirely false rumors the chain is about to collapse, hoping to depress the stock price and make a quick profit. Saunders won't have it. He cajoles a wide swath of southern bankers to loan him enough money to buy every single Piggly Wiggly share out there—to "corner" the market—and break the shorts by raising price. At this, he is unbelievably successful, pulling off what is generally recognized as the last true corner on Wall Street. The price of Piggly Wiggly shoots from $39 per share to $60, then—in a single morning—when Saunders demands delivery of all outstanding shorts—from $75 to $124. The shorts are ruined. The "boob from Tennessee" is triumphant. Right up to the moment the New York Stock Exchange decides to change the rules and bail out the shorts—many of whom likely sit on its

board—by announcing a complete halt on all Piggly Wiggly trading. This gives the short traders a chance to track down the few outstanding shares Saunders hasn't cornered. Agents are dispatched to faraway locations—the attic trunks of Albuquerque, safe deposit boxes in Sioux City—all while Saunders's backers begin to panic and demand payback on his initial loans. The result is a complete reversal. Despite beating the shorts fair and square, Saunders loses not only his Pink Palace but the Piggly Wiggly chain as a whole. It will limp forward in name to the present day, but without the energy or innovation of its founder.

31 **Cullen is working at the then midsized chain Kroger:** Max M. Zimmerman, *The Super Market: A Revolution in Distribution* (New York: McGraw-Hill, 1955).

31 **"I would be the 'miracle man' of the grocery business":** Ibid.

31 **This is the blueprint:** Big stores had been tried before, from the gimmicky, no-doubt-enraging Alpha Beta in Los Angeles, which insisted on stocking every item in its gargantuan twelve-thousand-square-foot shop in alphabetical order, to famous department stores stretching back to Le Bon Marché in France. But using size to lower price? And to lower price to such a degree as to create actual vertiginous hysteria? And then to rely on the increased sales volume to fuel profits? This was Cullen's great genius.

31 **He drafts a letter of almost fantastical specificity:** Max M. Zimmerman, *The Super Market: A Revolution in Distribution* (New York: McGraw-Hill, 1955).

32 **Nobody had ever seen anything like it . . . Housewives:** Thomas Hine, *The Total Package: The Evolution and Secret Meaning of Boxes, Bottles, Cans, and Tubes* (New York: Back Bay Books, 1997).

32 **in-store mascots and costumes, parades:** Rachel Bowlby, *Carried Away: The Invention of Modern Shopping* (New York: Columbia University Press, 2002).

32n **Rachel Bowlby refers . . . as a "happy infantilization":** Ibid.

33 **a spot-check in 1934:** Max M. Zimmerman, *The Super Market: A Revolution in Distribution* (New York: McGraw Hill, 1955).

33 **"Mass! Mass! That's the key":** I. M. Baker, "Steps to Success in Self-Service Store," *Chain Store Age*, January 1941.

33 **By 1940, the average store had grown to 9,000 square feet:** Max M. Zimmerman, *The Super Market: A Revolution in Distribution* (New York: McGraw-Hill, 1955).

33 **Today a Costco or Walmart can easily reach 200,000 square feet:** Jasen Lee, "Salt Lake City Costco becomes largest in the world," *Deseret News*, October 31, 2015.

33 **Sylvan Goldman . . . introduced the shopping cart in 1937:** Terry P. Wilson, *The Cart That Changed the World* (Tulsa: University of Oklahoma Press, 1978).

33 **By 1952, you had the Nest Cart Junior:** Ibid.

34 **the 1956 International Food Congress in Rome:** Tracey Deutsch, *Building a Housewife's Paradise: Gender, Politics, and American Grocery Stores in the Twentieth Century* (Chapel Hill: University of North Carolina Press, 2010).

34 **the Italian women went berserk:** Paul Hoffman, "Roman matrons fall for one stop shop," *Business Week*, July 7, 1956; "Crowds Throng American Supermarket," *Chain Store Age*, July 1956, as found through Deutsch, 2010.

34 **Pope Pius XII himself weighed in:** Pius PP. XII, *Address of Pope Pius XII to the Third International Congress on the Distribution of Food Products*, July 22, 1956.

34 **when Khrushchev toured Washington, D.C.:** Tracey Deutsch, *Building a Housewife's Paradise: Gender, Politics, and American Grocery Stores in the Twentieth Century* (Chapel Hill: University of North Carolina Press, 2010).

34n **Later, when Boris Yeltsin made an unscheduled stop at a Randalls:** Stefanie Asin, "Yeltsin Loves the Free Market," *Houston Chronicle*, September 17, 1989.

35   **the store Joe would go on to create:** The following narrative is based on several different sources, most prominently: Joe Coulombe and Alice Coulombe, who sat for separate interviews; Joe Coulombe's unpublished autobiography *The Wages of Success: How Trader Joe Coulombe Made It Happen* made available by its author; multiple interviews with early Trader Joe's employees, including LeRoy Watson (Joe's first employee at Pronto Markets), Robin Guentert (former president of Trader Joe's West), and Doug Rauch (former president of Trader Joe's), each of whom stayed with the chain for thirty-plus years. These interviews were supplemented by current and former TJ's employees who prefer to remain anonymous, as well as current and former suppliers to the chain who prefer to remain anonymous. Numerous trade write-ups on the chain were also invaluable. I'd particularly call out a 2005 interview with Joe Coulombe by Tim Morris of Coriolis Research as extremely helpful in getting my feet on the ground and providing context so others would talk to me.

36   **He commodified individuality itself:** Although I had already made this connection with the help of Trader Joe himself, hat tip to Timothy Noah of *Slate*, whose 1999 article on TJ's and Restoration Hardware makes a very similar point all on its own without (presumably) the benefit of having the Trader lay it out for him.

36   **When it comes to sales per foot for chains:** Ashley Lutz in "How Trader Joe's Sells Twice as Much as Whole Foods," *Business Insider*, October 7, 2014, puts TJ's sales per square foot at $1,730 and nearest grocery competitor Whole Foods at $930 per square foot. In comparing the chain to Apple and Tiffany, I am making a trickier comparison in that TJ's as a privately owned firm is not included in many of the broader lists that year (nor are its numbers updated year to year). But if its 2014 numbers are placed on *Fortune*'s 2015 list, it ranks third or fourth, and granting TJ's moderate growth in the 2015 year, this claim feels more than

reasonable. But regardless of precise positioning, the larger point about absolute awesome sales per square foot for a grocer seems inarguable. (Phil Wahba, "Apple extends lead in U.S. top 10 retailers by sales per square foot," *Fortune*, March 13, 2015.)

36 **It is consistently listed as one of Glassdoor and *Fortune*'s 100 Best Companies to Work For:** Aine Cain, "Trader Joe's is one of the best places to work in the US," *Business Insider*, July 12, 2018; Elaine Watson, "Quality and price propel Trader Joe's to the top of dunnhumby's retailer preference index," https://www .foodnavigator-usa.com/Article/2018/01/16/Trader-Joe-s-tops -dunnhumby-retailer-preference-index, January 16, 2018.

36 **For the entire twenty-five years of Joe's term, net worth grew:** Joe Coulombe to author.

36 **a thriving import-export business known as Pirate Joe's opened in response:** Chester Dawson, "This Pirate Sells Treasures from Trader Joe's to Canadians," *Wall Street Journal*, March 7, 2015.

36 **invented modern consumer staples like almond butter:** Multiple TJ's buyers and executives described their foray into almond butter as an invention, attributing it to buyer Doug Rauch in the early 1970s. This is a hard claim to verify. At the time, almond butter was not being sold by supermarkets (or health food stores), nor produced by any other major manufacturer. It required a novel grinding process distinct from peanut butter that TJ's had to develop, and then find a manufacturer—in this case a small religious sect in Oregon—to pilot. That said, there are references to using almonds to make "butter" dating back to the 1920s in trade magazines, and I find it hard to believe that someone in the Middle East didn't dabble with a similar process in the centuries preceding, so at the very least it seems like a case of multiple discovery. What does seem clear is TJ's was the first to mass-produce and commercialize the stuff in a way that led to its current prominent position on our shelves.

36   **sold excellent Brie from France cheaper than Velveeta in America:**
     To get this price, Trader Joe's had to reinvent the cheese supply
     chain so radically they almost undermined their own effort,
     presenting a product too fresh for its customers to recognize. At
     the time, in 1977, all Brie was shipped through New York—
     because that was the shortest distance from Europe—where it
     would then be trucked west, touched and transferred several
     times in the process. Given these opportunities for spoilage, New
     York cheese importers never shipped their freshest stuff west,
     instead filling out California orders with lower grades. "We had
     employees circle the store with samples," LeRoy Watkins, the
     buyer in charge of the deal, told me. "But if we told people it was
     Brie, they'd say, 'Oh I can't stand that stuff, it smells like wet
     diapers.' And because we were selling it for $1.99 per pound,
     when every other places sold it for $8.99 per pound, all our
     customers naturally assumed we had an inferior version of a
     product they already hated!" About to lose money on a high-
     quality product they had invested considerable resources into, the
     chain shifted gears and started advertising it as a *new* cheese from
     France. "Sales picked up from there," LeRoy explained. "By the
     end we were selling more Brie in our tiny number of stores than
     the entire rest of the country combined. But it took reformulating
     the supply chain, two years of research, refining the timing so it
     aged en route to us—all just for this one item."

37   **The produce is hit-or-miss:** This is probably the number one
     question I got while writing this book: Why is the produce at
     Trader Joe's so shoddy when everything else there is so great?
     Without commenting on the latter portion of the question, my
     guess on the former is that it's entirely intentional. In grocery,
     perishables are sold in tiers that reflect freshness. The shorter the
     shelf life, the cheaper it is. Traditional retailers won't touch "short
     code" perishables; they will literally rot on their shelves. But by

maximizing in-store turnover, i.e., the speed they flip their inventory, TJ's can load up on it and offer unmatchable prices in the process. If it all goes well, the customer experience is flawless. Of course, even minor hiccups, and the short code stuff gets uneven quick. This emphasis on turnover also completes a largely hidden design feature of the chain: the crowded stores, the massive lines, the shelves that look ransacked in a pre-snowstorm, postapocalyptic manner at the end of an ordinary day, the extreme attention to demographics, even the stinginess of not opening a new store in an area that is begging for one, all begin to make sense. To function properly, a Trader Joe's depends on extreme turnover: a base of shoppers intent on flooding its stores and devouring its entire inventory daily.

41 **The Borderland was a single-lane gravel road:** Thomas R. Beeman, "Road Building Under Fire," *Western Highways Builder,* July 31, 1920.

41 **In one stretch, a surveyor counted five:** Ibid.

41 **gasoline was generally bought out of a barrel:** American Museum of Natural History, "Fill 'er Up!," https://americanhistory.si.edu /america-on-the-move/fill-up, accessed August 30, 2018; John A. Jakle and Keith A. Sculle, *The Gas Station in America* (Baltimore: Johns Hopkins University Press, 1994).

41 **The great naturalist Aldo Leopold once said, "Game is":** Aldo Leopold, *Game Management* (New York: C. Scribner Sons, 1933).

43 **Pronto will pay employees $7,000 per year . . . the precise union equivalent:** Joe Coulombe to Tim Morris, "A conversation with Joe Coulombe," *Coriolis Research,* March 2005.

45 **"Certified was everything . . . All our product came from":** Robin Guentert to author.

48 **the first "jumbo" jet, would take four years, and the labor of fifty thousand mechanics:** Ed Van Jinte, "The Unexpected Success of the Boeing 747," *Works That Work,* December 2017.

49 **In 1937, the average airplane carried only 6.5 passengers:** Federal Aviation Administration, *Economic Impact Report 2015*, January 2015.

49 **The 747 could hold nearly five hundred . . . two and a half times its immediate predecessor:** Van Jinte, "The Unexpected Success of the Boeing 747," *Works That Work*, December 2017.

49 **In 1937, a flight from New York to Los Angeles took over eighteen hours:** Henry Ladd Smith, *Airways: The History of Commercial Aviation in the United States* (New York: Knopf, 1942).

49 **for the pleasure you would pay:** The National Air and Space Museum, "America By Air," https://airandspace.si.edu/exhibitions /america-by-air/online/, accessed August 30, 2018.

49 **over 80 percent of Americans had still not set foot:** Henry Ladd Smith, *Airways: The History of Commercial Aviation in the United States* (New York: Knopf, 1942).

49 **Within a year, the 747 had cut the cost of flying in half:** Howard Slutsken, "Five ways Boeing's 747 jumbo jet changed travel," www .cnn.com/travel/article/boeing-747-jumbo-jet-travel/index.html, November 7, 2017; updated February 8, 2019.

51n **The first TJ's would open with one hundred brands of scotch:** Joe Coulombe to author.

51 **It's hard to imagine tiki as sincere:** Thoughts on tiki informed by Wayne Curtis's *And a Bottle of Rum: A History of the New World in Ten Cocktails* (New York: Broadway Books, 2018); Sven A. Kirsten's *The Book of Tiki* (New York: Taschen Books, 2000); and Tim Glazner's *Mai-Kai: History and Mystery of the Iconic Tiki Restaurant* (Atglen, PA: Schiffer Publishing, 2016).

52 **Jungle Cruise at Disneyland:** Descriptions informed by archival video of the ride and Joe Coulombe.

52 **The perfect refuge from the encroaching, very real threats of a complex multicultural society:** Richard Nixon would validate this theory a few years later when he announced that iconic tiki spot Trader Vic's was his favorite restaurant in the world.

54 **the manager of that first store was a semi-functional alcoholic:** Robin Guentert to author.

62 **"Of course the rhetoric is nice," one buyer tells me:** Doug Rauch to author.

63 **When Whole Foods launched its 365 brand:** Joe Coulombe to Tim Morris, "A Conversation with Joe Coulombe," *Coriolis Research*, March 2005.

63 **In a series of internal memos:** These being Theory Paper No. 24—Intensive Buying ("Any fool with buying power . . ."); Theory Paper No. 23—Trader Joe's as a Hunter Forager ("What distinguishes our products . . ."); and Theory Paper No. 20— Value Added Retailing ("Bringing information to bear . . .").

66 **"Dyslexia lurks in the brain of every left-hander, which means we see the world differently":** Joe Coulombe, *The Wages of Success: How Trader Joe Coulombe Made It Happen* (unpublished, 2007).

68 **Karl and Theo Albrecht were born:** Dieter Brandis, *Bare Essentials: The Aldi Way of Retailing* (New York: Cyan Communications, 2004).

69 **The boys . . . came of age selling baked bread:** Dennis Hevesi and Jack Ewing, "Karl Albrecht, a Founder of Aldi Stores, Dies at 94," *New York Times*, July 21, 2014.

69 **Block by block, Essen was reduced:** Allied bombers dropped 36,429 imperial tons of explosives on Essen, leaving 90 percent of the city center destroyed, along with the majority of the suburbs. A single night raid in March 1943 left fifty thousand people homeless.

69 **1,200 workers sleeping in a space with only ten toilets:** William Shirer, *The Rise and Fall of the Third Reich* (New York: Simon and Schuster, 1959).

70 **A typical ALDI was 6,000 square feet but held only 280 SKUs:** Dieter Brandis, *Bare Essentials: The Aldi Way of Retailing* (New York: Cyan Communications, 2004).

70 **after a heated discussion about carrying cigarettes:** Joe Coulombe to author.

Part II. Distribution of Responsibility

75 **"Emerson, in his spare stony New England":** Randall Jarrell, *A Sad Heart at the Supermarket: Essays and Fables* (New York: Atheneum Press, 1967).

81 **The vents gush A/C:** There are laws against this idling with endless A/C. But they are so proudly ignored, with truckers bragging about their willingness to pay the fine, that the A/C becomes one of those acts of personal liberty that is meaningful precisely because it's not at all symbolic, i.e., a tiny comfort in a life that is plenty hard enough without also sweating yourself to sleep at night.

84 **10.7 billion tons of freight per year:** Bureau of Transportation Statistics, Table 2-1: Weight of Shipments of Transportation Mode: 2012, 2015, 2045 (Washington D.C.: U.S. G.P.O., 2017).

84 **350 pounds per man, woman, and child. Per day:** Steve Viscelli, *The Big Rig: Trucking and the Decline of the American Dream* (Oakland: University of California Press, 2016).

84 **It is the most common form of employment:** Quoctrung Bui, "The Most Common Job in Every State," https://www.npr.org/sections/money/2015/02/05/382664837/map-the-most-common-job-in-every-state, February 5, 2015.

85 **it is one of the most dangerous jobs:** Bureau of Labor Statistics, *Hours-based fatal injury rates by industry, occupation, 2016* (Washington D.C.: U.S. G.P.O., 2018).

89 **For this Lynne gets $1,231 gross:** The figures in this section and the following all come from my conversation with Lynne as described in the text. I did not ask for, nor did I view, receipts. But the figures and deductions seem well in line with industry norms and were completely unsurprising to the truckers I ran them by to triangulate during fact-checking.

90 **Some of which she can't completely explain even as they bleed her paycheck:** All of these deductions are pulled automatically before

Lynne receives a cent. This adds a further hurdle: if you notice a discrepancy, contesting it isn't so easy as taking time on your lunch break to go down to HR and talk it over. Truckers are on the road constantly; they have little relationship with their carrier other than their dispatcher or load planner, both of whom exist in a different time zone, and who likely have seen so much turnover they view you as disposable. This doesn't mean it is impossible to contest something; it means that if you find yourself working for an unscrupulous company they can make that process so difficult that you almost always give up. And it is one of the inviolate laws of humanity that if an opportunity for unscrupulousness exists, nasty people will notice and gravitate toward it. Which is precisely the larger problem of trucking.

94 **Lease-to-own programs in OTR trucking seem like both to me:** The conclusions in this section were informed by a wide array of sources ranging from the human voices I met on the road with Lynne to academic ethnographies on the OTR trucking industry. In particular this section would not have been possible without the academic work of Steve Viscelli, *The Big Rig: Trucking and the Decline of the American Dream* (Oakland: University of California Press, 2016); Michael Belzer, *Sweatshops on Wheels: Winners and Losers in Trucking Deregulation* (New York: Oxford University Press, 2000); and Shane Hamilton, *Trucking Country: The Road to America's Wal-Mart Economy* (Princeton, NJ: Princeton University Press, 2014). Additionally, Aubrey Smith's *The Truth About Trucking*, 2009, a self-published book by a thirty-year trucking veteran, and Desiree Wood's *TruckerDesiree* (blog) were beyond helpful, full of insight, wisdom, and difficult gray truths often left out of the more academic books.

94 **who cruise for drivers from homeless shelters:** From the second amended brief for *Roberts and McKay v. C.R. England*, No. 3:11-cv-02586 (U.S. Dist. Court, 2011): "Defendants also employ

recruiters that cruise for Drivers in such places as homeless shelters and soup kitchens."

94 **"Guaranteed jobs!" "No experience? No problem!":** Robert Boulter, lawyer specializing in trucker law, to author; Desiree Wood, trucking advocate and former trucker, to author.

95 **they are pounded with further praise for seizing this chance to control their own destiny:** There is a disturbing religiosity to many of these programs, where the language of self-sufficiency is overlaid with Jesus, and the decision to give a second chance to someone in recovery is presented, not as a business decision, but as a mission. "The message was Jesus loved us and so we should do exactly what our trainer said," one trucker tells me of his training with Covenant Transport.

95 **"They told me to ease up on the honesty speech":** *Dan Rather Reports,* "Queen of the Road," Season 4, Episode 32, October 20, 2009. Not a small problem either. A 2019 survey determined that over 300,000 truck drivers would likely fail a drug test, Alliance for Driver Safety & Security, 2019.

96 **Trucking used to be a middle-class job:** Steve Viscelli, *The Big Rig: Trucking and the Decline of the American Dream* (Oakland: University of California Press, 2016).

98 **over the last ten years industry turnover in trucking:** Burney Simpson, "Fleet Seek Drivers as Turnover Rate Hits 95%," *Transport Topics,* December 7, 2017; Eric Miller, "Driver Turnover Rates Decline, but Trucking Expects Reversal," *Transport Topics,* June 23, 2008.

98 **The turnover at a top law firm is 17 percent . . . deemed a crisis:** Mark Levin and Bruce MacEwen, "Assessing Lawyer Traits and Finding a Fit for Success," therightprofile.com, accessed August 30, 2018; "The Hidden Costs of Law Firm Attrition," *Beyond Billables* (blog), www.beyondbillables.com/blog/the-hidden-costs -of-law-firm-attrition, April 20, 2018.

98 **The turnover at Starbucks is around 65 percent:** Bijan Shahrokhi, "Escaping the Burn and Churn Employee Treadmill," *QSR*, August, 2014.

98 **the industry has figured out . . . make money off their replacement:** Desiree Wood to author.

99 **Moving freight from California to D.C. takes seven to ten days on the rails:** Ibid.

100 **Large trucking companies have one hundred new recruits coming in every week:** In *CRST v. J. B. Hunt Transport*, U.S. District Court, 2006. Both companies agreed on the consequences of the driver shortage, noting that "Hunt accordingly has to hire an average of 300 drivers each week . . . CRST must hire, on average, nearly 100 drivers per week."

101 **CRST . . . brings in approximately ten thousand new drivers each year alone:** Desiree Wood to author, and completely in line with the figures from the above lawsuit assuming a healthy proportion of recruits do not complete training.

102 **A recent class action suit certified against trucking giant C.R. England in 2017 alleges:** *Charles Roberts and Kenneth McKay v. C.R. England*, No. 2:12-cv-00302-RJS-BCW (U.S. District Court, 2018).

103 **Drivers who report on-the-job injuries might find a no-fault accident suddenly shifted into 50 percent fault on their DAC:** Robert Boulter, "Blacklisted Truck Driver Awarded over $100,000 for False DAC Report," http://www.boulter-law.com/2016/01/29 /blacklisted-truck-driver-awarded-over-100000-for-false-dac -report/, January 29, 2016.

103 **abandonment of equipment might appear on his DAC . . . refuses an overweight load:** "Marten Transport ordered to pay 51k to driver for refusing overweight load," http://www.boulter-law.com /2016/02/29/marten-transport-ordered-to-pay-51k-to-driver-for -refusing-overweight-load/, February 29, 2016; "Refusal to Drive

Unsafe truck—Driver Awarded $55k," www.boulter-law.com, March 14, 2016.

103 **a profession where being tossed off a truck is a common:** "Getting thrown off the truck in the middle of nowhere? Physically pulled out of a cab, having a gun waved in your face and then having your bags tossed out the side? Oh, I don't think most people would think twice about that . . . That doesn't mean that's right. But I think most people will defend that as normal," Desiree Wood, a longtime observer and trucking advocate, tells me. As if to underscore the point, Desiree—the advocate—has a post on her personal blog, "When is it okay to throw a student off the truck?"

106 **A massive 270-person civil discrimination case:** *EEOC v. CRST Van Expedited, Inc.,* No. 09-3764 (8th Cir. 2012).

106 **The case ultimately hinged not on the veracity of the allegations but on whether the EEOC had properly honored a statutory obligation before filing the lawsuit:** A statutory obligation that grows more maddening the longer you consider it. As a federal agency, the EEOC is required by law to try to settle all claims without going to trial. And after its initial investigation, the EEOC did just this with the first cohort of victims it uncovered. But as the case proceeded, and word got out, the number of women alleging abuse kept expanding—crucially during pretrial discovery when CRST's own internal records detailed another 150 victims it knew about but hadn't previously disclosed. This outpouring, woman after woman coming to light, as clear a sign of the urgency behind the case as you could get, became its legal undoing. The court ruled the EEOC needed to attempt settlement with each new victim *before* bringing a lawsuit—and since the EEOC obviously wasn't doing that, the case currently moving forward as they accumulated—the judge dismissed the whole thing out of hand.

108 **At the various distribution centers I visit:** In addition to the warehouses I snuck in with truckers, I attended an industry

tour of the Hunts Point Produce Market in the Bronx via the New York Produce Show and Conference, which informed these descriptions.

109 **That fresh apple you bite into has typically been sitting in dormancy for close to a year:** Multiple apple vendors at New York Produce Show and Conference to author.

109 **Red cherries . . . Bananas, avocados, tomatoes, and limes:** Hassan R. El-Ramady, Éva Domokos-Szabolcsy, Neama A. Abdalla, Hussein S. Taha, and Miklós Fári, "Postharvest Management of Fruits and Vegetables Storage," *Sustainable Agriculture Reviews*, Springer International Publishing, 2015; Mohammed Wasim Siddiqui, *Postharvest Management of Horticultural Crops: Practices for Quality Preservation* (Ontario: Apple Academic Press, 2017).

109 **our nation's storage facilities can build for that:** At one point, Michael Pollan asks about Twinkies, "How can the supermarket possibly sell a pair of these synthetic cream-filled pseudocakes for less than a bunch of roots?" His answer is the farm bill and cheap corn subsidies. That is a portion of the truth. But another answer lies here, in the warehouse—and the intrinsic properties of perishability that haunt fresh produce. All those cryogenic rooms cost money. How much would broccoli cost if it had the shelf life of pasta? Cheap indeed.

109 **a jack stretches off its base, extending maybe fifteen feet:** None other than the Big Joe 3,500-pound Counterbalanced Forklift, a 7,500-pound beast, riding on solid pneumatic tires, and capable of extending its mast just over nineteen vertical feet before ripping off down the aisle at forty feet per minute.

Part III. Self-Realization Through Snack

113 **"Men who Achieve—with hands or brain":** James McMillan, *The Way We Were: 1900–1914* (London: Kimber, 1978).

113 **"Gradually I began to realize":** T. J. Jackson Lears, *Fables of Abundance: A Cultural History of Advertising in America* (New York: Basic Books, 1995).

113 **five straight miles of newly laid fuzzy gray carpet:** This is an honest to god estimate based on scrunching over the floor plan of the event with a ruler, counting up the square feet.

114 **Three hundred thousand square feet of demonstration space, eighty thousand products:** Louise Kramer, Public Relations Director of the Fancy Food Show, to author.

117 **whether Paleo is a "trend" or a "fad":** For the curious, a "trend" is a more robust phenomenon lasting decades, while a "fad" tends toward the fleeting, implying a flimsy base. At this particular lecture, we determine Paleo is a fad, though "low-carb" and "meat-centric," two core Paleo concepts, are likely trends. One lecturer explains, you'll know it's a trend when you walk into a gas station and see it marked on every bag of chips in the place.

123 **Slawsa as a food was the creation of a gentleman I'll call Jerome Odell:** Brian Ries, "A little bit slaw, a little bit salsa," *The Sarasota Herald-Tribune*, August 15, 2012, updated August 18, 2012.

124 **And when he brought the stuff out . . . pushing him to make a business:** Carey O'Neil, "Slawsa family recipe launches Chattanooga business," *Times Free Press*, April 3, 2012.

125 **Neither will say a bad word . . . because they won't even say a single word:** All information on Jerome (and Julie's relationship with him) comes from publicly available news reports and blog posts, from his original attempt to get Slawsa on the shelf, available on the web today, and through the Wayback Machine–Internet Archive. I have elected to change his name in the text because he did not desire to participate in the book and I can't think of a good reason why including it would strengthen the book.

126 **they are made up of ideas that seem special to their creators:** Or worse than not special enough, ideas that are *too* special. If your product relies on a completely brilliant new ingredient—say,

chocolate sweetened with low-calorie, high-nutrient lucuma,
another goopy orange superfruit of the Andes—you will be
responsible for consumer education lest they walk right past your
bar without realizing the specialness you have put before them.

126 **prepared foods with the 40 to 50 percent markup that entails:**
Errol Schweizer to author.

133 **A buyer . . . tells me he averages thirty to forty cold calls per day:**
Arthur Ackles, buyer with Roche Bros. Supermarkets, to author.

133 **"Buyers at Whole Foods national are sent five hundred new
products per month":** Errol Schweizer to author.

134 **To make sense of this, let's return to our buyer:** A quick note on
terminology. I am using the word "buyer" here for narrative
continuity as that was the word used by both Ian (of Peeled) and
Annette (the agribusiness consultant). However, at most major
retail chains, the correct term for the person responsible for
these buying decisions is the "category manager"—who oversees
a team that includes analysts (to capture trends), designers (to
arrange the space), and replenishment buyers (to execute deals
already established). The best of these category managers are
part "philosopher, anthropologist, analyst, and architect," in
the phrasing of Errol Schweizer, while the worst are "total
hacks, some obese guy punching the clock deciding what you
should eat."

136 **These payments amount to $9 billion a year in industry profit:**
David Burch and Geoff Lawrence, "Own Brands, Supply Chains
and the Transformation of the Agri-Food System," in
*Supermarket and Agri-food Supply Chains: Transformations in
Production and Consumption* (London: Edward Elgar Pub, 2007).

136 **one national retailer was charging $55,000 for 22 x 12 inches:** Ian
Kelleher to author.

137 **In 2015, trade spend added up to about $76 billion taken in by
retailers:** "The truth is most retailers don't know what *anything*
costs," Kevin Coupe, an industry consultant, explains to me.

"There are so many hidden fees and back-and-forth of money."
This makes calculating trade spend a very murky thing. In his
prescient book *Agentry Agenda*, Glen Terbeek makes the case
that in 1999, intake from trade spend was likely equivalent to
total profits in all of grocery! My 76 billion number is simply the
result of applying the average of 12 to 15 percent for trade spend
to total reported gross revenue. (Bob Cristofono, "CPG Trade
Rate in 2014 at 13.4%," National Promotion Reports, January 30,
2015.)

138 **trade spend . . . was the number two cost for an entrepreneur:**
Blacksmith Applications, "6 Facts about Trade Spending," April
2017; Junaid Qureshi, "A comprehensive guide to pricing and
trade promotion management," www.actionableinsights.online,
April 8, 2017. To be sure, however, this was another stat I heard
frequently but that getting methodologically sound data on was
hard.

138 **And a 2011 Nielsen study suggests that 55 percent of this spending
is extractive:** Eddie Yoon, "See More with Smarter Trade
Promotions," *Harvard Business Review,* July 19, 2012.

138 **Endcaps . . . have been shown to increase sales more than 500
percent:** Barbara Kahn, *Grocery Revolution: The New Focus on the
Consumer* (London: Pearson Press, 1997).

138 ***Frozen & Refrigerated Buyer* . . . estimates the cost of national
rollout:** Warren Thayer, "Vendors Push Back on Slotting," *Frozen
& Refrigerated Buyer,* May 2015.

138 **It pushes retailers away from the Joe Coulombe model of building
food expertise:** For those keeping score, Joe and Trader Joe's hated
these fees. A defining feature of the chain, and a reason it was so
highly regarded by manufacturers, was his refusal to indulge in
them.

141 **the day I am writing this, November 1, is National Calzone Day:**
See nationaldaycalendar.com for the full doozy.

142 **Tony bought a small canning operation in 1972:** "The Golding Farms Story," www.goldingfarms.com, accessed August 30, 2018.

154 **"89 percent who get on the shelf and still fail":** Eighty-nine percent is a number I hear frequently from all sorts of people (including Julie). I believe that it originates from Burt Schorr's April 5, 1961, *Wall Street Journal* article, "Many new products fizzle despite careful planning, publicity." Newer Nielsen data indicates the figure is probably still pretty close to accurate. See Elaine Watson, "Why do 85% of new CPG products fail within two years?" www.foodnavigator-usa.com/Article/2014/07/31/Why -do-85-of-new-CPG-products-fail-within-two-years, July 31, 2014, or John T. Gourville, "Eager Sellers and Stony Buyers: Understanding the Psychology of New-Product Adoption," *Harvard Business Review*, June 2006.

Part IV. The Retail Experience

157 **"What does it mean to have and display a consumer attitude?":** Zygmunt Bauman, *Think Sociologically: An Introduction for Everyone* (Cambridge: Basil Blackwell, 1990).

157 **Orientation begins in a drab corner of the second floor:** Unlike every other section of the book, this portion was written without the knowledge or permission of the various people I met. Further, since I was actually on the job and thus beholden to things beyond my own neurosis, it also leans heavily on handwritten notes and memory rather than audio files. For those reasons, I've changed the names of several people to help protect their identity.

166 **In produce, where I do a brief stint for a Whole Foods competitor:** In the winter of 2015, I also worked for Gristedes for a blink.

169 **the *New York Times* published an exposé of sorts about Trader Joe's:** Noam Scheiber, "At Trader Joe's, Good Cheer May Hide Complaints," *New York Times*, November 3, 2016.

170 **Walter's day begins at four a.m.:** Re-created with the help of Walter. I did not actually sleep over and creep alongside him at four a.m.

175 **A typical automobile plant contains:** Marshall Fisher and Ananth Raman, *The New Science of Retailing* (New York: Harvard Business Review Press, 2010).

175 **Even by the early 1920s, assembly lines:** James Womack, Daniel Jones, and Daniel Roos, *The Machine That Changed the World* (New York: The Free Press, 2007).

175 **Henry Ford's River Rouge plant was an actual kingdom, with sixteen million feet:** Steven Watts, *The People's Tycoon: Henry Ford and the American Century* (New York: Vintage, 2006).

176 **Prior to mass production, cars were crafted by hand, one by one, the exterior metal beaten:** James Womack, Daniel Jones, and Daniel Roos, *The Machine That Changed the World* (New York: The Free Press, 2007).

176 **In 1950, it was a small family-run business:** Eiji Toyoda, *Toyota: Fifty Years in Motion* (New York: Kodansha USA, 1987); Jeffery Liker, *The Toyota Way: 14 Management Principles from the World's Greatest Manufacturer* (New York: McGraw-Hill, 2004).

177 **Taiichi Ohno, went to the United States . . . had a vision:** Taiichi Ohno, *Toyota Production System: Beyond Large Scale Production* (Boca: Productivity Press, 1988).

177 **it made Toyota the most profitable automaker:** Graham Rapier, "These are the 15 most valuable car brands in the world," *Business Insider*, September 25, 2017.

177 **its net margins grew to be over eight times higher:** Alexander Styhre, *The Innovative Bureaucracy: Bureaucracy in an Age of Fluidity* (New York: Routledge, 2007).

179 ***HR Daily Advisor*, a chirpy blog on the subject, explains:** Steven Bruce, "Just-in-Time Scheduling—Good News and Bad News," *HR Daily Advisor* (blog), December 19, 2016.

179-80 **workers in these conditions had hours that varied month to month from "usual" by almost 50 percent:** Susan Lambert, Peter Fugiel, and Julia Henly, *Schedule Unpredictability Among Early Career Workers in the US Labor Market: A National Snapshot* (Chicago: EINet, 2014).

180 **60 percent of retail workers said . . . available to fulfill *every* work schedule:** Ari Schwartz, Michael Wasser, Merrit Gillard, and Michael Paarlberg, *Unpredictable, Unsustainable: The Impact of Employers' Scheduling Practices in D.C.*, Fiscal Policy Institute, June 2015; Josh Choper, Daniel Schneider, and Kristen Harknett, "Uncertain Time: Precarious Schedules and Job Turnover in the U.S. Service Sector," The Shift Project, 2019.

180 **Amazon . . . recently patented a wristband:** Ceylan Yeginsu, "If Workers Slack Off, the Wristband Will Know. (And Amazon Has a Patent for It.)," *New York Times*, February 1, 2018.

182 **one 2006 study:** Marshall Fisher, Jayanth Krishnan, and Serguei Netessine, "Retail Store Execution: An Empirical Study," papers .ssrn.com, January, 2001.

Part V. When I Look in My Window: Backstage at the Theater of Retail

185 **"The pleasure-seeker will naturally be pushed":** Colin Campbell, *The Romantic Ethic and the Spirit of Modern Consumerism* (New York: Palgrave, 2018).

190 **To give some small context:** I hope it goes without saying that I am simplifying something that is achingly complex. Unfortunately, details of this regulation—from the accuracy of food labels to federal recall abilities to general administrative cultures of independence versus industry suck-ups—is out of the scope of this book. But, suffice to say, they represent a giant, convoluted, actively shifting maze, which functions pretty well in

some areas (food safety) and pretty horrendous in others (fraud), and which has all been weakened by the Trump administration with its stated goal of "deconstruction of the administrative state." For better or worse, food regulation is the administrative state.

190 **in 2009, the Government Accountability Office estimated:** "Seafood Fraud: FDA Program Changes and Better Collaboration Among Federal Agencies Could Improve Detection and Prevention," Government Accountability Office, 2009; Gil Paterson, Kaylee Errecaborde, Nicholas Phelps, "Seafood Fraud in the United States: Current Science and Policy Options," University of Minnesota Food Policy Research Center, 2015.

190 **50 percent of all fresh fruits and 80 percent of all seafood are in fact imported:** Commissioner Margaret Hamburg, "Food Safety Modernization Act: Putting the Focus on Prevention, Food and Drug Administration," https://obamawhitehouse.archives.gov /blog/2011/01/03/food-safety-modernization-act-putting-focus -prevention, accessed August 30, 2018.

190 **found fraud in over 40 percent of the products submitted to it:** Harold Upton, "Seafood Fraud," Congressional Research Service, April 7, 2015.

190 **a whopping 4.5 percent of domestic food production facilities:** Marion Nestle, "The FDA's Food Inspection Problem: One Reason Our Food Isn't Safe," *The Atlantic*, December, 2011.

190 **Bill Marler, the biggest, strongest, and savviest of these tort crusaders:** Wil S. Hylton, "A Bug in the System," *New Yorker*, February 2, 2015.

191 **the Gap would be attacked for its labor:** N. Craig Smith, Sean Ansett, and Lior Erez, "How Gap Inc. Engaged with Its Stakeholders," *MIT Sloan Management Review*, June 22, 2011.

191 ***LIFE* magazine would publish a photo essay:** "Six Cents an Hour," *LIFE*, 1996.

191   **Kathie Lee Gifford would bawl the mascara right out:** ABC, "Kathie Lee Gifford—Transcript #455-2," *Primetime Live*, May 22, 1996.

191   **during a special pre-taped prime-time segment, Kathie Lee:** Ibid.

192   **Price Waterhouse conducted exactly zero supply chain audits. By 1998:** Michael Power, "Evaluating the Audit Explosion," *Law and Policy* 25, no. 3 (July 2003); Timothy Lytton and Lesley McAllister, "Oversight in Private Food Safety Auditing: Addressing Auditor Conflict of Interest," *Wisconsin Law Review*, April 7, 2014.

192   **$50 billion-per-year bucket that is the for-profit auditing industry:** "Auditing Working Conditions: Breaking Through the Conspiracy of Silence," Ethical Trade Initiative, 2015; Genevieve LeBaron, Jane Lister, and Peter Dauvergne, "Governing Global Supply Chain Sustainability Through the Ethical Audit Regime," *Globalizations* 14, no. 6 (2017).

193   **five main export facilities for seafood processor Thai Union:** Andy Hall to author.

193-94n **Top standards organizations are issuing certifications ... but ... "the auditors who certified them were experts in car batteries:** Richard Stiler, "Third Party Audits: What the Food Industry Really Needs," *Food Safety Magazine*, October 2009.

194   **In 1999, there were sizable recalls for meat occurring:** Bill Marler to author.

194   **instead unfolding with all the spontaneity of a doctor's appointment:** Repeated oblivious imposition is a unique form of aggression. It is also one of the few places the audit truly excels. It is not uncommon for larger producers to have two audits a week, every week, the entire year. The result of this haunting is known as "audit fatigue" and it is in its own way a big contributor to gaming standards, encouraging Kabuki theater, generally preventing an authentic culture of trust. LeBaron et al. tell the delightful story of a manufacturer audited to two different standards by two different

retailers. "In one audit the fire extinguisher needs to be 36 inches from the ground. In the next audit, it needs to be 32 inches"—that was eventually resolved by hiring a former auditor as a consultant who recommended the factory "install two hooks and rotate the extinguisher back-and-forth." Your private sector at work! Sonali Rammohan, "Toward a More Responsible Supply Chain: The HP Story," *Supply Chain Management Review*, July 2009; Genevieve LeBaron, Jane Lister, and Peter Dauvergne, "Governing Global Supply Chain Sustainability Through the Ethical Audit Regime," *Globalizations* 14, no. 6 (2017).

194 **A date is set. Inspection questions previewed:** As hinted in the text, the conflicts of interest here are truly impressive. The same auditing firm sent to evaluate the companies will also offer to help them prepare to ensure they will pass. These fees run high—from $5,000 to $30,000—adding lucrative money to the auditing firm's bottom line, keeping everyone excited about keeping the system running. One former auditor reports visiting a manufacturing plant that had "shut down for a full week to prepare." Naturally, "it always passed with flying colors and high scores." Joe Fassier, "Welcome to Certification Nation," *New Food Economy*, October 29, 2015; Richard Stier, "Third Party Audits: What the Food Industry Really Needs," *Food Safety Magazine*, October 2009.

194 **They cannot open locked doors:** Genevieve LeBaron, Jane Lister, and Peter Dauvergne, "Governing Global Supply Chain Sustainability through the Ethical Audit Regime," *Globalizations* 14, no. 6 (2017).

194-95 **Retail brands often give auditing firms strict instructions:** Ibid.

195 **they are duty bound to tell only you:** Ibid.

195 **Factory managers in China can buy software:** Kathy Chu, "A Look at How Some Chinese Factories Lie to Pass Audits," *China Labor Watch*, April 30, 2012.

195 **Li Qiang, founder of the China Labor Watch, explains:** David Barboza, "Questions for Li Quiang of China Labor Watch," *New York Times*, January 26, 2012.

203 **Sociologist Colin Campbell traces this ethic back to the Romantic poets:** Colin Campbell, *The Romantic Ethic and the Spirit of Modern Consumerism: New Extended Edition* (Cham: Palgrave Macmillan, 2018).

203 **instructing the writer to "express what he thinks and feels":** William Wordsworth, *Preface to Lyrical Ballads*, 1801.

203 **Anthropologist Daniel Miller studied purchasing:** Daniel Miller quoted in *Elusive Consumption in Retrospect: Report from the Conference*, edited by Karin M. Ekstrom and Helene Brembeck, Center for Consumer Science, School of Economics and Commercial Law, Goteborg University, 2002.

204 **Cultural theorist Grant McCracken grappled with:** Grant McCracken, *Culture and Consumption: New Approaches to the Symbolic Character of Consumer Goods and Activities* (Bloomington: Indiana University Press, 1990).

205 **supplying content to compete with around twenty-one thousand food-centric blogs:** Sourced from blog directory Technorati in March 2014, via www.besthospitalitydegrees.com, accessed August 20, 2018.

205 **"The dark side of this aspect of consumption":** Grant McCracken, *Culture and Consumption: New Approaches to the Symbolic Character of Consumer Goods and Activities* (Bloomington: Indiana University Press, 1990).

Part VI. The Bottom of the Commodity Chain

213 **"Homo sum: humani nihil a me":** Terence, *Heauton Timorumenos*, act 1, scene 1, line 77.

213 **steel anchor weights concussing the ecosystem:** This description of the benthic trawl is based on conversations with Thai and

Burmese fishermen, descriptions of typical trawl gear from the Food and Agriculture Organization of the United Nations, and conversations with marine biologists and fishery experts.

214 **Fish are attracted by the noise:** J. Main and G. I. Sangster, "A Study of the Fish Capture Process in a Bottom Trawl by Direct Observation from a Towed Underwater Vehicle," *Scottish Fisheries Research Report* 23 (1981).

214 **Tun-Lin is on his knees:** This scene is based on a series of extended interviews with Tun-Lin himself. However, getting the necessary nuance, context, and direction in those interviews would have been impossible without conversations with Phil Robertson, the deputy director of Human Rights Watch Asia Division, Daniel Murphy of Environmental Justice Foundation, Lisa Rende-Taylor of Project Issara, Katrina Nakamura of Sustainability Indicator, and Patima Tungpuchayakul of Labour Protection Network. Additionally, Tun-Lin's interviews were cross-referenced and informed by interviews with at least seven other trafficked migrants held in similar conditions.

215-16 **NGOs estimate 17 to 60 percent of Thai shrimp includes slave labor:** U.S. Department of State Trafficking in Persons Report, Country Narratives, T–Z and Special Cases, Washington, D.C.: U.S. G.P.O., 2014.

216 **The smallest fish, of which there are the most these days:** Daniel Murphy of Environmental Justice Foundation to author; Steven Trent, Daniel Murphy, and Josh Stride, "Pirates and Slaves: How Overfishing in Thailand Fuels Human Trafficking and the Plundering of Our Oceans," Environmental Justice Foundation, February 25, 2015.

217 **Thus is the beginning of the Thai shrimp industry:** This section draws largely on my own experiences in Thailand, including a week-long, cross-country tour of the Thai aquaculture sector designed for overseas investors. However, that lived experience was supplemented invaluably by interviews with Thai seafood

supply chain and aquaculture experts Corey Peet of the Monterey Aquarium, Robins McIntosh of CP Foods, David Kawahigashi of Vannamei 101, Darian McBain of Thai Union, as well as interviews with current managers, brokers, and migrants working in aquaculture facilities at all levels who preferred to remain anonymous.

217 **350,000 metric tons . . . just under 10 percent of the total global supply:** James Anderson, Diego Valderrama, and Darryl Jory, "Shrimp Production Review," Global Aquaculture Alliance, June 2017. From 2011 to 2017, Thai shrimp production has shifted from 650,000 tons to 350,000 tons during the writing of this book. It may rise again after getting disease under control or it may fall because the cost of reforms push industry elsewhere.

217 **the second- or fifth-largest producer after China:** Ibid.

217 **a top supplier to the United States:** Xiaojin Wang, Michael Reed, "Estimation of U.S. Demand for Imported Shrimp," presented at the Southern Agricultural Economics Association Annual Meeting, February 1, 2014; James Anderson, Diego Valderrama, and Darryl Jory, "Shrimp Production Review," Global Aquaculture Alliance, June 2017.

217 **Shrimp are the single most popular, profitable, and widely consumed:** Lynsee Fowler, "Top Ten List Highlights Seafood Consumption Progress," National Fisheries Institute, November 2, 2017.

220 **ponds are packed dense with shrimp, up to ninety per square meter:** Brian Hunter, "A Brief History and Current Status of Shrimp Farming in Thailand," *Shrimp News International,* November 23, 2011; Brian Montrose et al., "Farm Gate Cost of Penaeus vannamei Production (Plus Farming Strategies, Nurseries, and Stocking Densities)," *Shrimp News International,* December 23, 2012.

221 **an immediate and final spasm to each shrimp heart:** Yayra Aku Gbotsyo, "The Effect of Cold Stress on Heat Shock Proteins in

Larvae of the Brine Shrimp," (master's thesis, Saint Mary's University, April 2017).

221 **bag frozen to –30°F:** Raul M. M. Madrid and Harold Philips, "Post-Harvest Handling and Processing," in *Freshwater Prawn Culture* (Oxford: Blackwell Science, 2000).

221 **Each hour of delay . . . lost shelf life:** Theofania Tsironi, Efimia Dermesonlouglou, Maria Giannakourou, and Petros Taokis, "Shelf life modeling of frozen shrimp at variable temperature conditions," *LWT-Food Science and Technology* 42 (2009).

222n **in one of the few investigated cases:** Margie Mason, Robin McDowell, Martha Mendoza, and Esther Htusan, "Global supermarkets selling shrimp peeled by slaves," Associated Press, December 14, 2015.

225 **These shrimp were not grown but caught:** Taras Grescoe, *Bottomfeeder* (New York: Bloomsbury USA, 2008).

225 **ensnaring five pounds of unwanted bycatch for every one pound of salable shrimp:** M. Hall, D. Alverson, and K. Metuzalas, "By-Catch: Problems and Solutions," *Marine Pollution Bulletin* 41 (2000).

225 **prices have fallen while production has increased some 3,000 percent:** E. C. Ashton, "The impact of shrimp farming on mangrove ecosystems," *CAB Reviews: Perspectives in Agriculture, Veterinary Science, Nutrition and Natural Resources*, 2010.

226 **Historically, coastal communities seized on and enhanced tide:** Ibid.

226 **The single great breakthrough came:** Robins MacIntosh to author.

226 **female shrimp who loses a single eyeball:** Umaporn Uawisetwathana, Rungnapa Leelatanawit et al., "Insights into Eyestalk Ablation Mechanism to Induce Ovarian Maturation in the Black Tiger Shrimp," *PLOS ONE*, 2011.

227 **Mangroves razed. Seawalls torn down to allow:** Alfredo Quarto and Sara Lavenhar, "Industrial Aquaculture: Human

Intervention in Natural Law," in *International Food Law and Policy* (New York: Springer Press, 2017).

227 **"You would think, gee, if we can produce them in farms":** Steve Cowan and Barry Schienberg, *Empty Oceans, Empty Nets,* Bullfrog Films, 2002.

227 **It takes two pounds of wild-caught fish to create one pound of shrimp:** A very conservative, industry-friendly ratio. During interviews I was quoted ratios ranging from 3:1 to 6:1.

228n **the horrid ecological:** Steven Trent, Daniel Murphy, and Josh Stride, "Pirates and Slaves: How Overfishing in Thailand Fuels Human Trafficking and the Plundering of Our Oceans," Environmental Justice Foundation, February 25, 2015.

228 **the next day . . . all is rot:** The risk is so great and the tools so limited, it encourages a recklessness of desperation that has given the industry a poor reputation. A smallholder farmer who is going down in a blaze of white spot syndrome can either dump antibiotics and cleaning agents at the problem or lose everything. The responsible option—halt production, eat a crushing loss, and modernize the production facility—is not financially viable. The best shrimp farming has therefore evolved into something requiring considerable wealth and expertise, essentially eliminating the original smallholder. And once those seawalls have come down—and the local fresh water is contaminated with salt—it is impossible for the smallholder to go back to rice. Industry only begets more industry and we can't wish it away.

228-29 **Jonathan Shepherd . . . has estimated the collective toll as ranging up to $20 billion and calls shrimp aquaculture "virtually uninsurable":** *Undercurrent News* (blog), "'Virtually uninsurable' shrimp industry has lost billions to disease since 1990s," https://www.undercurrentnews.com/?s=uninsurable&post_types=post, September 28, 2017.

230 **He tells me he is from Mwabi:** This section is based on a series of
extended interviews with Tun-Lin. It is further informed by my
own reporting in Thailand and Myanmar, including traveling to
Mwabi village, crossing back to Thailand at Myawaddy/Mae Sot,
and attempting to trace portions of Tun-Lin's route to Samut
Sakhon (albeit obviously years after the fact). Finally, details were
cross-referenced and informed by interviews with at least seven
other trafficked migrants held in similar conditions, as well as
experts on trafficked labor such as Patima Tungpuchayakul of the
Labour Protection Network, Andy Hall of the Migrant Workers
Rights Network, Daniel Murphy of Environmental Justice
Foundation, Phil Robertson, the deputy director of Human Rights
Watch Asia Division, and Lisa Rende-Taylor of Project Issara.

239 **At this point, he is twenty-two years old:** As I've tried to indicate
in the main text, Tun-Lin's story did not emerge linearly, and it
was often very difficult to pin down a firm chronology of events.
The twenty-two years of age here is based on an age of fourteen to
sixteen for leaving Myanmar (depending on the interview), five
years on his first boat (consistent across interviews), six months in
the fish processing plant (a detail not even included in all
interviews), as well as accounting for the time of his migration
and captivity. I bring this up not to question Tun-Lin's veracity—
there are no perfect victims; his story need not add up to outside
eyes—but to surface the limitations in forming a coherent
journalistic narrative from a human memory torn by trauma,
time, modesty, and shame.

240 **Up through the 1980s much of the fishing in Thailand:** I'm
indebted to Phil Robertson for laying out this progression so
clearly, an extension of his argument in "From the Tiger to the
Crocodile: Abuse of Migrant Workers in Thailand," Human
Rights Watch, 2010.

240 **rapidly intensifies into Typhoon Gay:** G. S. Mandal and Akhilesh
Gupta, "The Wind Structure, Size, and Damage Potential of

Recent Hurricane Intensity in the North Indian Ocean,"
Advances in Tropical Meteorology (New Delhi, India: Indian
Meteorological Society, 1996).

241 **talk of ghosts at sea . . . Many in the northeast stop eating seafood:**
Phil Robertson to author.

241 **catch volume in the Gulf of Thailand flatlines:** Steven Trent,
Daniel Murphy, and Josh Stride, "Pirates and Slaves: How
Overfishing in Thailand Fuels Human Trafficking and the
Plundering of Our Oceans," Environmental Justice Foundation,
February 25, 2015.

242 **Nationalist politicians in Thailand seize on this and call migrants:**
Phil Robertson, "From the Tiger to the Crocodile: Abuse of
Migrant Workers in Thailand," Human Rights Watch, 2010.

242 **Legal migrants are stopped for papers when they go out:** The
difficulties faced by legal migrants are directly related to the
pressure on illegals. "The system is so convoluted, even companies
that want legal workers need to use recruitment agencies," Lisa
Rende-Taylor, a Thai supply chain expert, tells me. "These
recruitment agencies then use sub-brokers to handle the work.
From there, no matter what the intentions, it gets shady quickly."
But, even if recruited perfectly, legal migrants live a marginalized
existence. The ID cards they need to travel are often kept with
employers and can obviously be abused and used as leverage.
Above all, legal migrants are treated as a commodity, not as
humans: companies are given a quota they can hire, and then can
sell or trade that quota to other companies without ever telling
the workers until it is done and they are about to be shipped away.

247 **A Pulitzer Prize–winning journalist:** Margie Mason of the
Associated Press to author.

248 **they uncovered some of the first cases of human trafficking:**
Several other grassroots NGOs, such as the Stella Maris
Seafarers' Center, reported cases of human trafficking
contemporaneously, and several international aid groups/

individuals like IOM (Phil Robertson in particular), Human Rights Watch, and the Environmental Justice Foundation (Steve Trent) rang their respective alarm bells as hard as they could. Further scattered news stories reported on the sector prior to the *Guardian*'s 2014 exposé, including Al Jazeera and National Public Radio. However, it also became clear reporting this that the 2012 NPR piece and 2014 *Guardian* piece had an outsized impact on international attention, and that the LPN had an outsized impact on both of them. As such the LPN appears to exist as a crucial common factor behind many of the major steps that led to Thai seafood slavery moving from an ignorable regional story to media crises heard round the world.

249 **Founded in 2008 by eBay billionaires:** Clare O'Connor, "Inside eBay billionaire Pierre Omidyar's battle to End Human Slavery," *Forbes*, November 19, 2012.

249 **searching for a cause:** Michael Gentilucci, "Can't Get a Grip on Omyidar Philanthropy? You're Not Alone, So Take This Guided Tour," *Inside Philanthropy*, March 27, 2014.

249 **After a 2010 feature in *National Geographic*:** Clare O'Connor, "Inside eBay Billionaire Pierre Omidyar's Battle to End Human Slavery," *Forbes*, November 8, 2012.

249 **Over 35 million people per year work under coercion:** "Profits and Poverty: The Economics of Forced Labour," International Labour Office, 2014.

249 **labor is responsible for some $150 billion in profits:** Ibid.

250 **Sex slaves . . . less than a quarter:** Stefan Gold, Alexander Trautrim, and Zoe Trodd, "Modern slavery challenges to supply chain management," *Supply Chain Management* 20 (2015).

250 **what they called a "strategic vetting process":** The following depiction of the Humanity United process was compiled with help from Lori Bishop, Brian Edge, Katrina Nakamura.

251 the *Guardian* leverage the Humanity United report to publish their own massive exposé: Kate Hodal, Chris Kelly, and Felicity Lawrence, "Revealed: Asian Slave Labor Producing Prawns for Supermarkets in US, UK," *The Guardian*, June 10, 2014.

252 he sized up those very normal, non-sensational, non-media-friendly conditions: Occasionally it is necessary to make an implied comparison glow red like a signal flare. So let's look at those conditions once more, the very normal ones whose combination allowed seafood slavery to rise and flourish in Thailand. Thailand is foremost an extremely wealthy country, a regional economic powerhouse, but bordered by far poorer nations. That border is both heavily policed but porous, laced with crossings that are equally dangerous as they are attainable. The migrants who decide to cross it are fleeing violence and seeking a better life. They make arduous multiday treks, employ dubious coyotes and snakeheads to broker their passage, and act on faith and desperation as much as reason. They don't speak the language, don't have money, and don't fully understand the laws of the country they are crossing into. They are, however, willing to do the jobs their richer neighbors have forsaken. Thailand is also a country where casual racism toward those darker-skinned neighbors is tolerated, where a nationalistic, jingoistic political party plays off those tensions to make them a popular scapegoat, and where both police action and official policy have driven those migrants even further underground, transforming them into illegal aliens, even as they have spent most of their lives fantasizing about Thailand and the Thai lifestyle . . . I hope at this point the parallels for North American readers are inescapable, and any hope that the behavior and conditions I've described in this chapter "could never happen here" is recognized as either a form of exceptionalism that signals lack of imagination or the type of wishful thinking that abuts denial.

252 **"The focus on Thailand has brought so many resources":** Simon Baker to author.

252 **"This labor is 100 percent necessary across the globe":** Jackie Pollock, of ILO, to author.

252 **"There is nothing special about Thailand":** Daniel Murphy to author.

252 **"I do think the boats are extreme. But only in the violence":** Andy Hall to author.

252 **"What I can say is that production has shifted to India":** Josh Stride to author.

254 **"catering to the aesthetic sense of consumers":** Jim Prevor, *Jim Prevor's Perishable Pundit* (blog), August 25, 2015.

255 **They found a private prison system:** Subsequently documented by brilliant reporters at the Associated Press who joined along with P'Aon during follow-up trips.

Afterword: The Long Road from P'Aon to Amazon–Whole Foods

259 **"That corpse you planted last year":** T. S. Eliot, *The Waste Land* (London: Hogarth Press, 1922).

259 **"You! Hypocrite reader! My fellow! My brother!":** Claude Baudelaire, *Les Fleurs du Mal*, 1857. As quoted in the original French in *The Waste Land* but translated into English here.

362 **Andy . . . along with five thousand other employees who got the ax:** Errol Schweizer to author. *See also* Tom Huddleston Jr., "Whole Foods Cutting 1500 Jobs," *Fortune*, September 28, 2015.

362n **John Mackey came out against universal health care:** Emma G. Keller, "Whole Foods CEO John Mackey calling Obamacare fascist is tip of the iceberg," *The Guardian*, January 18, 2013.

270 **Whole Foods–Amazon takes the next logical step . . . cuts medical benefits for its part-time workers:** Hayley Peterson, "Whole Foods is cutting medical benefits for part-time workers," *Business Insider*, September 12, 2019.

INDEX